10.95

GROWTH AND CHANGE OF SCHIZOPHRENIC CHILDREN :

A LONGITUDINAL STUDY

GROWTH AND CHANGE OF SCHIZOPHRENIC CHILDREN:

A LONGITUDINAL STUDY

WILLIAM GOLDFARB, M.D., Ph.D.
HENRY ITTLESON CENTER FOR CHILD RESEARCH

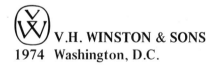 V.H. WINSTON & SONS
1974 Washington, D.C.

A HALSTED PRESS BOOK

JOHN WILEY & SONS
New York   Toronto   London   Sydney

V. H. Winston & Sons, Inc., Publishers
1511 K St. N.W., Washington, D.C. 20005

Distributed solely by Halsted Press Division, John Wiley & Sons, Inc., New York.

Library of Congress Cataloging in Publication Data:

Goldfarb, William, 1915-
 Growth and change of schizophrenic children.

 Bibliography: p.
 1. Schizophrenia in children. I. Title.
[DNLM: 1. Schizophrenic psychology–In infancy and childhood. WM203 G618g]
RJ506.S3G58   618.9′28′982   74-13824
ISBN 0-470-31102-9

Printed in the United States of America

Contents

Acknowledgment

The longitudinal research herein developed has been supported since 1962 by the National Institute of Mental Health (NIMH Grant MH 05753). However, we also wish to acknowledge the encouragement and support of the Ittleson Family Foundation, whose practical interest could always be stimulated by the promise of exploration and new pathways of research.

While the author is responsible for the written report, the research it discusses represents the cooperative efforts of an intensely devoted and technically skilled group of workers. These equal partners in the investigative journey we have been traveling since 1962 include:

Herbert Cohen, M.D.
Judy Florsheim

Nathan Goldfarb, Ph.D.
Shirley Hoberman (1961–1963)
David M. Levy, M.D.
Donald I. Meyers, M.D.
Ruth Pollack (1957–1969)
Hannah Scholl, Ph.D. (1963–1968)
Lawrence Taft, M.D. (1957–1967)
Elaine Yudkovitz

For many years the logistical organization of the longitudinal program was the responsibility of Mrs. Ruth Pollack. Mrs. Pollack died prematurely in 1969 and the present report may be seen as a memorial to her unusual commitment.

It is essential to record Dr. Nathan Goldfarb's special role in the design of the experiment and in programming the very complex analysis of the data. His statistical analysis of longitudinal changes in behavior has much to contribute to the broad methodology of developmental analysis.

The burdensome collection of data for many years has required the careful efforts of a large number of research and technical assistants. The list is too long to mention each of the individuals; but they know we are grateful to all of them. The business of investigation makes enormous demands on our clerical and administrative staffs to whom we express gratitude.

One must also keep in mind that the laboratory for the investigation was the Henry Ittleson Center for Child Research, a subdivision of the Jewish Board of Guardians. Meaningful in-depth studies of children in living situations and over long periods of time are possible only in child centered treatment facilities like the Ittleson Center committed to intensive treatment and individualized management of disturbed children. Our research effort has always elicited the interest and cooperation of our entire therapeutic staff, whom we gratefully acknowledge.

Preface

This is a report of longitudinal change in a group of schizophrenic children while in residential treatment at the Henry Ittleson Center for Child Research in New York City. The period of observation of severely disturbed children—three years between the ages of 7 and 10 years—is only a brief interval in the entire life-span; but three years is a large segment of early childhood and certainly represents a long period of inpatient treatment and observation. In addition, the early school age period is universally regarded as a time when children are particularly accessible to educational and social experience.

Our research interest in behavioral and psychological changes in schizophrenic children reflects our therapeutic objectives, i.e., the enhancement of their psychological growth and integrity and the careful delineation of the changes effected in these children. We have always recognized that psychotic children grow and change. On completion of the study, we felt that our early conviction regarding the merits, indeed the necessity of systematic longitudinal study of schizophrenia, had received support; on the other hand, we were reminded of the distinct limitations of this kind of study and of its limited generalizability. The project needs to be seen in broad perspective. In this regard, we have always felt that our own perspective with regard to a statistical study was deepened and enlarged because the study was carried out in a psychiatric center dedicated to the comprehensive treatment of individual psychotic children. This kind of therapeutic background with individual children assists both in the design and appraisal of results of a group study.

The Center's therapeutic program provides longitudinal data which are uniquely useful in the study of individual change. These data are also used in our research program. In our research, we wish to generalize from the data on individual children so that hypotheses may be developed and tested and also to improve the ability to predict change in individual schizophrenic children. We, therefore, find it necessary to supplement the qualitative, individual case histories (provided by our therapeutic program) with statistical processings which provide the quantitative summaries, trends, and measures of precision that may be used for generalizations and predictions. These statistical processes, in turn, provide the therapist with important, new information not directly apparent in the individual case histories. In this fashion the programs of therapy and research are mutually sustained and enriched.

The case histories and the derived statistical data make available for therapy and research two types of longitudinal data: the original case history for each child, and the derived statistical tables for each individual child and for groups of these children. Although these two types of longitudinal data have a common origin in the therapy of individual children, they differ in the amount and kinds of information which they make available.

The statistical processing of case history data may clarify and otherwise add to the usefulness of the data. However, in so doing, it diminishes the case information to the degree that there is a loss of content, complexity, and information of interrelationships which the individual case history can provide. The statistical summary of longitudinal data develops with stated precision new understanding of tendencies, ranges, and relationships among carefully defined variables, and thereby provides new perspectives regarding individual children and groups of children. But, as therapists, we are acutely aware that these summaries sacrifice valuable information for each child which the therapist accumulates. Case histories describe the evolution, development and interplay of forces and relationships in individual children that are too complex to be defined, codified, and measured in statistical terms. The statistical tables may augment appreciation of the range and variability of the factors with which the therapist works. However, these statistical data are too simple and too limited to provide the information needed by the therapist to work effectively in the treatment of a particular child and to predict the unique course of development for this child.

Statistical summary of longitudinal changes may assist the therapist with hints of new methods, with perspectives in the development rates of his own patients as compared with other children, or with similar perspectives on specific functions such as perception, motor coordination, and intelligence. The therapist is helped to see where and when he may expect change in a child.

We are alert to those statistical processes which carefully select variables for study and thereby exclude from consideration the much more comprehensive information available in our case histories. Because such selection is carefully controlled, the statistical project is limited by research objectives, by the need to express the findings in quantitative fashion, and by the need to work only with those quantitative measures which are sensitive enough to distinguish among individual children. In these statistical processes, the data describing motivations and social relationships are limited or even excluded. For example, our statistical data demonstrate changes in functional intelligence which we believe will be of interest but these data do not demonstrate how changes in intelligence quotient are linked to conscience, motivation, changing identification, and the family organization.

The shrinkage of case content imposed by the statistical method is, of course, present in this statistical study even though it examines changes as measured by as many as 40 scores and ratings. Although these statistical data include a large number of dimensions, we never assumed that we were studying the "total personality." Certainly we did not believe that the statistical data were adequate to appraise each child's unique characteristics in sufficient depth. Indeed, we consciously excluded the detailed motivational and interactional data which could best be presented on an individual and qualitative basis. As will be noted, our selection of variables for study was influenced by the psychoanalytic concept of the ego. In accord with an adaptational emphasis, we focused our attention on functions involved in self regulation and self direction. These functions are dramatically impaired in psychotic children. We presumed that changes in adaptive status would be expressed in changes in level of self regulative competence. In the present statistical design, however, we deliberately reduced our attention to motivational and drive factors even though they organize and give continuity to self regulative functions such as perception, memory, and psychomotor response. Similarly, we did not try to pinpoint interactional factors that crucially influence the self regulative expressions of each of the children as individuals. In contrast to the functional emphasis of our present statistical summations, the organizing influence of dynamic, motivational, and interactional factors is considered in our treatment program in very detailed and careful fashion for each individual child as he is exposed to a wide gamut of treatment modalities including individual psychoanalytic methods, milieu therapy, family therapy, and individually designed functional remediation. Motivational and interactional data derived from treatment are thus described in the individual case history.

An example of the different uses of case histories and their derived statistical data may be found in our consideration of the child's communication. Although the issue of communication has been given very serious consideration in this volume of statistical data, it focuses only on appraisals of levels of communication skills of the children. Only a small portion of the relevant communication data appearing in the case files of the children in the Ittleson Center have been codified and tabulated for statistical handling. Certainly, a profound appreciation of the patterns of psychosocial organization and communication within the families of schizophrenic children,·the specific modes of communication between the children and their mothers and fathers, and especially each child's internal fantasies and emotions regarding human relationship and his highly idiosyncratic expression in verbal-gestural behavior, rest upon qualitative information which exceeds in scope and complexity the communication information which we have been able to present in statistical form. Thus, it will continue to be important to present careful case descriptions of the evolution of individual schizophrenic children, with detailed attention to motivational and relational factors.

Finally, although attention to emotional and motivational factors was limited in the present report of longitudinal changes in adaptive equipment, we did study the children longitudinally with a variety of projective tests. An analysis of the longitudinal Rorschach Test data is now in process. It promises to fill in some of the gaps in our descriptive understanding of schizophrenic children, since the Rorschach Test attempts to probe the affective as well as the intellectual life of the individual and to define some aspects of the dynamics and inner patterning of his personality structure.

CHAPTER I
Objectives and Background

We wish to study the psychological growth of schizophrenic children. That is to say, our objective is to evaluate changes in crucial aspects of their behavior and psychological organization. Under a definable set of conditions, for example, while receiving as comprehensive a program of psychiatric treatment as we are able to offer, do these children regress? Do they improve? Do they even become normal? Do the changes take a long time to become evident? In other words, employing a selected set of operationally defined variables, can we delineate rates of change in schizophrenic children? It may be reasoned that measurable improvement in these specified responses can be employed as evidence of more general clinical improvement since childhood schizophrenia is an entity diagnosed on the basis of observed deviancies in behavioral responses which are measurable.

Furthermore, study of schizophrenic children in terms of carefully selected and relevant variables may bring to light previously undisclosed characteristics associated with childhood schizophrenia. Or longitudinal study may demonstrate that these dimensions become more manifest at certain times than at others in the maturation of a schizophrenic child. Such study should thus make the description of childhood schizophrenia more precise and objective.

We also wish to study these changes in schizophrenic children viewed individually. We have become increasingly conscious that there is maximum validity in observing "the schizophrenic child" with sharp focus on his individual uniqueness, and that appraisal of group changes alone is insufficient. Group findings regarding change are particularly hazardous for inferences about individual children in view of the behavioral and psychological diversity of the children included in most samples of schizophrenic children. Averaging procedures may hide true individual patterns. Available samples are also not likely to be generally representative of the entire population of schizophrenic children. However, careful studies of change in schizophrenic children, which embody suitable techniques for appraising and classifying changes over time in each of the individual schizophrenic children in the sample under study, do manifestly provide data which are representative of the individual child. Appropriate grouping of individual patterns of change and growth for homogeneous clusters of children should lead to more valid generalization about other samples and populations.

In considering factors linked to change in schizophrenic children, it is feasible and profitable to subdivide the large sample of children into homogeneous groups on the basis of a number of appropriate variables. Thus, we have already found it profitable to subdivide schizophrenic children on the basis of sex, level of neurological integrity, social class, and age of admission to the psychiatric treatment program. When so categorized, the subclusters may be described in terms of a variety of dependent variables and age changes in these variables.

In planning the study of how schizophrenic children change, we decided to employ a prospective longitudinal design rather than one based on cross sectional or retrospective modes of data collection. Clearly, prospective longitudinal study of children is extremely difficult to design and carry through to completion. The task of maintaining the experimental sample is back breaking—a large professional staff is required, and there are continuous problems in maintaining staff stability and commitment over long periods of time. Also, procedures for studying changes in children are difficult to define operationally. Even before making operational and procedural decisions, the delineation of dimensions which are relevant and feasible for longitudinal assay in childhood is in itself a complex challenge. The orderly collection of useful longitudinal information is thus a massive, incredibly difficult and risky undertaking.

Why, then, did we initiate an ambitious program of longitudinal study, despite our full awareness of the inevitable frustrations of developmental study of an aberrant group of children, the complexities of longitudinal analysis, and the high risk of failure? It seemed to us that maturational studies of schizophrenic children are fundamental to a comprehensive understanding of their behavioral disorders. Such studies are, of course, clearly necessary to spell out what happens to individual schizophrenic children as they grow older and to show the variety in individual patterns of growth. The information relative to individual growth patterns is, in itself, helpful in subclassifying the children into homogeneous groupings required for experimental and observational investigation. Most important of all, longitudinal appraisal is essential to spell out the subtle interplay of factors responsible for those child attributes which account for the class of disorders termed "childhood schizophrenia." It has not been feasible to establish the etiology of childhood psychosis by observing the emergence of its earliest expressions. However, the investigation of individual changes in diagnosed schizophrenic children as they mature in childhood promises to cast light on factors contributing to their key aberrations. In a sense, all investigations of schizophrenic children—whether descriptive, or experimental, or therapeutic—represent efforts to define how they change and what influences are responsible for observed change in their life course. The investigations usually do not observe these changes directly and are limited in what can be learned about changes in individual children. Prospective longitudinal assay, however, offers the most direct, and therefore more precise and accurate, measure of individual change.

The residential treatment center is particularly suited for longitudinal observation in depth of individual children. They are observed intensively for long periods of time each day in a broad variety of therapeutic encounters, both group and individual. The families participate in the therapeutic program and there are many opportunities for observing the psychosocial behavior of the families as functional units. The part played by intrinsic deviations in the child, such as cerebral dysfunction, in their psychological adaptation is also most accessible to study under conditions of intensive study and treatment. Furthermore, the relative stability of the institution provides a fairly stable climate which makes individual differences more apparent than would a changing social environment.

In view of obvious individual differences in patterns of individual change, it was also decided to apply the longitudinal method of assay to a great variety of dimensions considered of key significance in the description of schizophrenic children. Such attention to a wide range of traits was considered essential in order to expose the patterns of development peculiar to each schizophrenic child.

This, then, is our first comprehensive report summarizing data derived from systematic longitudinal study of a group of 40 early school age schizophrenic children while they were in residential treatment and after they were discharged from therapeutic residence. The collection of longitudinal data gathered while the children were in residential treatment has been completed, while post discharge data are still being gathered. For this reason, and because the environmental impact of the therapeutic residence is so different from that of the child's environment after his discharge from the residence, the data of the treatment and post discharge phases of study will be analyzed separately. The present report restricts itself to the description of in-treatment changes only.

In presenting the longitudinal data, our precise purpose is to describe how this sample of 40 schizophrenic children changed—if indeed they did change—in a number of adaptive functions over a three year period between 7 and 10 years of age while in a therapeutic residence. Our intent is not to explain why they change. Rather, we ask are the functions stable in expression or do they alter significantly? Do the changes represent improvements or decline in these functions? Are there wide individual differences in level and rate of change? The factors contributing to the change are more elusive. We might, for example, question if the changes to be noted are due in large part to aging per se or to the environmental and therapeutic influence of the residential center. The answer to this important question will have to await replication of the present study with control groups of schizophrenic children treated by alternative methods or by use of a totally untreated group of schizophrenic children who parallel the Ittleson children in essential attributes.

The present interest in longitudinal observation of schizophrenic children, the dimensions selected for prospective study, and the approach to subclassification of schizophrenic children for purposes of analysis reflect the historical approach to childhood psychosis at the Ittleson Center for Child Research since 1953. From the beginning, it has seemed clear that the most important investigative objective is the comprehensive description of schizophrenic children. The large question is: Who are the children designated to be suffering from childhood schizophrenia? How do they differ from normal children in their perception and construction of reality? Do they change in adaptive strengths as they grow older?

Historically, in order to answer these questions, our studies have moved in sequence from detailed behavioral observation of schizophrenic children (Goldfarb, 1961) to appraisal of contributory factors (including cerebral and environmental factors) and transactional analysis of the schizophrenic child in interaction with his environment (Behrens & Goldfarb, 1958; Goldfarb, 1961; Goldfarb, 1962; Meyers & Goldfarb, 1962; Goldfarb, Levy, & Meyers, 1966, 1972), and—most recently—to longitudinal observations of their growth patterns (Goldfarb & Pollack, 1964; Goldfarb, Goldfarb, & Pollack, 1966, 1969).

The description of schizophrenic children continued to be the most essential objective—and ever increasingly so—inasmuch as the most important conclusion to be drawn from clinical and research evidence, as one studies them in greater and greater depth, is the heterogeneous character of schizophrenic children and the multiplicity of factors contributing to their aberrations. For example, as one explores their neurological organization with increasing sophistication and refinement, primary atypism in neurophysiologic organization becomes apparent in a large percentage of the children (Goldfarb, 1961); yet, as one learns to observe communication and family functioning, it becomes equally apparent that deviancy in the psychosocial organization of the families is a factor warranting primary consideration (Goldfarb, 1961, 1962; Meyers & Goldfarb, 1961). Finally, recently completed follow-up investigations have confirmed the wide differences among schizophrenic children in the natural course of their growth and development (Goldfarb, 1970).

Such diversity among schizophrenic children in behavior, life course, and contributing influences may seem paradoxical since the criteria for diagnosis of childhood schizophrenia are definable and clear and psychiatric observers are in general agreement regarding these criteria. Thus, a review of the criteria for the diagnosis of childhood schizophrenics admitted to the Ittleson Center during the first ten years of its operation has confirmed that all the criteria employed are subsumed in the following nine criteria, as defined by a British working group (Creak, 1961):

(1) Gross and sustained impairment of emotional relationships with people;

(2) Apparent unawareness of his own personal identity to a degree inappropriate to his age;

(3) Pathological preoccupation with particular objects or certain characteristics of them without regard to their accepted functions;

(4) Sustained resistance to change in the environment and a striving to maintain or restore sameness;

(5) Abnormal perceptual experience (in the absence of discernible sensory abnormality);

(6) Acute, excessive and seemingly illogical anxiety as a frequent phenomenon;

(7) Speech either lost, or never acquired, or showing failure to develop beyond a level appropriate to an earlier age;

(8) Distortion in motility patterns;

(9) Background of serious retardation in which islets of normal, near normal or exceptional intellectual function or skill may appear.

All the Ittleson Center children showed at least five of the nine criteria. Further, every child showed four adaptational errors, i.e. (a) an impairment in human relationships, (b) a defect in personal identity, (c) excessive anxiety provoked by change, and (d) speech and language disturbance.

The diagnostic criteria for childhood schizophrenia would thus seem to be precise enough and to define a reasonable descriptive entity. However, detailed studies of the children demonstrate that these criteria serve as a very gross filter which separates out a class of children who are in fact still highly diversified. They differ widely among themselves in adaptive capacities, neurological organization, and family background (Goldfarb, 1961).

It is not surprising, therefore, that observers differ in the qualities of the samples of schizophrenic children under their observation since the samplings may be very selective in their choice of subjects. As we have suggested previously (Goldfarb,

1970), observers have tended to overgeneralize their findings to represent all schizophrenic children, whereas they have only described their own special samples of children.

Such specificity and limitations of sampling can be demonstrated in observations of characteristics of children under study in a single laboratory or treatment center. Thus, although the Ittleson Center sample of schizophrenic children in the present investigation is not representative of those other samples of schizophrenic children in residential treatment in other centers, we also considered the possibility that the present study population even differed from the total Ittleson Center population of schizophrenic children. For example, the tabulations of our study refer to 40 children in residence who were tested at admission and then annually for at least three years while in residential treatment. It is of interest to know whether those children who had sufficient treatment data to be included in a three year longitudinal study were similar to earlier Ittleson Center admissions. The study children were compared with another group of 46 children treated previous to the study. Historically, the sample included in the study represented admissions to the Ittleson Center since 1962, while the contrast children were under care at the Ittleson Center from 1953 to 1962.

When the earlier sample was compared with the children under study, there were no significant differences in race and religion. There were also no significant differences in the neurologist's appraisal of the neurological status of the children in the two groups. However, the later group participating in the study had significantly more female children than did the earlier group. In addition, employing the Hollingshead-Redlich Index of Social Position, the children in the study included more children from low income families than did the earlier children. Also, the children in the study were reared in families with poorer psychosocial functioning than the earlier children, as evaluated by the Ittleson Center Family Interaction Scales. This latter finding reflects our own general observation that in recent years the children admitted to the

Center came, more often, from families which are organized at lower levels of psychosocial functioning than in the previous period of the Center's history.

It may be said, even before we report the detailed findings, that of specific relevance in our present consideration is the evidence that the individual schizophrenic children differ among themselves in longitudinal course as well as in attributes at any special point in time. They range widely in responsiveness to education (Goldfarb & Pollack, 1964) and in ultimate clinical status (Goldfarb, 1970). We have seen that some start as totally lacking in capacity for self care, language, and school response, and remain so throughout life. Others show remarkable improvements in social and psychological functions, respond to school as well as normal children (Goldfarb & Pollack, 1964), and are ultimately able to accommodate to the ordinary demands of community living (Goldfarb, 1970).

Pragmatically speaking, the diagnosis of childhood schizophrenia does not in itself suggest a single and universal therapeutic plan. This is not surprising, since, as we have suggested, each schizophrenic child is a unique individual—as unique as any normal child in his personality organization, his strengths and weaknesses, his family, his life experiences, and his developmental history. For this reason the individual case method remains the major tool for diagnosis and treatment of individual schizophrenic children.

The answer to a question such as "What are schizophrenic children like?" needs to include the study of homogeneous subdivisions of schizophrenic children, and the study especially of individual schizophrenic children with an eye on the intrinsic behavioral organization of each child and on his transactional relationship to his environment. The children also need to be studied longitudinally over time as well as at any single point in time. In this longitudinal analysis of groups or samples of schizophrenic children, it is particularly necessary to recognize the range of individual variation in growth and development and to provide operationally for the appraisal of individuals. Descriptive generalizations regarding these children should be ultimately based on summaries of individual growth summaries.

Longitudinal evaluation of the development of schizophrenic children even as they grow is essential to determine their potentialities for change. Just as it might help to find how much change might be expected in individual schizophrenic children, it could also pinpoint which specific behavioral attributes change and which remain stable. Along with the emergence of the range of individual differences in growth patterns, factors in the child and his psychosocial environment which are linked to these individual differences should become clearer.

Aside from the obvious value of descriptions of schizophrenic children with reference to changes over time, the evaluation of methods and programs for treating schizophrenic children and for modifying their behavior requires the specialized techniques of prospective longitudinal observation and analysis of children under such treatment. It is anticipated that the findings of the present longitudinal investigation will ultimately enable us to compare our mode of treatment with alternative modes. For example, by employing the developmental curves of the children treated in residence at the Ittleson Center, and by establishing suitable controls, it should be possible to compare the growth of these children with that of schizophrenic children treated in the Ittleson Center Day Center, or of schizophrenic children in the custodial care of large ward services with smaller adult-child ratios and less adequate provisions for treatment. It should ultimately even be possible to spell out those crucial intervals in the individual child's growth curve when therapeutic intrusion is most likely to effect desirable shifts in development. Provided suitable assays are employed, it should be possible to test ways for facilitating the fullest development of some specific attributes and for reducing and transforming other traits.

In planning the longitudinal investigation we have had to decide what attributes and patterns of behavior to study. In previous systematic descriptive study of schizophrenic children, we have emphasized the importance of those purposeful functions which every individual requires for adaptation and survival (Goldfarb, 1961). These functions are crucial in self direction and self regulation in light of shifting environmental demands. and embody a broad repertoire of receptive, integrative, and executive capacities. In simplest terms, we have assumed that the major criteria for the diagnosis of childhood schizophrenia refer to deficits in these key purposeful functions.[1]

In longitudinal studies of schizophrenic children, the most profitable approach is to learn what changes occur over time in specific and important self regulative functions rather than in a global "schizophrenic state"—the latter a very ambiguous construct, at best. Observers have little difficulty agreeing on measures of changes in a child's social responsiveness, cognitive skills, psychomotor coordination, speech, or even in such general attributes of ego as attentiveness, activity level, and persistence; they do have difficulty evaluating alterations in a presumptive unitary entity or state termed "schizophrenia." For this reason, we have for many years studied changes in a large series of definable attributes of behavior (activity level, attention, effort), perceptual behavior, conceptual behavior, psychomotor behavior, and speech and language. Finally, the children have been observed for changes in neurological organization, and evaluated by staff psychiatrists as well as the entire clinical staff for changes in clinical status.

The present longitudinal study, therefore, is based on several presumptions. It may be presumed that the entity of childhood schizophrenia is a construct of the psychiatric observer based on gross disabilities in a given cluster of self regulative functions. We have also maintained that the clear definition of these adaptive

---

[1] For practical purposes as well, the description of individual schizophrenic children ordinarily requires analysis of these adaptive strengths and weaknesses and the unique organization of the child's self regulative functions.

functions is feasible and that there is more profit in studying stability and change in these specific and well delineated functions than in the gross entity we have termed "childhood schizo-phrenia." It must be stressed additionally that there is profit in studying a large number and variety of functions, as there is wide individual variation among schizophrenic children in regard to which functions change and which remain stable. Individual variation applies to both qualitative and quantitative aspects of longitudinal change. Although in some children functional changes are extensive enough and of a quality to warrant the judgment of alteration in total clinical status, changes in some specific adaptive functions may occur without observable significant change in global status of a child. An illustration of the latter circumstance is to be found in the remarkable educability of some schizophrenic children who nevertheless remain markedly deviant in crucial aspects of behavior.

Lastly, it is the major proposition of this report that the longitudinal study of adaptive functions in schizophrenic children over sufficiently large intervals of time will cast significant light on their individual development. When these individual curves of growth in self regulative function are summarized and categorized with reference to relevant variables, the data should illuminate the larger issue of growth and development of schizophrenic children as a group.

CHAPTER II
Environment of Children

Environmental influence on the longitudinal changes to be described will not be evaluated. However, the climate within which the children were treated and observed needs to be delineated because of our conviction that all behavioral expressions of the schizophrenic child—even those regarded as strongly suggestive of deviant somatic organization—have a transactional significance and reflect, in part, the level and quality of external stimulation.

It is safe to presume more generally that a child's environment influences change in his personal characteristics. As evidence, environmental alterations have been paralleled by changes in specific attributes and the environment does affect the extent to which the characteristics of identical twins are the same or different (Newman, Freeman, & Holzinger, 1937). There is general agreement that the social and psychological environment is a major determinant of the changes shown by children in psychological characteristics over time (Bloom, 1966). This is of significance in the present investigation of longitudinal changes in schizophrenic children treated at the Ittleson Center, since the children were studied at a point of great environmental shift from home to therapeutic residence and thereafter in a longitudinal fashion while in residence.

From the point of view of influence on data, the environmental factor is controlled in that all the children were exposed to the same social setting. This setting (the therapeutic residence of the Ittleson Center) is definable and, indeed, its fundamental therapeutic principles have been described in some depth (Goldfarb, Mintz, & Stroock, 1969). It is also likely that the psychosocial environments of the children's own families are less homogeneous than that provided the children at the Ittleson Center. The children in the study, whatever their differences, were subjected to a relatively similar social experience, and a great deal of continuity and stability has been built into the therapeutic environment by conscious design. In other words, all the children were exposed broadly to the same patterns of time, space, and role relationship. Within each child's experience, too, there was a strong continuity in extent and quality of social exposure.

The dramatic change in life climate from home to treatment residence was sharp in quality and intense in degree, and was based on the therapeutic presumption that a major shift in psychosocial climate was a prerequisite for psychological and behavioral improvement in the children. This presumption is reflected in the concept of the therapeutic milieu as a mode of treatment for psychotic children. However, it is even more totally and precisely embodied in the systematic approach to the treatment of psychotic children developed at the Ittleson Center—an approach we have termed "corrective socialization" (Goldfarb, 1965; Goldfarb, Mintz, & Stroock, 1969). This approach focuses sharply on the adaptive deficits of the children and attempts to achieve a responsive human environment which is specifically and uniquely suited to meet the ego needs of each child. Precise efforts, for example, are made to improve such characteristics as attachment behavior, ego control, attention, persistence, accessibility to auditory and visual stimuli, and more specific functional capacities such as perceptual ability, orientation, educational achievement, speech, and communication. To do so, we have employed an extensive range of therapeutic instruments including individual psychotherapy, milieu therapy, group therapy, family therapy, education including specialized remedial work, and more recently, a program to improve the children's capacity to communicate.

The therapeutic design is thus very ambitious and incorporates a variety of instrumentalities for correcting distortions in the schizophrenic child's self regulative equipment and for building in ego functions which he obviously lacks. It involves extremely detailed and round-the-clock attention to the active qualitative and quantitative reorganization of the child's environment so as to facilitate the development of desirable adaptive characteristics. There is always an enormous difference in psychosocial attributes between the child's family, which has been unable to cope with its disturbed child, and the therapeutic residence which proposes to bring about self regulative improvements in the child. In a general way, the difference in climate between the child's family and the Ittleson Center may be illustrated by the contrast between the paralysis in parental function noted in many families of schizophrenic children (Goldfarb, Sibulkin, Behrens, & Jahoda, 1958; Meyers & Goldfarb, 1961) and the deliberately structured character of the therapeutic residence (Goldfarb, Mintz, & Stroock, 1969).

The residence, therefore, is a highly intrusive environment which does not at any point abdicate its responsibility to educate, to respond to appropriate contingencies, to enlarge the range of potential influences and reinforcements for each child, and to expand his construction of reality. Whereas the great majority of the children, for example, had been excluded from school and were considered uneducable before admission to the

Center, all the children were required to be and, in fact, are successfully maintained in the classroom while at the Center.[2]

Rather precise illustration of the planned and highly individualized shift in environment for individual children is demonstrated by the practical application of our research findings in the area of communication. Failures in communication characterize all schizophrenic children (Goldfarb, 1970) although the failures are highly diversified in kind as well as in degree. In reference to communication, our therapeutic objective is the improvement of the schizophrenic child's motivation and capacity to communicate meaning and mood to others. To meet this objective, each child's speech and communication are carefully evaluated. In addition, his family's style of communication is appraised. We are particularly interested in the link between the interactional conduct and pattern of communication of the family and the child's distortions and limitations in speech. In turn, therapy includes direct remediation of the child's communication errors. However, of additional interest in our present discussion is the great investment in improving the capacity of the child's human environment to communicate with clarity and to facilitate the development of his capacity to bridge the gap between himself and others by speech and gesture. The development of a clear and responsive environment which seizes on all contingencies to reinforce the child's drive and capacity to communicate requires extensive involvement with the styles of communication of the child's family and of the child caring personnel at the Center as well. In regard to communication, therefore, we are very certain that we have succeeded in producing a major qualitative shift in the child's environment.

Although it may be presumed that environmental improvement produces improvement in relevant functions and characteristics, the manner of such change is highly complex. Certainly, in the case of psychotic children, the task of deliberate environmental

---

[2]In the latter circumstances, most of the children have evidenced significant educational response (Goldfarb & Pollack, 1964).

change in order to undo the deviant manifestations of childhood psychosis involves more than simple quantitative enrichment. Thus, again in regard to communication, the therapeutic emphasis is on dispelling the contradictory, confusing, and ofttimes extremely ambiguous verbal and cognitive climate to which the child has been desperately striving to accommodate. In the process, however, the motivational factors underlying the confusing styles of communication quickly come to view. These motivational processes which act to interfere with communication may be very broad in significance, and are comparable to those psychodynamic processes which have traditionally been illuminated by the comprehensive efforts of psychoanalysis. After all, the ability and inclination to talk is understandably connected with the affective aspects of acceptable attachment behavior. At every point, therefore, when an effort is made to improve a specific adaptive function in a schizophrenic child, one frequently finds oneself involved in a reverberating fashion with a host of other functions and associated motivations.

It is also true, however, that environmental shifts can be specific and thus affect many changes in characteristics which are themselves quite specific. A rather dramatic example is to be found in the data regarding the relationship between growth in educational attainment and more general clinical and emotional improvement. Thus, although many children show good school response, even to levels superior to normal (Goldfarb & Pollack, 1964), fewer schizophrenic children show clinical improvement and the attainment of total normalcy is a rarity (Goldfarb, 1970). In other words, while good educational response requires improvement in general qualities of ego (such as attention, concentration, persistence and perceptual organization), the fact is that many schizophrenic children become well educated but remain quite schizophrenic by all presently accepted criteria.

Response to environmental enrichment is not necessarily automatic; and parallel improvement in the child's behavior is not inevitable since the child's own intrinsic capacity to change is a significant factor. The child's responsiveness is, in turn, influenced by the state of development during which the environmental shift occurs. For example, in studies of normal children there is firm evidence that many of the most stable characteristics in all children show most rapid growth in the early years, followed by periods of slower growth. Influences on growth of these characteristics are likely to be most pronounced during the periods of most rapid development (Bloom, 1966). For many important traits, the most rapid period of development is during the first five years of life. One would expect, therefore, that as with normal children, the consequences of any influences which affect growth of behavioral attributes in schizophrenic children are likely to be greatest during periods of most rapid development of such characteristics. Beyond this, however, it is clear that schizophrenic children vary widely as individuals in potentiality for change. For example, follow-up studies (e.g., Eisenberg, 1956; Goldfarb, 1970; Rutter, 1965) demonstrate that the larger universe of schizophrenic children contains a highly diversified group of individuals, including some who show virtually no potentiality for significant improvement in purposeful behavior and others who demonstrate impressive improvement in such behavior. In addition, our own clinical experience has suggested that the psychosocial climate of the child's family before his entrance to the Center may be a factor in determining the child's responsiveness to the new environment at the Center. This hunch has emerged from systematic longitudinal studies of changes in self regulative behavior in schizophrenic children while in residential treatment. For example, there is suggestive evidence that a cluster of schizophrenic children from families which are extremely deviant are more delayed in their responsiveness to therapy than another cluster of schizophrenic children from a broader range of families including some families which are quite normal in interactional conduct. It is true that the two clusters of children are not strictly comparable. For example, the former contains children free of neurological dysfunction (nonorganic) and the latter, children with evidence of neurological dysfunction (organic). The nonorganic children also show higher levels of intellectual capacity and integration than the organic. However, these differences between organic and nonorganic children would tend to support our hunch that the markedly deviant family is linked to delay in the child's responsiveness to treatment, inasmuch as the brighter, less neurologically impaired children (who came from the more deviant families on the average) are slower in manifesting first signs of intellectual (Goldfarb, Goldfarb, & Pollack, 1969) and adaptive (Goldfarb, 1968) improvement.

CHAPTER III
The Sample and Methodologic Issues

Sample Selection and Stratification

Beginning in 1962, all schizophrenic children admitted to the Ittleson Center for residential treatment became subjects for longitudinal study. Additions of children to the study sample were completed in 1967. In every case the diagnosis of childhood schizophrenia was agreed upon by two child psychiatrists. Totally independently, each child was also evaluated for neurological integrity by a child neurologist who had no access to psychiatric case material; he reached his judgment on the basis of his own neurological history and examination. Neurological history and physical examination were rated separately with scores ranging from 1 to 5 (scores 2 and 4 were interpolated appropriately) as follows: (1) unequivocally positive, (3) equivocally positive, (5) unequivocally negative. Children who received ratings (1) to (3) in either examination or history were considered to be manifesting neurological dysfunction and placed in the organic subcluster of schizophrenic children. The remainder were children who presented no positive evidence of neurological dysfunction and they were placed in the nonorganic subcluster.

Every child in the study sample was administered the experimental battery of tests at admission to the residence and annually thereafter while in residence. After discharge from the residence, he was administered the battery of tests biannually. For purposes of present analysis of changes while in residential treatment, children who had been in treatment for at least three years were chosen for study. These children thus presented four scores for each characteristic studied, including admission scores and annual scores obtained for three years after admission.

Techniques for psychological testing and for eliciting the fullest cooperation of these most disturbed children had been refined for many years by the research staff of the Ittleson Center. This involved careful integration of the research staff into the total life of the Center with extensive efforts to enhance their relationships to the children. The children became very accustomed to the research personnel and moved freely through the research areas. They came to expect regular contact with the personnel and frequently evidenced pleasure with the experimental experience and, especially, the attention shown them. For purposes of testing, they were, of course, seen as frequently as they needed to be in order to obtain their fullest cooperation and effort. Repeated observation of the same child was very common. Because of the observers' extensive familiarity with the children outside the test situation, and the patience and care with which the tests were administered, the test results may be regarded as valid measures of the child's best functioning level at the time of observation.

In 1969, out of the reservoir of children in residence who had been under longitudinal study, all children with at least three years of residential treatment were selected for inclusion in the present analysis. This selection insured that the same children would be represented in the three year study at each year of treatment. The data to follow, therefore, describe a group of 40 schizophrenic children who had at least three years of continuous residential treatment and should not be generalized to those other schizophrenic children in the Ittleson Center residential treatment program who have experienced less than three years of treatment.

Moreover, it must be noted that the population sample consisted of children who had entered the Center at different times within a general period of approximately ten years. However, the study was initiated at a time when the climate and staff had been well stabilized, so that we may assume the treatment and environment were approximately the same for all children in the study at each year of treatment.

At admission to the residential program, the mean age of the children was 6.9 years.[3] (The standard deviation was 1.1 years.) Their ages at admission and subsequent three years of treatment, therefore, were approximately as in Table 3.1.

We knew that some of the variables to be studied are largely independent of age because of the manner in which they are derived, for example, WISC IQ and Vineland Social Quotient. Other measures, however, are direct assays of capacity level and are strongly affected by the age factor, for example, social age and strength of grip. We can only speculate on the extent to which observations derived in the 7 to 10 year period may be expected to show changes in development. It was our presumption that although it is a period of important growth, this age group is relatively free of the sudden accelerated and dramatic changes associated with infancy, preschool ages, and the adolescence period.

Changes in the first three years of treatment are reported inasmuch as all of the children had at least three years of

---

[3]In selecting a population of schizophrenic children for purposes of clinical and experimental investigation, we consciously made a decision to observe children between the ages of 7 and 10 years.

Table 3.1 Average Age at Admission and at Each Year of Treatment

Year of treatment	Average age (years)
Admission	7
First year	8
Second year	9
Third year	10

Table 3.2 Children by Sex

Sex	Number	Percent
Male	27	67.5
Female	13	32.5
Total	40	100.0

Table 3.3 Children by Evidence of Impairment in Neurological Status

Status	Number	Percent
Organic*	26	65.0
Nonorganic**	14	35.0
Total	40	100.0

*Organic–based on evidence of neurological dysfunction in either physical examination or history.
**Nonorganic–based on absence of such evidence.

treatment. However, available data for individual children in the study cover more than three years of residential treatment. Indeed, mean duration of treatment was 4.2 years. (The standard deviation was 0.8 years of treatment.)

Approximately twice as many boys as girls were included in the study, as indicated in Table 3.2.

As previously stated, the children were evaluated independently by a child neurologist using history and neurological examination. If there was evidence of deficient neurological integration either in the history or neurological examination, the children were termed organic. Children free of such positive findings were termed nonorganic. Table 3.3 indicates that organic children were almost twice as numerous as nonorganic children.

Psychiatrists also classified the children in terms of neurological integrity. While the neurologists made judgments on the basis of their own neurological evaluations and had no access to any other material, the psychiatrists utilized all available data including neurological diagnosis; and, of particular interest, they also used the information derived from comprehensive treatment observation of the children as individuals, as members of the group and of the family. In this fashion, the psychiatrists classified 28 children as manifesting disturbances in neurological integrity, in contrast to 26 children classified similarly by neurologists. Then, considering all the information, the psychiatrists attempted to weigh qualitatively the contribution of neurological and psychosocial factors to the ego deficiencies of the 28 children they had placed in the organic group. The distribution of the 28 children by relative dominance of these factors as judged by the psychiatrists on the basis of all diagnostic and therapeutic information is presented in Table 3.4.

While cerebral dysfunction was judged to be the dominant and primary contributing factor to the deficits of the children in the largest of the three subgroups in Table 3.4, these children contributed less than half of the entire organic group (39.3%). Indeed, it was the psychiatrists' judgment that psychosocial factors were primary agents contributing to the children's

Table 3.4 Contribution of Neurological and Psychosocial Factors to Adaptive Deficits of Organic Children

Dominant factors	Number	Percent
Neurological factor	11	39.3
Psychosocial factor	9	32.1
Both neurological and psychosocial	8	28.6
Total	28	100.0

aberrations in a conspicuous proportion (32.1%) of the organic children and that they were also as crucial as the deficiencies in neurological integrity in a sizable proportion (28.6%) of the children. In the clinical judgment of the psychiatrists, psychosocial influences needed to be considered in a primary fashion in about 60.7% of the organic children. Psychosocial aberrations were conspicuously evident also in the families and histories of every one of the nonorganic children. If one therefore refers to the total experimental population of 40 children, it was the considered psychiatric judgment that emotional and psychosocial influences were linked in a key fashion to the ego deficits of 73.0%, or the large majority of the children, including those who presented evidence of cerebral dysfunction.

The social class position of the families (Table 3.5) was evaluated with the Hollingshead-Redlich Index of Social Position (Hollingshead & Redlich, 1962). This index, based on occupation and education of the parents, is the basis for dividing families into five social classes. But for purposes of the present study, the classes were then regrouped into three categories. Classes I and II were combined into a social group which, for convenience, is termed "upper class," Class III was retained as "middle class," and Classes IV and V were combined and termed "lower class." A comparison of the percentage of households in each of these three class groups in the New Haven population studied by Hollingshead and Redlich with those in the present study of families of schizophrenic children shows that the Ittleson Center population

Table 3.5 Percentage Distribution of Households by Social Class for Ittleson Sample and Standardization Population

Social class	Experimental sample (Ittleson Center)	Standardization population (Hollingshead-Redlich)
Upper	12.5	9.9
Middle	37.5	16.9
Lower	50.0	73.3
Total	100.0	100.0

has a smaller representation in the lower social class category and a correspondingly larger representation in the middle category.

The children were classified into two categories by age at admission, that is, children who were seven years or less and those who were at least eight years of age. The distribution of children into these two age categories is shown in Table 3.6.

Classification of the children by the Wechsler Full Intelligence Quotient at admission demonstrates the range of children in functional adaptive level (Table 3.7). The children vary from extremely retarded to superior intellectual functioning. The greatest bulk of the children (75.0%) were below IQ 90.

There is a good deal of association among the variables noted above. For example, a greater portion of the schizophrenic children who had been admitted to treatment at less than 8 years of age came from the middle and upper classes (Table 3.8). Similarly, a greater proportion of the children admitted to

Table 3.6 Age at Admission to Treatment

Age at admission	Number	Percent
Less than 8 years	25	62.5
8 years or older	15	37.5
Total	40	100.0

Table 3.7 Wechsler (WISC) Full Intelligence Quotients (FIQ)

Full Intelligence Quotients	Number	Percent
Unscorable	6	15.0
46–69	10	25.0
70–89	14	35.0
90–109	6	15.0
110 or more	4	10.0
Total	40	100.00

treatment after 8 years of age came from the lower classes ($p < .04$, two-tailed test).

The Wechsler Full Intelligence Quotient was also related to admission age in an interesting fashion. Of particular note, as can be seen in Table 3.9, all of the six children whose FIQs were too low to be scorable were among the younger children at admission.

Organicity as diagnosed by the neurologist was linked to a number of important variables, such as sexual distribution of the children (Table 3.10). Among the organic schizophrenic children, there were more than three times as many boys than girls. These findings support previous descriptive studies of the psychotic children at the Ittleson Center. As has been suggested in the past, the well known finding of a higher ratio of boys to girls among

Table 3.8 Age at Admission by Social Class

Social class	Age at admission			
	Less than 8 years		8 years or older	
	Number	Percent	Number	Percent
Upper	5	20.0	0	0.0
Middle	11	44.0	4	26.6
Lower	9	36.0	11	73.4
Total	25	100.0	15	100.0

Table 3.9 Wechsler Full Intelligence Quotient and Age at Admission

Age at admission	FIQ					
	Unscorable		46–89		90 and over	
	Number	Percent	Number	Percent	Number	Percent
Less than 8 years	6	100.0	14	58.3	5	50.0
8 years or older	0	0.0	10	41.7	5	50.0
Total	6	100.0	10	100.0	10	100.0

schizophrenic children may reflect most prominently the processes and events associated with brain damage and reproductive trauma rather than childhood psychosis per se, inasmuch as psychotic children who are free of observable neurological dysfunction tend to show an equal proportion of boys and girls ($p < .05$, one-tailed test).

There are also major differences between organic and non-organic children in FIQ at admission. Thus all but one of the unscorable children were found among the organic schizophrenic children. In addition, very few of the children whose IQs at admission were in the normal and higher range were found among the organic children. Indeed, the great bulk of organic children had FIQs below 90 while the majority of nonorganic children had FIQs of 90 or over.

Table 3.10 Sex and Neurological Status

Sex	Organic*		Nonorganic**	
	Number	Percent	Number	Percent
Boys	20	76.9	7	50.0
Girls	6	23.1	7	50.0
Total	26	100.0	14	100.0

*Organic—based on evidence of neurological dys-function in either physical examination or history.
**Nonorganic—based on absence of such evidence.

Appraisal Procedures

In planning for the study of schizophrenic children as they grew, selection of specific appraisal procedures reflected our empirical experience in the course of their comprehensive treatment. As previously noted, planning also was influenced by our theoretic convictions regarding childhood schizophrenia. Finally, in accord with investigative design, the longitudinal study followed an earlier cross sectional study which had compared schizophrenic and normal children and anticipated in a practical fashion the present longitudinal investigation (Goldfarb, 1961). In the cross sectional study, an effort was made to select techniques for behavioral observation which were specifically relevant for study of early school age schizophrenic children in residential treatment and thereafter. That is to say, they were age appropriate and also referred to aspects of behavior that are crucial in the phenomenology and dynamics of childhood psychosis. Intercorrelational and factorial analyses of the test results were employed to discover the underlying variables so as to eliminate test redundancy and thereby reduce the number of procedures in the test battery.

To elaborate further, practical experience in the therapeutic management of schizophrenic children had called our attention to the importance of their response to schooling in the evaluation of treatment response. The children have, therefore, been tested regularly with a standardized series of educational achievement tests. Clinically, too, we have been impressed with schizophrenic children's deficiencies in self care and independence, and the correlation between improvement in social competence and broad clinical improvement. For this reason, the systematic appraisal of social maturity was employed as one of the procedures in the program of longitudinal evaluation.

Our theoretic model for the study of childhood schizophrenics especially influenced our selection of appraisal procedures (Goldfarb, 1961). In this theoretic model, the most productive concepts were those derived from the psychoanalytic construct of the ego. For example, as already noted, we have proposed that the major criteria for the diagnosis of childhood schizophrenia refer to serious deficits in a broad array of purposeful functions necessary for adaptation and survival. There are large gaps in these children in all major self regulative aspects of ego, including receptive, integrative, and executive functions. These lacunae include defects in self monitoring processes, language, relational responses, and communication behavior. Linked to these deficits are the disabilities in self awareness and in the sharp differentiation of self from the non-self. Accordingly, in planning evaluative techniques for descriptive and longitudinal study, we asked: What is the schizophrenic child's overall level of ego organization? What is his capacity in such specific functions as perception, conceptualization, and motor-executive response? How well does he communicate? What is his level of neurological organization and integrity?

This approach to childhood schizophrenia has been implemented in our psychiatric evaluations of the children's therapeutic progress. Thus the psychiatric evaluation of clinical progress which is presented in this report is based on psychiatric judgments of each child's ego status. These judgments utilized the very detailed and valid data of comprehensive round-the-clock residential treatment. Entirely independent clinical judgments of the child's neurological status by a pediatric neurologist were also employed.

Apart from these clinical judgments, however, the bulk of our data (used to describe the behavioral organization of the children) came from a very extensive series of tests and observations of the children under standardized conditions. It is clear that appraisal of a specific attribute of behavior over time required observation at stated intervals of the same child as he grew, and the observation methods needed to be standardized so as to assure the observer that he was probing the same function with each assay. Standardized testing and observation were particularly suited to the evaluation of the purposeful functions of most significance in this study of schizophrenic children. Aside from the advantage of feasibility and availability of observational instruments for evaluating various aspects of the ego, these standardized tests and observational procedures were considered essential for quantitative description of change, since they permitted the observer to focus on the same facets of adaptive response at different times in growth. They assured a high level of observer reliability. Whatever contaminative effects may conceivably derive from the chance encounters between the child and the research staff outside the test situation were also reduced by the standardization of test and observation procedures. Frequently, too, they provided data for normal children with which the present data for schizophrenic children could be contrasted.

The longitudinal information to be reported has been derived from the following procedures:

A. *Psychiatric evaluation of ego status.* Rating of global ego status based on observations of the child's ability to differentiate people, his inclination to engage with others, his level of communication and of cognition, his receptor behavior, his social maturity, and his educational response.

B. *Education evaluation.* The Metropolitan Achievement Tests—tests of reading, arithmetic, and total educational attainment.

C. *Vineland Social Maturity Scale.* Test of social competence.

D. *Global aspects of ego.* Scales of behavior during psychological tests.

(1) *Activity level.* Rating of the level of physical energy exerted by the child during examination.

(2) *Attention.* Rating of the degree to which the child attends to the task at hand or is distracted by extraneous stimuli.

(3) *Sustained effort.* Rating of the child's application to the task at hand.

E. *Neurological tests and ratings.*

(1) *Muscle tone.* Rating of the elastic tension of the muscles when they are passively stretched and of general body and postural tone in resistance to gravity.

(2) *Double simultaneous stimulation.* Test of the child's ability to perceive and locate two simultaneous tactile stimuli

applied to the face and hand under homologous conditions (both cheeks or both hands) and heterologous conditions (cheek and hand) and also under conditions of eyes open and closed.

(3) *Oculomotor functioning.* Test of eye and head movement when a child is required to move his eyes with reference to his own body (schematic movement), a target in outer space (command), a moving target (pursuit), and a target moving toward and away from the child (convergence-divergence).

(4) *Whirling.* Two tests of the child's tendency to whirl under conditions of passive head turning with arms at side, and outstretched and parallel.

(5) *Romberg.* Two tests based on the classic neurologic test of position sense. The child's posture is observed to appraise his ability to maintain posture with eyes closed, hands at side, and feet together for one minute—and with arms outstretched and parallel.

(6) *Finger to finger and finger to nose test.* Neurologic tests of motor coordination in which the child is asked to bring the index fingers of each hand together from a position of extended arms, and then to bring the index finger of each hand to his nose from an extended arm position.

F. *Receptor behavior.*

(1) *Auditory startle.* Rating of the child's behavior in response to a sudden, unexpected loud sound.

(2) *Delayed auditory feedback.* Rating of the child's voice and speech, his language and level of communication, and his behavior in response to interference with normal reception of his own voice by artificial delay of the return of his voice.

G. *Perceptual.*

(1) *Gottschaldt Embedded Figures Test.* A figure ground discrimination test in which the subject is asked to locate a stimulus figure in a more complex one.

(2) *Street Gestalt Completion Test.* Test of perception of wholes when fragmented stimuli are presented.

(3) *Bender Gestalt Test.* Test of the child's capacity to copy a group of visual patterns. Although included in this class of perceptual tests, it is actually a test of perceptuo-motor response.

H. *Conceptual.*

(1) *Weigl Color Form Sorting Test.* Test requiring the categorizing of objects by color and shape.

(2) *Orientation test.* Test of the child's orientation to time, place, and person.

I. *Motor.*

(1) *Lincoln-Oseretsky Motor Development Scale.* Comprehensive scale of coordination in many motor tests.

(2) *Railwalking.* Test of motor coordination and balance.

(3) *Dynamometer.* Test of strength of grip.

J. *Global intellectual functioning.* Wechsler Intelligence Scale for Children.

K. *Speech and language.* Ratings of speech and language on the basis of the presumptive norm by a speech pathologist.

A total of 40 measures have been derived from all these tests and observations for purposes of longitudinal study. As will be seen, when describing changes in these 40 measures, it will frequently be possible to refer to normal data derived either from original test standardization populations or from a sample of 65 normal public school children to whom we administered all tests and observations which we ourselves originated and for which, therefore, there were no standardization data.[4]

Administration of Tests

Although the tests and other evaluative methods were carefully selected to yield desired information, it was also necessary to assure competency and integrity in the adults who applied the evaluation procedures. All scores used in this report were obtained under direct supervision of a single highly trained observer who

[4]Three years of longitudinal data for schizophrenic children and cross sectional data for the normal children appear in the Appendix in 40 sets of tables.

also did most of the testing. Tests were always administered to each child individually. Every attempt was made to exclude the adverse effects of fatigue and anxiety upon scores by giving the tests only under suitable conditions. Since the child was generally acquainted with the evaluator and test setting, and since there was always enough time to permit the testing to go on only when the child was in good health and in the proper frame of mind, test data reflected the child's highest level of functioning.

Reliability coefficients are available for all tests which were constructed for purposes of present investigation (they will be reported in the course of the discussion). It can be assumed that whatever might be the test dependability reflected in these coefficients, possible factors of incompetency of the observer or limitations imposed by physical conditions under which the tests were administered were not important sources of error.

Methodologic Considerations

A major purpose of the study was to determine whether children change in connection with those measurable variables which reflect the essential characteristics of schizophrenic children. Evidence of the sheer presence or absence of change would be sought. At this stage of investigation in the field, a measure of the size of change, though extremely useful, is not the major objective since the nature of such change is perhaps, in part, a reflection of the particular environment of the children in this sample. But, on the other hand, evidence indicating growth and improvement in the sample would suggest that future effort be directed towards determining whether such changes do actually show the effects of treatment and, if so, how treatment might be improved. Certainly if no improvements could be demonstrated, then the functions of a treatment center would have to be examined accordingly.

With the decision made to determine whether schizophrenic children improve, at least in the Ittleson sample, other methodologic decisions were then made, including the determination to study individual children over a three year period—a three year longitudinal study of 40 children in residence at the Ittleson Center. This assumed that three years would probably provide sufficient time for an approximately 7-year-old child to reflect significant changes in relevant conditions. (There was some previous evidence of significant change in this age range in physical and other characteristics.) A prospective longitudinal design was used because, in so doing, a more accurate measure of individual changes could be expected than from cross sectional or retrospective collections of data. Also, as previously stated, a decision was made to observe a wide range of variables.

The longitudinal approach could also be expected to indicate whether developmental patterns for each child are indeed peculiar to the child, and whether such patterns should therefore be distinguished from summary group curves which might mask such diversity and thereby fail to serve as standards in assessing change in individual children. Also, there was the awareness that since a unit change in a variable need not have the same significance for all children, the numerical expression of such changes should not be treated equally for all individual children as is done in group summaries. Although we had no intention of developing general curve forms to conform to the data in our files, or their mathematical expression, we did hope to learn how schizophrenic children differ from normal children in their development—differing perhaps in the rate of change with regard to characteristics.

We also assumed that group curves can furnish us with at least gross information of the nature of change in individual schizophrenic children. However, in seeking standards for predicting change rather than for describing past changes in the individual child, many factors in addition to those included in the study need to be considered. For predictive purposes too, data for individual children should no doubt supplement the group curves. Of course, when there is significant uniformity in development among children, the group curves may show important features of development that may be missed in individual observations because of chance conditions affecting these individual children.

For this reason, it was decided to obtain summary curves for selected subgroups where the relative homogeneity of the included children would offset the sampling error of individual curves while preserving the significant patterns of individual change. Although the basis for the subgroup classifications used in this report are easily described, it should be noted that the Ittleson population is unique in some important respects and that subgroup summaries must therefore be used cautiously in predicting changes of schizophrenic children in other settings and circumstances. Whether individual or grouped data are used, the range and mix in the Ittleson sample of such characteristics as intellect and brain damage, the fact that all Ittleson children come from intact families, and other such individual, social and environmental factors, require judicious use of the data when applied to other schizophrenic children. However, with these limitations properly considered, the data do provide information on changes and rate of change for a group of children who are representative of a large number of schizophrenic children in the general population.

Since all children in the study reflect the generally same pervasive Ittleson environment, we are permitted to compare individual children without the greater complexity which would arise should each child live in a completely different setting. This is not meant to exclude consideration of the infinite variety of events and factors which still provided each Ittleson child with his own peculiar living space; it only means that there were nevertheless broad constraints and institutional patterns which affected all of the children in this sample and did, therefore, provide for some common experiences.

Standard Data Format

With the objective in mind of measuring growth in a wide range of variables, we had to consider how to summarize the findings so that in some practicable fashion, and within the limitations of our resources, we would describe the behavior of 40 individual children. Although the importance of studying each child separately to obtain a sense of the range of individual growth patterns was recognized, we had to consider also the complexity of analyzing about 40 different growth patterns for 40 different variables and the problem of presentation of so much information. Beyond this we saw the advantage for the observer and the general public of standardizing the statistical presentation by providing standard tables and common methods of analysis for all variables. This was complicated by the range in the precision of measurement in the different test procedures, ranging in precision from the high level of IQ scores to results expressed in ranks ranging over three or four broad intervals of response. For practical purposes, based largely upon computerized processing of the data, the same statistical techniques were applied in all cases but the consequent analysis took into account the differences in precision and scoring.

All basic statistical data for the 40 variables is contained in the Appendix in 40 sets of tables, each set comprising three to five tables. Thus for each of the 40 variables there is a set of three tables which contain the longitudinal data and significance tests for the schizophrenic children and also, where available, two additional tables with annual data for the normal children.

For the schizophrenics as a group and for 14 subgroups of these children, arithmetic means and standard deviations at the time of admission to treatment and at three points in time at the end of each year of treatment are included in the first table of each set.

In addition, separately for each of these 15 groupings, a linear regression is shown by providing the estimated score at admission and the estimated average annual increase. Also provided is the probability that the trend line may be assumed to arise by chance alone. (Although a second degree curve might sometimes have been useful, they are not shown because they most often do not account for significantly more of the trend than a straight line.) Then, in order to determine whether the children in each of the 15 groupings showed change over the four points in time, there are presented the results of the Friedman Analysis of Variance, wherein the probability given indicates the chance that the recorded changes in individual annual scores may have arisen for each group by chance alone. Finally, the table shows the probabilities that the slopes of the trend lines for relevant subgroups (e.g., males and females) are similar, as well as the probabilities that the trend lines are alike for these related subgroups. The scores for many of the variables are in the form of ranks and are not on an interval level of measurement; therefore, they do not meet the assumptions required for use of such trend analysis. These probabilities are nevertheless useful guides in comparing relevant subgroups such as males with females, organics with nonorganics, or for comparing groupings based on social position.

Standardized Analysis

In our analytic procedure for each of the 40 variables, the total group of 40 children (in the first table of each of the 40 sets) was first examined to see whether there was significant change over the three year period; for this purpose, the Friedman Analysis of Variance test was used. Where this test indicated significant change over the entire period of time, we were interested in determining in which of the three years this change was significant. Thus, while the Friedman tests showed whether there was any change at all for the particular group, the Wilcoxon matched-pairs signed-ranks test was used to select the particular years in which significant annual change occurred and also to compare admission rating with final third year rating. This interested us because we wanted to know the pattern of group changes in terms of when the change started (in the three year period), how long it continued, and when it leveled off. For example, did most of the change occur in the first year of treatment? Or did it begin to change significantly in the second year? Or was there significant change in all three years? The Wilcoxon results appear in the second table in each of the 40 sets.

Deviation from our standardized sequence for analyzing data was sometimes required by the fact, as stated, that the many different types of test data varied from the relatively high level of measurement and wide range of scores represented in the intelligence tests to the lower level of measurement (where the scores show only relative rank and a restricted range of scores) represented in our broad classification of ego level. Correlation and regression analysis of the individual curves was not useful where only a narrow range of scores was available for the four points of time. In such instances the analysis took into account the fact that although the individual child's scores for a variable such as ego status did not ordinarily vary by more than a single unit, any variation at all was in practice so important as to be considered a significant change by the analyst.

Although the study of change in individual children was intended to be the primary focus, and although statistical data were made available for the purpose, we found it to be impractical to study each of the approximately 40 children separately in connection with each of the 40 variables. We therefore followed the procedure of first analyzing the overall group of children and then examining 14 separate and relatively homogeneous subgroups to see whether the overall pattern was also generally descriptive of these subgroups. Where subgroups were similar, they were not discussed separately. Even though individual histories of the children in the subgroups were likely to resemble their subgroup trends, these individual histories were also examined where it was thought that they were sufficiently unique to add to the understanding of individual trends. On the other hand, where analysis of individual curves did not appear to add to the understanding of how the schizophrenic children changed in connection with the variable under study, the report was restricted to description of the total group and those subgroups which differed from the overall group in their development.

The third table in each of the 40 sets of tables provides frequency distributions and was used to supplement the analysis of the group averages of schizophrenic children in the first table of each set.

Use of Data from Normal Children

The fourth and fifth tables in each set (numbered A-4 and A-5) contain frequency distributions as well as means and standard deviations for a control group of normal children based on a sample of 65 children between the ages of 6 to 11 years—where such normative data was obtained by us. They may be compared with previously described tables for schizophrenic children (the first, second, and third tables in each set numbered A-1, A-2, and A-3). Information for the 65 normal children is embodied in cross sectional data which were derived from a sample of children attending a New York City school with approximately the same racial, religious, and social characteristics as the children in the longitudinal study. The statistics for these normal children are used in the report to compare the levels and changes in schizophrenic children with comparable data for normal children—particularly useful since normative data for the variables represented in the table are not generally available. The data for normals may, therefore, be used profitably for comparison by other observers and therapists.

Since these normative data are cross sectional in nature, that is, the six age groups consist of separate samples of children, they are useful for providing estimates of annual age averages, but are not as informative as longitudinal data in providing estimates of annual changes in individuals.

For our own analysis of the normative cross sectional data we utilized the Kruskal-Wallis One Way Analysis of Variance Tests and the Duncan Multiple Range Test to see which of these age groups differed from each other significantly, thereby indicating whether there were age trends. It was then practicable to compare, in a general way, the normative cross sectional data with the longitudinal data for schizophrenic children. Comparisons were simplified by the fact that often the data for schizophrenic children, even at the highest levels of accomplishment, showed with great consistency that their scores were below the lowest levels of the normal children.

True Change Versus Practice Effect

The use of longitudinal data introduces the risk that gains derived from practice effect may be mistakenly viewed as true improvement. In this regard, our objectives simplify the analysis since we are more interested in determining whether any changes occur at all than in determining in a precise way the size of the changes. We did make the presumption that the curves of change derived from annual retests represented true changes rather than mere practice effect, because of the long interval of time between tests. Not only was the impact of memory minimized by the long interval, but in most cases the increase in age required the introduction of new content into the tests. In addition, we were aware that some of the tests could be only minimally affected by practice. We refer, here, to observations where the memory of a child could not possibly be a factor—such as in observation of activity level, whirling tendency, or speech capacity. In the case of some tests, as in the measure of strength of grip and school achievement tests, on the face of it, improvements noted could hardly be due to practice effect. Finally, as will be noted, the tendency toward change and improvement in scores was consistent among most of the tests, including those where we were more uncertain about the role of practice effect.

Apart from considerations of practice effect, we determined to make a very powerful effort to elicit the best score at every testing. This would minimize changes resulting merely from the fact that during a particular testing the child was not feeling well or was not at ease. We hoped, thereby, to reduce fluctuations resulting from environmental factors, testing conditions, and alterations in the children's anxiety levels.

Significance Levels for Measures of Change

Consideration of the purpose of the study and nature of the data led us to the decision of using .10 as the probability of error in rejecting the hypothesis of no differences, rather than the more rigorous and commonly used probabilities. We did so because we wished also to avoid the significant error of accepting the hypothesis of no change when in fact there is true change. We did not want to obscure real differences. We were far less concerned with the exact value of the probabilities than we were with the issue of whether the various hypotheses should be doubted at this stage of research.

The major reason for doing so is based on our belief that the broad field of study of childhood schizophrenia requires considerable amounts of new, objective information and consideration of alternative principles and theories. Therefore, the purpose of this report is to supply data and suggestions rather than rigorous tests of hypotheses. It is hoped that the factual acceptibility of the data may be tested by other investigations, and the truth of the hypotheses tested by later investigations with the support of careful experimental controls. We attempted also to provide information which might limit useless speculative thinking and stagnation deriving from lack of objective information. For these reasons, we wanted to limit, in reasonable fashion, the chances for rejecting without further testing those hypotheses which our experience and findings suggest to us.

There are also other statistical considerations which led to consideration of a less rigorous test of significance cut-off than we would apply in other situations. We recognize that there is a very wide variation in measurement levels of our data, ranging from interval level measurement to measurement which at best is only a device for ranking. We cannot assume either normality in the populations, or equality of variances as may be required; and our sample is perhaps too small to disregard these assumptions. Therefore, we have depended upon nonparametric tests which are of lesser power than those parametric tests which are often applied with smaller Type I error probabilities. These considerations plus our willingness to accept a greater risk of Type I error in order to assist in the development of theory have entered into our decision to use a .10 probability of error arising from chance variations.

There is still another consideration which the users of these data must recognize. Because of the considerable number of variables and subgroups of children which were involved and because of the obviously correlated relationships which were noted, a fair number of the so called significant differences must be minimized and assumed to be caused by chance. This inflation of probabilities provides still another reason for confirmation of the findings by additional samples and studies.

CHAPTER IV
Changes in the
Total Group

Our first question asks whether growth in key functions manifests itself in our schizophrenic children when the entire group is considered over time. If, as we hypothesized, changes are found to occur, and especially if they represent adaptive improvements, this would tend to contradict the notion—sometimes explicit and sometimes implicit—that schizophrenic children are unalterably fixed in their disordered patterns of response. In this study we are primarily interested in whether improvements are at all possible, rather than in determining the size of changes. We shall not even attempt to delineate the reason for the improvements, an objective that cannot be met with sufficient precision and control with our data. It would seem sufficient in itself to discover if improvements, even if small, are possible under the general conditions of residence in the Ittleson Center. Nevertheless, we shall try to supply some hints of influential factors in our description of subdivisions of schizophrenic children and individual children. Subdivisions do strongly suggest independent variables that might be explored further in future controlled investigations.

As we have stressed, it is necessary to consider changes of individual children as well as average changes in groups. It is our intention, therefore, to examine longitudinal curves of each child in each dimension. In accord with this intention, our analysis will proceed as follows. We shall appraise and report overall group changes first. Changes in subgroups and individual changes will then be appraised to determine if the mean overall group data strongly parallels subgroup and individual data. For reasons of brevity and feasibility, reference to subgroup and individual data will emphasize variations of subgroups and individuals from the overall group phenomena.

Psychiatric Evaluation of Ego Status

Psychiatrists at the Ittleson Center are particularly well supplied with information to appraise the integrative level of each child at the Center because of their intimate and intensive therapeutic contact with the children. Each child is rated annually on the Ego Status Scale. To do so, the rating psychiatrist makes use of all data available in a therapeutic residence, including the unique information of direct psychotherapy and the comprehensive, daily 24 hour observations of the child caring and educational personnel. The Scale itself reflects the proposition that delineation of the psychoses of childhood should take into account the serious deficits in many aspects of ego organization, especially in relational response, cognition, social maturity, and educational response.

Figure 4.1 summarizes the definitions of each of the five levels in the Ego Status Scale. It will be noted that each level is a summed judgment based on observations of the child's ability to differentiate the important people in his life, his

Level of impairment	Definition	Rating
Very severe	No differentiation of important persons, e.g., mother from others; makes no contact with anybody; no speech or gestural communication; total or near total avoidance of looking and listening; indiscriminate mouthing and smelling; near-total absence of self-care; no educability.	1
Severe	Human preferences observable but misidentifications of important persons occur often; limited contact; speech and gestural communication below level of 3 year old (echoic, pronouns confused, comprehensibility below 90%); mouthing and smelling still prominent; self care below that of 3 year old; minimal educability (at preschool level).	2
Moderate	Recognition of and responses to important persons, contacting behavior (approaching, talking to others); speech and gestural communication above that of 3 year old; responds to school education above grade 1; yet gross distortions of reality (body image, capacities, etc.) and psychotic behavior.	3
Mild	Mild eccentricity and no friends but functions acceptably in relation to school (including community school and with or without special adjustment such as ungraded class or special tutoring) and in relation to the external environment; or no longer manifestly outlandish or bizarre relationship to people, school, and the external environment but neurotic defenses present (e.g., obsessional or phobic).	4
Normal	By ordinary observation.	5

FIG. 4.1 Scale for Psychiatric Appraisal of Ego Status.

human contacting behavior, his level of communication, his receptor behavior, his self care, and his response to schooling. The judgments refer to observable behaviors and have demonstrated their feasibility and value in the study of changes in a child's adaptive organization over time. The ratings are also very reliable. For example, in one test of reliability two psychiatrists agreed on 34 of 35 judgments and deviated by one step interval in one case.

On admission, all children fell between step levels 1 and 3 which describe very severe to moderate levels of impairment (Table 4.1). This range of impairment embodies the defects of children with manifest psychotic behavior and disabilities of such seriousness as to warrant residential treatment or comparable forms of comprehensive care. At admission, the largest proportion of the children (55%) were at level 2, representing severe impairment. Levels 4 and 5 in the Ego Status Scale (mild impairment to normal) are attained by children who show higher levels of adaptive integration and who are able to cope with the requirements of life in the community and of the ordinary community school program.

The step intervals of the Ego Status Scale are not equal in range. For example, in our practical experience the shift from level 3 to level 4 is more difficult for a schizophrenic child to accomplish than from level 2 to level 3. On the other hand, a change of one step interval at any level in the Ego Status Scale reflects a large and obvious shift in level of ego organization.

As noted in Appendix Tables A variable 1, the mean scores of the group as a whole rose in a significant fashion during the three years of observation, the greatest improvement occurring in the first year. If we study the individual children for clinical estimate of ego status and utilize as a criterion of change a shift of at least one step interval in the Ego Status Scale, we may conclude that slightly over half the children (52.5%) showed improvement within the three years. A somewhat smaller percentage (45.0%) remained unchanged, and clinically one child (2.5%) declined. Only one child improved more than one step in the scale. During the three year period of observation, one child (2.5%)

Table 4.1 Distribution of Schizophrenic Children by Rating on Ego Status at Admission

Rating	Level of impairment	Frequency	Percent
1	Very severe	8	20.0
2	Severe	22	55.0
3	Moderate	10	25.0
4	Mild	0	0.0
5	Normal	0	0.0
Totals		40	100.0

reached level 4 (mild impairment), a level designating an acceptable capacity to live in the community and to cope with a community school.[5]

Educational Evaluation: The Metropolitan Achievement Tests

The schizophrenic child's response to schooling is a key determinant of clinical plans for him. More than anything else, it influences whether he will remain in his family and the community or whether he will be separated from them. When the ordinary school in the community cannot cope with him because of his aberrant behavior or if the school finds the child uneducable, placement in a psychiatric residence away from the family is frequently advised for the psychotic child. At this time, too, the family is more disposed to accept a drastic plan for his institutional placement away from home. In actual fact, while virtually all children admitted to the Ittleson Center have been of school age, they had typically

---

[5] This is paralleled by other data indicating that children in the study had an average of 4.2 years of residential treatment, and that the dominant clinical judgment of the professional staff was that the great majority required more than three years of treatment. The present study, of course, does not evaluate the behavioral changes to be noted after three years of treatment.

been excluded from the community schools and had been considered uneducable prior to admission to the residence. Similarly, clinical decision to discharge a given child from therapeutic residence and to return him to the community has frequently been determined, in large part, by his capacity to adapt to the requirements of a school for normal children. More specifically, such a discharge plan has reflected a level of educational attainment and a qualitative accessibility to educational influence which enables the child to be educated in community schools.

Even beyond this very practical requirement for discharge, all experiences embodied in the schizophrenic child's "learning to learn" are key aspects of his treatment more broadly. Schooling has been utilized to enhance the ego growth and social responsiveness of schizophrenic children even more, perhaps, than to improve their competence in the "three 'Rs'." Indeed, we have assumed that learning to read or do arithmetic, where such learning had previously been impossible, is always associated with growth in accessibility to the influences of pain, pleasure, and an array of secondary reinforcing stimuli, in human relational response, in receptor response, in self awareness, in self esteem, and in such global functions as attention, concentration, and persistence.

For the above reasons, the children have been tested regularly (every six months) with the Metropolitan Achievement Tests, a series of educational achievement tests standardized for New York City children. The Metropolitan Achievement Tests include tests of the basic skill subjects which interest us most, that is, reading and arithmetic. The Test series is also very comprehensive and contains five batteries covering the entire range of elementary grades, including Primary I (grades 1, 2), Primary II (grades 2, 3), Elementary (grades 3, 4), Intermediate (grades 5, 6, 7), and Advanced (grades 7, 8, 9). For each child, the appropriate battery was used in accord with his educational level. In the present study, Primary Batteries I and II and the Elementary Battery were most often employed. Alternative test forms of the various batteries were available and were used to avoid the contaminating effects of repetition of the same test with a given child. Because different test forms as well as different batteries were administered, a variant of the standard score was used as the unit of measurement.[6] Use of standard scores permits one to move from one battery to another and to record longitudinal curves of educational growth for the children as individuals and in groups.

As the child matures educationally, his competence in reading and arithmetic is assayed for somewhat varying groups of subtests appropriate for each level of skill. For example, while number concepts are emphasized in Arithmetic Test in the Primary I battery, arithmetic computation and reasoning are evaluated in the higher test batteries. The score used in the present study is based on an average of subtest scores.

In the data to be presented, if a child was unable to read, he was assigned a score of 65, and if unable to show any arithmetic attainment, a score of 105. These assigned scores are one unit below the lowest recorded score for any of the schizophrenic children in residence. Reading and arithmetic curves of the normal standardization population are available to contrast with the longitudinal curves of the schizophrenic children.[7]

Reading Achievement. As a total group, the schizophrenic children demonstrated a consistent improvement in reading achievement each year between admission and third year of treatment. Indeed, they showed significant improvement in

[6]The standard scores in the Metropolitan Tests are normalized, scaled scores based upon the distribution of raw scores for a selected, precisely defined population. This population was the modal group at grade 6. The mean was arbitrarily set at 200 and the standard deviation at 20 points (Metropolitan Achievement Tests Manual, 1948).

[7]The educational curves of the normal standardization population can only be related to age. The standardization curve for normals at age 7 are thus to be compared to those of our schizophrenic children at admission when they were about seven years of age; and each year thereafter. Curves for normal children at ages eight, nine and ten years are compared with curves for schizophrenic children in their first, second and third years of treatment.

reading for the three year period and also each of the three years of treatment (Tables A variable 2). This trend is confirmed by analysis of most subclasses of the children utilized in the present study and by appraisal of individual curves of change. All subdivisions of the children, by our method of subclassification, showed a similar trend except children with a WISC FIQ below 46 at admission to treatment. The latter do not demonstrate significant growth in reading over three years. Twenty-seven of the 38 children (71.1%) showed significant improvement over the three year period. Twenty-six of the children, that is, a majority of the children (68.4%), were unable to read at onset of residential treatment. After three years of treatment, most of these nonreading children demonstrated a measurable degree of reading accomplishment and only four children (15.4%) were still nonreaders.

While the schizophrenic children improved consistently in mean reading scores, they began below the level of the normal population and remained so throughout treatment. If the mean scores are expressed in terms of grade equivalent, after three years of treatment and at a mean age of 10 years, the schizophrenic children were approximately 1½ years below the mean grade (grade 4.6) of normal 10-year-olds in the standardization population.

The following criteria have been used in appraising the absolute educational status of individual children after three years of treatment. A child was considered at grade in his reading if his grade equivalent score in reading was within one half year of the grade norm for his age. He was considered retarded if his grade equivalent score was more than a half year below the norm for his age; and he was considered accelerated if his grade equivalent score was more than a half year in advance of his age norm. On this basis 13 of the 38 children (34.2%) were at normal grade level or higher in reading accomplishment after three years of treatment; and the remaining children (65.8%) were thus still retarded.

Arithmetic Achievement. The children showed longitudinal changes in arithmetic achievement similar to those described above in reference to reading (Tables A variable 3). Thus, they improved in mean arithmetic attainment between admission and the third year of treatment. They also showed significant improvement each year of observation. Twenty-four (63.2%) showed significant improvement over the three year period. Twenty-six of the 38 evaluated (68.4%) evidenced no measurable accomplishment in arithmetic on admission; after three years, only four (10.5%) still were nonachievers in arithmetic. As in reading, the children may be compared individually in arithmetic grade with normal children. Using the criteria described above for reading, 26.3% of the children were at normal grade or higher for their age after three years of treatment; 73.7% were retarded in grade level.

While the schizophrenic children improved as a group in mean arithmetic attainment, and while a majority of the children as individuals improved, they tended to be inferior to normal children at comparable ages. After three years, for example, their mean arithmetic performance was 1.3 years below that of a normal standardization population of comparable age. As noted above, too, the majority of children who had improved after three years of treatment were nevertheless still retarded in grade in comparison to normal children.

Total Achievement. Not surprisingly, the total achievement scores (Tables A variable 4) showed trends similar to those in reading and arithmetic, since the latter are subsumed along with other attainments in the total estimate. Thus the children showed significant improvement over the three year period. There was also significant improvement in each of the three years of observation. Similarly as individuals, the great majority (73.7%) of the testable children showed significant improvement over the three years, and none showed a trend to decline.

Vineland Social Maturity Scale

The Vineland Social Maturity Scale reflects the social competence of the child; social competence, in turn, is defined as "a functional composite of human traits which subsumes usefulness as reflected in self sufficiency and in service to others" (Doll, 1953). This scale is uniquely suited to study the schizophrenic child as a whole, since the ultimate manifestation of his many ego aberrations is his extreme social incompetence. Similarly, when he improves significantly in purposeful function, he demonstrates improvement in level of social competence. In our empirical experience, the Vineland Social Maturity Scale has reflected alterations in social competence in a sensitive fashion.

Information is gathered from interviews with adult observers of the child. In the present study, child care workers responsible for the daily round-the-clock care of the children supplied the necessary information. Their reports are viewed as highly valid since the data are derived from extensive, detailed, and very attentive observation. The results may be expressed in a number of ways, including social age equivalent and social quotient. The latter is the ratio of age equivalent to chronological age representing the child's social maturity relative to normal children of his age. We are, of course, interested in the schizophrenic child's growth in absolute level of social competence, such as exemplified in the age equivalent score. In addition, since all normal children grow in the functions embodied in global social competence, we want to determine if the schizophrenic children change at a pace which will make them more or less like normal children of comparable age. For this reason, we employ the social quotient as a primary unit of measurement.

The Vineland Scale units of measurement parallel those of the Stanford-Binet test of intelligence. That is, the Vineland age equivalent score is a measure of altitude or level of social competence and, in this regard, it is comparable to the mental age score of the Binet test. Similarly, the social quotient delineates the child's status in social competence relative to normal children his own age, in the same way that IQ defines his brightness relative to normal children his own age.

On admission, the children were very retarded in mean age equivalent score and in mean age social quotient. Thus, at admission, the children averaged 82 months of age, whereas their mean social age was only 60 months. Similarly, their mean social quotient was 70.9, and all the children but one had social quotients below 100, the presumed normal average.

Social Age. Employing social age as a measure of level of social competence, the children as a whole improved significantly during each of the three years of observation (Tables A variable 5), demonstrating their greatest improvement during the first year of treatment. Indeed, the change during this 12 month period represented 14 months of improvement in absolute level of social competence. Thereafter, they showed an average of 11 months of improvement in social competence during the second year of care, and seven months during the third. It is of interest that they improved significantly in social age as a group during each of the three years of treatment. Not a single child declined significantly, while 15 children improved significantly as individuals over the three year period.

Social Quotient. Apart from mean level of social competence, we are interested in how the children compared to normal children their own age at each point of observation. Their status relative to normal children is expressed in the social quotient (Tables A variable 6). As noted, the children were retarded in mean social quotient at admission (mean social quotient, 70.9); they remained below the normal social quotient of 100 throughout treatment in spite of rises in social quotient. They improved significantly in mean social quotient over the three year period and there was significant annual improvement the first year. A study of the individual curves of the children reveals that a majority of the children (62.5%) attained their highest social quotient within the first two years of treatment. The range of change in social competence is very great. Thus, relative to admission, social quotient rises of up to 50 points were noted. Similarly, falls in social quotient up to 39 points were observed. It must be understood that these falls in social quotient did not necessarily mean that the children declined in social age. Indeed, none of the children showed a significant downward trend in social competence as represented in social age for the three year period.

It is clear, therefore, that while the children as a group grew in altitude of social competence (mean social age) throughout the three years of observation, their competence relative to normal children (as represented in mean social quotient) showed a significant improvement only in the first year. As will be seen, a number of subclusters of the children actually showed no significant improvement in social quotient between admission and third year. This finding would seem to us to reflect, in part, the substantive content of the Vineland Scale itself and the kinds of socializing experiences to which the children have been exposed in the treatment milieu.

The items of the Vineland Scale have been categorized as follows:

(1) Self help general—*examples*—cares for self at toilet, tells time to quarter hour;

(2) Self help dressing—*examples*—goes to bed unassisted, bathes self unaided, exercises complete care of dress;

(3) Self help eating—*examples*—uses table knife for cutting, cares for self at table;

(4) Communication—*examples*—reads on own initiative, makes telephone calls;

(5) Self direction—*examples*—makes minor purchases, cares for self or others;

(6) Socialization—*examples*—participates in preadolescent play, plays difficult games;

(7) Locomotion—*examples*—goes to school unattended, goes about home town freely;

(8) Occupation—*examples*—does routine household tasks, does small remunerative work.

It is noteworthy that the self help items are found in the test at the earlier ages. Indeed, all but one are listed at ages below 10 years. In contrast, the items pertaining to communication, self direction, locomotion, and occupation appear at later years. This distribution of items rationally reflects the shift in substantive content of socialization processes between early childhood, prepubescence, and adolescence. Significant improvement of the children's responses in the categories of self help is easily accomplished in an intimate residential climate, even within the first two years of treatment. However, we have recognized for some time that it is far more difficult to enhance the children's attainments in other categories of social competence delineated in the Vineland Scale, such as communication, self direction, socialization, locomotion, and occupation. This might explain, in a measure, the improvement in average social quotient during the first year and the failure to sustain similar improvement in social quotient during the next two years of treatment. In a subtle fashion we might well be observing the limiting consequences of institutional experience and the constraints placed on the education of the children's social capacities by the institutional environment. We are currently embarked on a comprehensive effort to improve the communication and social competence of the children. It will ultimately be possible to see if the longitudinal curves of social maturity are different in the future in response to the environmental changes being introduced. If our conviction is confirmed, the longitudinal curve of social maturity based on the social quotient should then show continuous improvement throughout the entire period of therapeutic observation.

Global Aspects of Ego

Psychological examinations offered an opportunity to observe the children for extended periods of time (an average of five hours for each observation), enabling psychologists to appraise the children in significant overall characteristics of adaptive behavior. Each child was appraised for activity level, attentiveness, and sustained effort—attributes which powerfully influenced the efficiency of their learning, problem solving, and more total construction of reality. In the cross sectional comparison which preceded the present longitudinal study, schizophrenic children were highly differentiated from normal children in these behavioral attributes (Goldfarb, 1961). Compared to normal children, schizophrenics manifested aberrations in activity level (both hyperactivity and hypoactivity), reduced attention, and poorly sustained effort.

A measure of the schizophrenic child's deviations in overall characteristics of adaptive response can be obtained with the use of the definitions (and their associated ratings) (see Figure 4.2).

It is noted that ratings of attentiveness and of effort range from a low of 1 to a high of 5. Activity ratings refer to activity deviations and are represented in both extreme hyperactivity and hypoactivity. Activity ratings, therefore, range from ratings of 1 for either marked hyperactivity or hypoactivity to 3 for normal levels of activity. There is very strong agreement among observers in these ratings. Two observers of normal children agreed perfectly in their ratings.

The test behavior ratings assigned the 65 normal children, who, when tested, ranged between 6 and 11 years of age, are included in Tables A variable 7, A variable 8, and A variable 9. They show significant improvement over time in means of each of the behavior ratings. Study of the individual children confirm the inference that the most extreme deviations (rating 1 for activity level and ratings 1 and 2 for attentiveness and sustained effort) in each of the three variables were very infrequent and that the highest levels of behavioral response (rating 3 for activity level and ratings 4 and 5 for attentiveness and sustained effort) were highly characteristic, i.e., manifested by the majority of the children at each age. To illustrate further, only one 6-year-old child in the entire group of public school children had a rating of 1 in activity level, and no child in the public school group had a rating of 1 in attentiveness or sustained effort.

Activity level. The ratings of activity level are of primary importance since marked deviations in activity level have represented one of the important criteria for the diagnosis of childhood psychosis. It is therefore of interest that, in contrast to the other general characteristics of behavior, the schizophrenic children as a whole did not show significant changes in mean activity level over the three year period of treatment. This is confirmed by analysis of the children as individuals. For example,

Activity level	Rating
Hypoactive—exceptional absence of childish restlessness, lack of apparent energy, sits and stands very quietly, complains of or manifests fatigability.	1
Hyperactive—cannot sit or stand still, "perpetual motion," jumps up and down, runs, hops, excessive irrelevant motor activity.	1
Sits and stands quietly but not fatigued by tasks, exerts energy required to perform tasks but with less than average briskness.	2
Some excessive activity—occasional darting, wriggling, finger play, etc. but can sit and stand still most of the time.	2
Average self possession when sitting, standing, moves with normal alacrity, without excessive and irrelevant jumping, running or moving about.	3

Attentiveness	
Completely inattentive—fails to attend to examiner, very distractible, dances about room, or otherwise refuses to attend to examiner and task; so distractible, test cannot be carried out.	1
Requires great effort on part of examiner to maintain subject's attention to demonstrations and instructions; eyes wander; easily distracted by external and/or internal stimuli; continually interrupts demonstrations or instructions by asking irrelevant questions and turning attention to objects, other people, or self.	2
Attends but distracted by objects, unusual preoccupations or other people between tasks; has to be recalled to test situation before each new item, but attends to instructions and demonstrations without further interruptions.	3
Attentive but occasionally distracted by objects, people, or self-preoccupation; has to be recalled to task by examiner on not more than 1/10 of items.	4
Completely attentive—does not have to be recalled to task by examiner at any time; not distracted from task or demonstration at any time.	5

Sustained effort*	
Incapable of sustained effort—complains each task "too hard"; makes no sustained attempt on any task and completes none or only the easiest and simplest; may be emotional display (whining, crying) along with refusal even to attempt most tasks.	1
Child gives up easily—uses any excuse to reject or discontinue task; attempts many items only after continued urging and encouraging of examiner; frequently complains task too hard; unable to maintain effort for duration of trial.	2
Child attempts all items, but gives up readily on complex or difficult tasks without exerting real effort to accomplish act; can sustain effort for duration of trials with continued urging and encouragement from examiner.	3
Maintains effort for duration of trials on all tasks and attempts all tasks; moves on to next item willingly even though not completely successful in executing tasks; is realistic in willingness and gives up on tasks when beyond his ability.	4
Capable of exceptionally sustained effort—persistent; continues to practice failed items beyond requirements of examiner or until he is satisfied with his own achievement; never gives up; protests against moving on to new items until he has correctly executed task even though no further trials can be scored.	5

*Response to encouragement.

FIG. 4.2 Behavior scales.

as shown below, the children did not show significant improvement in percentage of children assigned the highest rating 3, representing normal patterns of motility:

Admission	20.0%
First year of treatment	17.5%
Second year of treatment	12.5%
Third year of treatment	22.5%

Attentiveness. The schizophrenic children evidence significant improvement in mean level of attentiveness from admission to third year of treatment. The most significant annual improvement for the group was in the second year of treatment. This trend to improvement is confirmed by the individual curves of change. Thus, paralleling this group trend was the rise in percentage of children who evidenced highest levels of attentiveness (rating 5) as follows:

Admission	2.5%
First year of treatment	7.5%
Second year of treatment	10.0%
Third year of treatment	20.0%

Although the schizophrenic children improved significantly in attentiveness, they tended to be inferior to normals in this regard throughout the period of observation. Their highest level was reached in the third year at an average age of 10 years. Even at this point of highest capacity for attentiveness in treatment, however, the schizophrenic children showed less capacity for attention than all the age groups of normal children, including normal 6-year-olds.

Sustained effort. The schizophrenic children improved significantly in capacity for sustained effort over the three year period. This trend is confirmed by appraisal of individual curves. Here, the trend is best demonstrated in the percentage of schizophrenic children who attained optimal levels of effort (ratings 4 and 5). There are practically no 5 ratings. The proportion of schizophrenic children who were given ratings of 4 and 5 is as follows:

Admission	27.5%
First year of treatment	30.0%
Second year of treatment	35.0%
Third year of treatment	52.5%

Again, although the schizophrenic children improved throughout treatment, they were inferior to normal children in the age groups of 6 to 11 years in mean ratings of sustained effort. In addition, no normal child in this age range showed the very lowest rating (rating 1), and only one child out of 65 was assigned rating 2. In contrast, throughout treatment a high percentage of the schizophrenic children tended to be assigned ratings 1 and 2, indicative of the most serious impairments in capacity for sustained effort, as follows:

Admission	45.0%
First year of treatment	45.0%
Second year of treatment	37.5%
Third year of treatment	30.0%

The schizophrenic children as a whole, therefore, improved between admission and the third year of treatment in attentiveness and sustained effort. However, they showed no significant shift in activity level over the three year period. As noted in the cross sectional study, normal children showed improvement in all three behavioral characteristics between 6 and 11 years of age. If the schizophrenic children between 7 and 10 years of age are compared with the normal children of the same ages in terms of mean scores, it is noteworthy that even the mean scores achieved by the schizophrenic children at 10 years of age, i.e., the third year of treatment, were below those of the normal 7-year-old children in each of the three ratings. This is confirmed by an analysis of the individual children. A high proportion of the schizophrenic children at admission and at each age were assigned to the lowest behavioral ratings—rating 1 in activity level, and ratings 1 and 2 in level of attentiveness and sustained effort. Similarly, after two or three years of treatment, a minority of the schizophrenic children showed optimal ratings, i.e., rating 3 in activity level and ratings 4 and 5 in level of attentiveness and sustained effort. In summary, although the children improved in some crucial overall aspects of behavior (attentiveness and sustained effort), after three years of treatment they remained inferior, even relative to normal children who were three years younger.

Neurological Tests

The present section describes changes noted, over time, in assays of the functional integrity of the nervous systems of schizophrenic children. Such changes will be inferred from their longitudinal responses in a series of biometric tests from the conventional, clinical, neurological examination.

Systematic neurological appraisal of children for purposes of longitudinal evaluation has been hindered by an absence of uniform criteria for diagnosis of neurological dysfunction, by lack of developmental standards for neurological functions which grow in childhood, and by the insensitivity of conventional procedures for neurological diagnosis. In the latter regard, it must also be recognized that children with unquestionable and unequivocal evidence of neurological dysfunction are most likely to find their way to neurological therapeutic services. If present, therefore, neurological impairments of children diagnosed as schizophrenic are likely to be considerably less obvious than the disabilities of children who are managed by neurological services. As a consequence, the standard neurological study which features unequivocal localizing signs (such as reflex changes, abnormal reflexes, and conspicuous motor and sensory asymmetries and dysfunctions) is not sufficiently sensitive to diagnose the range of neurological abnormality found in psychotic children.

More pertinent and refined indications of neurological disability in schizophrenic children are aberrations in patterned behavioral and psychological response, including impairments in gross and fine motor coordination, balance, gait, posture, muscle tone, perception, conceptualization, and speech. In assaying aberrations in coordination, for example, suitable weight is given to such subtle manifestations of defective differentiation of motor response as dysdiadokinesis, slowness, irregularity in amplitude, overshooting, undershooting, tremor, and other abnormal adventitious movement, overflow response, and immature postural response. Defects in the hierarchical organization of sensory response are best demonstrated in circumstances of multiple, simultaneous stimulation. Some general psychological manifestations of cerebral dysfunction are perhaps even less definitive, but may be of key diagnostic interest if very severe or if noted in combination with defects in the above patterned response. These manifestations include such general attributes of adaptive behavior as hyperactivity, brief attention span, distractibility and undifferentiated, unselective response to all stimuli, impulsiveness and, even, unfocused, undifferentiated expression of fear and rage.

The group of neurological deficits which refer to problems of patterning and differentiation in psychological areas—such as perception, conceptualization, psychomotor response, and communication—influence the results in virtually all the psychological tests of our present battery. In this sense, all the psychological tests of the experimental battery are neurological tests and appraise the level of neurological integrity. However, reference will be made to tests more specifically derived from established clinical neurological procedures.

In the past, these neurological tests have been employed to define focal neurological defects, and may still be so used. Thus, note may be taken of qualitative deficits of diagnostic import. For example, the spastic gait of upper motor neurone disease, or the ataxic and atonic manifestations of cerebellar disease, or their differentiation from posterior column disease, may be observed in the Romberg Test. The dyskinesis of basal ganglia disease—including jerky, fragmented choreiform movements or wormlike athetotic movements, or the tendencies to rigidity, tremulousness and the associated disorders of mimetic and background motion—may be weighed. Similarly, primitive righting and postural reactions are accessible to view in a number of the tests (e.g., oculomotor, whirling, and Romberg). However, the present section will employ units of measurement which summate the observations and are being employed as global measures of general level of neurological integrity.

The group of neurological signs which reflect defective patterning and differentiation of neurological response refer to neurological functions which vary in dimension and also mature as the child grows older. For purposes of longitudinal research, uniform diagnostic criteria and normal developmental standards are thus essential.

The tests and observations in the neurological battery included ratings of muscle tone, the double simultaneous stimulation tests, the oculomotor tests, the whirling tests, the Romberg tests, the finger to finger test, and the finger to nose test. For purposes of longitudinal analysis, a single summed score in each of the tests is used. (Longitudinal data are in the Appendix, Tables A variable 10 to A variable 23.)

To assist us in interpreting present longitudinal findings with schizophrenic children, we have available developmental information based on cross sectional data describing the responses of the group of 65 normal children to the same tests. As previously noted, these children were all average public school children, free of psychiatric disability and generally similar to our experimental group in social and cultural environment. Aside from 15 children at age 10, they included ten children at each year between 6 and 11 years. They thus offered data descriptive of children of early school age, such as the children in the experimental group. We employ these data from normal children with caution as an approximate contrast, inasmuch as the public school data are cross sectional in their derivation in contrast to the longitudinally based data describing the schizophrenic children.

Appendix Tables A variable 10 to A variable 23 include tables of means and derivations of neurological tests for normal children who ranged in age between 6 and 11 years at time of testing. Table 4.2 contains measures of reliability of the scoring of these variables based on judgments of two independent observers of 20 normal children. There was a high level of observer agreement in the tests.

Table 4.2 Correlations Between Two Observers for Neurological Test Ratings for Normal Children

Test	Correlation*
Muscle Tone	1.00
Double Simultaneous Stimuli	
With eyes open, homologous	1.00
With eyes open, heterologous	1.00
With eyes closed, homologous	1.00
With eyes closed, heterologous	1.00
Total score	1.00
Oculomotor Functioning	
Total	1.00
Postural adjustment	.93
Whirling, arms at sides	.89
Whirling, arms outstretched and parallel	.78
Romberg, arms at sides	.86
Romberg, arms outstretched and parallel	.96
Finger to finger	1.00
Finger to nose	1.00

*Based on Gamma Tests.

Muscle tone. An estimate is made of general body and postural tone in resistance to gravity, and of muscle tension in response to passive stretching of the limbs (Figure 4.3). Clinically, we have been impressed by deviation in muscle tone in schizophrenic children, more frequently in the direction of hypotonicity than hypertonicity. Evidence for such deviation is supported by the mean ratings for muscle tone of the children as a whole at admission and at each year of treatment (Tables A variable 10). It is also confirmed by the study of individual curves of change. All four mean ratings were consistently below the mean ratings of the normal public school children of comparable ages. Apart from age 7, the majority of normal public school children at each age between 6 and 11 years were assigned optimal rating 3 (80% of the total normal group

Level of muscle tone	Rating
Extreme hypotonicity: Extreme flaccidity of muscles; limp "ragdoll" body; virtually no resistance to passive motion; child collapses or leans against objects or person in environment.	1
Extreme hypertonicity: Extreme spasticity and rigidity (clasp knife, cogwheel), stiff trunk and limbs; wooden or robot like movement, scissors gait.	1
Moderate hypotonicity: Flaccidity of muscles; child habitually slumps and slouches; very slight resistance to passive motion.	2
Moderate hypertonicity: Muscular rigidity, jerkiness, above average resistance to passive motion.	2
Normal tone: Child maintains normal posture with ease; stands and sits straight; moves with fair ease and grace; slight muscle tension on passive motion and normally resilient.	3

FIG. 4.3 Muscle tone.

attained this rating). In contrast, at any single point in time during treatment, a minority of schizophrenic children were assigned normal rating 3 and a majority were given the lowest ratings (1 and 2). A review of the qualitative basis for the lowest ratings among the schizophrenic children confirmed that the muscle tone aberrations generally embodied marked hypotonicity.

Nor did the schizophrenic children as a whole change significantly in muscle tone over the three year period of treatment. As will be increasingly evident when other evidence is reviewed, stability of muscle tone in these children thus contrasts sharply with the changing character of most other attributes being evaluated longitudinally. It should be noted, too, that level of muscle tone showed no significant developmental alteration between the ages of 6 and 11 years in the normal public school group. It would seem that muscle tone is an attribute reflecting neurophysiologic organization, which is established early in life in both normal and schizophrenic children, and subsequently shows little developmental change or responsiveness to educational and therapeutic influence.

Double Simultaneous Stimulation Test. This test appraises the child's ability to perceive and locate two simultaneous tactile stimuli applied to the face and hand under homologous conditions (both cheeks or both hands) and heterologous conditions (cheek and hand) and also under conditions of eyes open and closed.

The test, also known as the face-hand test, was first presented by M. B. Bender as a test of cerebral dysfunction (Bender, 1952). When cheek and back of the hand are touched at the same time with eyes closed, brain damaged individuals are more likely than normals to make errors in pointing to the sites of stimulation. Typically, among the brain damaged, the cheek stimulus is reported correctly but the hand stimulus is either not reported at all or falsely located. Normal children less than 6 years of age (Fink & Bender, 1952) and mental defectives with mental age below 7 years of age (Fink, Green, & Bender, 1953) show similar patterns of error.

As used at the Ittleseon Center, the child is presented with ten heterologous face-hand touches (six contralateral and four ipsilateral) and four homologous touches (two face-face and two hand-hand)—a total of 14 touches. The child is given the series of 14 stimuli with eyes open and then closed.

The 14 specific double simultaneous stimuli are administered in order as follows:

(1) Right cheek, left hand   (8) Left cheek, right hand
(2) Left cheek, right hand   (9) Right cheek, right hand
(3) Right cheek, right hand   (10) Left cheek, left hand
(4) Left cheek, left hand   (11) Right cheek, left cheek
(5) Right cheek, left hand   (12) Right hand, left hand
(6) Right hand, left hand   (13) Right cheek, left hand
(7) Right cheek, left hand   (14) Left cheek, right hand.

The score is the number of correct responses. It is possible to record number of correct responses under each of four conditions, i.e., eyes open homologous, eyes open heterologous, eyes closed homologous, and eyes closed heterologous. With these four conditions, the maximum score is 28.

For purposes of describing longitudinal change in response to multiple simultaneous tactile stimulation, we shall first employ the total score in this test which summates successful response to homologous and heterologous stimuli with eyes open and eyes closed (Tables A variable 15). The schizophrenic children as a whole demonstrated a steady and unequivocal improvement in their discrimination of double simultaneous stimulation, and significant improvement occurred among them in all of the three years. Every subdivision of the children showed similar curves of improvement, whether classified by age of admission, sex, social class position, or IQ. (Children above FIQ 109 tended to begin with maximum scores so that improvement was not shown. In this regard, these children resembled normal children.)

In the main, changes in total scores paralleled changes in the scores which describe responses to homologous and heterologous stimuli with eyes open and closed (Tables A variable 11 to A variable 15). Exceptions in individual curves and in curves of sub-divisions of the entire group reflected variations in general capacity of the children and in difficulty of the task. For example, like normals, schizophrenic children as a whole did not change in response to homologous stimuli with eyes open, since most of the children were able to achieve complete success in this test at admission. On the other hand, even in this very easy task, there were some schizophrenic children (6 out of 38, or 15.7%) who failed completely at admission. This was in contrast to the normal public school children between 6 and 11 years of age, for none of them showed such total failure in response to homologous stimuli with eyes open. The schizophrenic children who failed totally at admission in this very easy tactile discrimination task, even where permitted to use their eyes, tended to be the children with WISC Full IQs below 46, but some of them did show improved response during the three years of treatment. With the more difficult, more discriminating tasks—that is, homologous stimuli with eyes closed and heterologous stimuli with eyes open and closed—the schizophrenic children demonstrated significant improvement over the three year period of observation. Normals also improved significantly in response to heterologous stimuli with eyes open or closed. They showed no improvement with homologous stimuli with eyes open, because so many of the younger children received maximum scores with eyes closed.

Inferences regarding the schizophrenic children's attention to and utilization of visual information may be drawn from a comparison of their response to heterologous tactile stimuli in the Double Simultaneous Stimulation Test when their eyes were open with their responses when their eyes were closed. As in a previous study (Goldfarb, 1961), normals always did better, or as well, in the discrimination of heterologous stimuli with eyes open over their performance with eyes closed. In contrast, although the schizophrenic children with eyes open at age 7 also performed better than with eyes closed ($p < .05$, 2-tailed test), they included a group of children (16% of the total) who actually performed better with eyes closed. We have interpreted this finding to mean that normal children utilized more consistently the visual information to improve their discrimination of the touch stimuli in the Double Simultaneous Stimulation Test, whereas the schizophrenic children did not always make similar use of visual information to improve their discriminative responses.

Oculomotor Functioning. These tests are designed to study voluntary eye movement and postural adjustments which accompany such ocular motion. Specifically, they appraise the child's capacity to move his eyes with reference to his own body (schematic movement), a target in outer space (command), a moving target (pursuit), and a target moving toward and away from the child (convergence-divergence).

Clinical examination of schizophrenic children has confirmed that, like normal children, they do not typically suffer from paralysis of the ocular muscles. However, previous studies confirmed that they are inferior to normal children in their performance in the standardized series of tests of ocular movement. We have presumed, therefore, that in their poor performance, the schizophrenic children are manifesting the consequences of deficiencies in attention, cooperation, persistence, comprehension, and conceptual deficiencies (especially disturbances in body integrity and directional discrimination). In addition to their direct limitations in voluntary eye movement as defined in the tests, schizophrenic children show unusual difficulties in dissociating eye and head movements; that is to say, they are more inclined than normal children to move their heads before or at the same time as their eyes (Pollack & Krieger, 1958; Goldfarb, 1961). This significant immaturity in postural adjustment in the course of voluntary looking, noted in a high proportion of schizophrenic children, is very infrequently observed in normals.

In the test of schematic movement, the child is asked to move his eyes in stated directions, without moving his head and by reference to his body. ("Look to your right, to your left, to the top of your head, to your feet.") In the command test, the child is asked to look at targets in extra-personal space. (These targets are affixed to the subject's right and above eye level, another to his left and above eye level, another to his right and below eye level, another to his left and below eye level, and one directly in front of him.) In the pursuit test, the child is asked to follow a pencil as it moves from his right to his left at eye level, then from above eye level to below eye level directly in front, then from his left to his right at eye level, and finally from below eye level to above eye level directly in front. In the convergence-divergence test, the examiner moves his pencil at the child's eye level from beyond far point toward the child to beyond near point and then in reverse movement outward.

In schematic and command tests, failure to move the eyes as commanded is scored 1 and successful ocular motion is scored 2. In the convergence-divergence and pursuit tests, failure is scored 1, following in one direction is scored 2, and total success in following the stimulus away from the subject and return is scored 3. Failure in all four tests is scored 4 and total success results in a score of 10.

Postural adjustment is appraised in three of the four tests (schematic, command, and pursuit). In each of the three tests a score of 1 is given if the child clearly dissociates head and body movements from eye movements. Maximum score is 3.

In the test of voluntary eye movements, the normal public school children showed near perfection of response at all ages between 6 and 11 years of age (Tables A variable 16). Developmental improvement is thus not evident normally in this age period and it may be presumed that if there is growth in oculomotor control, such maturation in ocular coordination occurred quite early in the preschool period. The schizophrenic children as a whole did show significant improvement between admission and the third year of treatment, although the improvement in eye coordination occurred significantly during the third year of treatment. It is also noteworthy that the highest mean score, attained after three years of treatment, is below those of the normal groups at all ages.

Normal ability to dissociate eye and head movements, as represented in mean number of successful eye-head dissociations, does have a developmental character during early school age. Thus, the fine differentiation of eye and head movement—a key aspect of postural orientation—improved between 6 and 11 years of age in the normal group of children (Tables A variable 17). Indeed, by age 11, the mean score represented maximal performance by all the normal children, that is to say, every child was able voluntarily to move his eyes in all directions without prior or simultaneous movement of his head. At every age between 6 and 11, a majority successfully dissociated eye and head movements in two of the three oculomotor tasks. By age 7, a majority showed such successful differentiation of eye and head movements in all three oculomotor tests. By age 10, 90% of the children achieved such successful head-eye dissociation.

The schizophrenic children improved in their ability to dissociate eye and head movement each year between admission and third year of treatment. However, they entered treatment with extremely primitive postural responses, and remained below normal throughout treatment; their mean number of successes after three years of treatment at about 10 years was below that of the normal 6-year-olds. Evaluation of the individual curves of change confirms the maturation of differentiated eye-head response in schizophrenic children. Thus, the number of children who failed totally decreased and the number who succeeded in all three tasks increased each year of treatment. However, individual impairments in postural adjustment were striking at all ages: 72.5% of the schizophrenic children showed total inability to dissociate eye and head movements at admission; after three years of treatment, 37.5% still showed total failure in all three tasks. Similarly, although a very small percentage of the children (15.0%) achieved total success on admission and a larger proportion (42.5%) did so after three years of treatment, it is clear that, at best, less than a majority achieved such total success in all three trials. Immaturity in postural adjustment to requirements for visual orientation was very conspicuous. Consequently, although the children improved during residential treatment, they remained strongly impaired.

Whirling Tests—Arms at Side. The child's tendency to whirl his entire body on his own body axis when his head is turned by the examiner is appraised. He is required to stand with feet together, hands at his side and eyes closed. Then his head is rotated under four conditions of pressure: very slight finger tip pressure, slight pressure so that head is moved 22½°, moderate pressure so that head is moved 45°, marked pressure so that head is moved 90° (detailed scoring criteria in Figure 4.4). It will be noted that weight is also given to spontaneous whirling by the child after the passive head rotation experiments. The score is the sum of the five subscores, the highest (score 24) representing the most normal response, i.e., the weakest inclination to whirl under conditions of passive head turning.

Normal public school children did not show significant change between 6 and 11 years of age; major developmental maturation would seem to have been consummated chiefly before 6 years of age. Schizophrenic children improved consistently in group means over the three years of treatment (Tables A variable 18). Most improvement occurred in the third year of treatment. Despite improvement at each year between 7 and 10 years of age, the

Description of movement	Score
Finger Tip Pressure	
Whole body (continuous)	1
Whole body (halting)	2
Head and shoulders	3
Head only	4
No movement	5
Slight Pressure	
Whole body (continuous)	1
Whole body (halting)	2
Head and shoulders	3
Head only	4
No movement	5
Moderate Pressure	
Whole body (continuous)	1
Whole body (halting)	2
Head and shoulders	3
Head only	4
No movement	5
Marked Pressure	
No movement	1
Whole body (continuous)	1
Whole body (halting)	2
Head and shoulders	3
Head only	4
Spontaneous Whirling	
Present	1
Absent	5

FIG. 4.4 Whirling Test, arms at side.

schizophrenic children remained below the normal children at age 6 in group means.

Arms Outstretched and Parallel. This test also appraises the child's tendency to whirl when his head is turned passively. However, an additional condition is introduced—the child is required to stand with his arms extended in front and parallel. This offers an opportunity to observe changes in arm position as

Description	Score
Height Relationship of Two Arms	
Drops one arm completely.	1
Chin arm lower than occipital arm; right arm consistently higher than left arm; left arm consistently higher than right arm.	2
Heights of two arms remain the same; chin arm higher than occipital arm.	3
Convergence-Divergence of Two Arms	
Both arms diverge markedly; both arms converge markedly.	1
Both arms diverge slightly; both arms converge slightly.	2
Both arms remain approximately parallel.	3
Arm Level	
The level of the outstretched arms rises markedly; the level of the outstretched arms lowers markedly.	1
The level of the outstretched arms rises or lowers slightly.	2
The level of the outstretched arms remains unchanged.	3
Movement Response	
Spontaneous whirling	0
Whole body (continuous)	1
Whole body (halting)	2
Head and shoulders	3
Head only	4

FIG. 4.5 Whirling Test, arms outstretched and in front.

an aspect of postural and righting response of the body. In this experiment, marked pressure only is employed (the head is moved 90°). Scoring criteria are described in Figure 4.5. Here too the score is the sum of subratings; the highest score of 13 represents the most mature righting response and the lowest score is 3.

Normal children did show a significant trend to developmental improvement in response in the age range of 6 to 11. Schizophrenic children also showed maturation in their postural and righting behavior in this test (Tables A variable 19). However, after three years of improvement and at 10 years of age, the mean rating of schizophrenic children was still below that of normal 6-year-olds.

Romberg Test—Arms at Side. This test is derived from the classical neurological test of postural balance, employed in the past to differentiate cerebellar and posterior column impairments. In the first part of the test, the child's posture is appraised with eyes closed, hands at side and feet together for one minute. Detailed observations are recorded of movements of the mouth, face, body, eyes, and extremities. As noted in the following description, the ratings reflect facial expression, postural adjustments of the body, eyelid control, vocalization, and movement of the extremities. (Maximum score is 28; poorest score, 6.)

Schizophrenic children as a whole demonstrated improvement in this test between admission and third year of treatment (Tables A variable 20). The improvement trend was manifested by most subdivisions of the group and confirmed by an analysis of individual children. Most obvious individual exceptions to this trend were the children with neurological dysfunction associated with most extreme deficits in capacity (ego status 1 and IQ below 46). The latter children remained severely impaired throughout treatment.

Normal public school children evaluated in the present study showed a rise in accomplishment in the Romberg Test with arms at side. Although the schizophrenic children also demonstrated improvement, their average level of response tended to be below that of normal children of comparable age. Their highest mean score, noted after three years of treatment when they were 10 years of age, was still below the mean score for normal 6-year-olds. There was thus no overlap between schizophrenic children and normals in mean ratings in this age range.

Romberg Test—Arms outstretched and parallel. The child's posture is appraised with eyes closed, feet together and arms extended in front and parallel. Ratings for this part of the test

Description	Score
Facial Grimaces	
Many facial grimaces present.	1
Few facial grimaces present.	2
No unusual facial grimaces observed.	3
Postural Adjustment—Movement	
Cannot ever stand still.	1
Marked swaying before ½ minute.	2
Slight swaying before ½ minute.	3
Marked swaying after ½ minute.	4
Slight swaying after ½ minute.	5
Stands still—minimal movements observed.	6
Stands still throughout minute.	7
Eye Movements	
Refuses to close eyes at all and refuses mask.	1
Refuses to close eyes at all but permits mask over eyes.	2
Eyes open before ½ minute and do not close on request.	3
Eyes open after ½ minute and do not close on request.	4
Eyes open before ½ minute but close on request.	5
Eyes open after ½ minute but close on request.	6
Eyes closed throughout minute or lashes flicker.	7
Vocalizations, Mouthing, Talking	
Vocalizations present—copious and intense.	1
Vocalizations present—copious and quiet.	2
Vocalizations present—few and intense.	3
Mouthing, vocalizations present few and quiet.	4
No mouthing, vocalizations absent.	5
Movements of Hands	
Marked movements present.	1
Moderate movements present.	2
Absent	3
Movement of Feet	
Marked movements present.	1
Moderate movements present.	2
Absent	3

FIG. 4.6 Romberg, arms at side.

Description	Score
Postural Control	
Marked movement of body	1
Moderate movement of body	2
Minimal movement of body	3
No movement of body	4
Arm Movements	
Adventitious Movements	
Marked	1
Moderate	2
Minimal	3
Absent	4
Converging or Diverging	
Divergence—outstretched arms:	
a. marked	1
b. moderate	2
c. slight	3
Outstretched arms remain parallel	4
Ascending or Descending	
Outstretched arms tend to rise or fall:	
a. markedly	1
b. moderately	2
c. slightly	3
Level of outstretched arms remains unchanged	4

FIG. 4.7 Romberg Test, arms outstretched and parallel.

are shown in Figure 4.7. It will be noted that here special attention is given to placement and movements of the arms. (Maximum score is 16; minimum, 4.)

Similar trends were noted in the Romberg Test, arms extended (Tables A variable 21). Normal children tended to improve. Schizophrenic children also improved. However, even after three years of improvement and at average age 10 years, the schizophrenic children were less proficient in this test than even 6-year-old normals.

Description	Score
Failure because of following: makes no attempt to bring fingers together to touch; refuses to close eyes; covers eyes or face with hands; marked degree of overshooting or incoordination.	0
Equivocal success modified as follows: A. Fingers touch top of head; all fingers touch; two hands touch. B. Fingers touch at level of forehead or over head; fingers touch at level of waist or below; fingers touch chest only, not each other.	1 2
Success modified as follows: fingers touch while arms are extended in front with arms parallel; fingers overlap while touching; fingers approach each other but do not touch with elbows flexed and arms extended; arms flexed, elbows close to body.	3
Clear success (tips of index fingers touch like this →←) → Response may be modified as follows: Moves slowly from $\overset{\rightarrow}{\leftarrow}$ to →←; nose or chest touched simultaneously with fingers.	4

FIG. 4.8 Finger to Finger Test.

Finger to Finger Test. The child is asked to extend his arms out to his sides and then to bring the tips of his index fingers together in front with his eyes closed. This test appraises motor control and fixation. (See Figure 4.8 for descriptions and scores.)

Finger to Nose Test. The child is asked to close his eyes and then to bring the tip of the index finger to each hand to his nose from an extended arm position. This test, like the finger to finger test, is designed to demonstrate deficits in motor fixation and control. Scorings in Figure 4.9 range from 4 (for clear success) to 0 (for failure).

In general clinical observation, we have noted that school age children of all ages and with normal integrity of the nervous system respond to the Finger to Finger and Finger to Nose Tests with facility and success. This is confirmed by the systematic

Description	Score
Failure because: refuses to close eyes; covers face or eyes with hands; marked difficulty in fixation and/or inco-ordination; makes no attempt to bring finger to nose.	0
Equivocal success modified as follows: A. Touches lip, not nose. B. Uses more than one finger; uses hand, not finger; uses both hands together; refuses to use more than one hand.	1 2
Success modified as follows: touches bridge of nose; touches side of nose and/or corner of eye; squashes or pinches nose, squeezes nose with two fingers; touches nose and mouth simultaneously.	3
Clear success (index finger touches tip of nose) modified as follows: uses other than index finger; touches mouth before touching nose; overshoots slightly, then corrects.	4

FIG. 4.9 Finger to Nose Test.

study of normal public school children. Thus, in the Finger to Finger Test (Tables A variable 22), the majority of the normal children at each age between 6 and 11 achieved total success (rating 4) as shown in Table 4.3. While mean scores rose, the rises were too small and the variability large so that the various age groups were

Table 4.3. Normal Children Achieving Complete Success in Finger to Finger Test

Age (years)	Percent
6	70.0
7	70.0
8	80.0
9	90.0
10	100.0
11	90.0

Table 4.4. Normal Children Achieving Complete Success in Finger to Nose Test

Age (years)	Percent
6	60.0
7	90.0
8	90.0
9	100.0
10	100.0
11	100.0

not significantly differentiated from each other. At each of these years, too, 90% to 100% of the normal children were given the highest ratings (3 or 4), designating total or slightly modified success.

In the Finger to Nose Test (Tables A variable 23), the normal children did show significant improvement in mean ratings between 6 and 11 years. Here too, however, the majority at each age achieved clear and total success (rating 4) as shown in Table 4.4. Only one child in the entire group of public school children was given a score below 3, representing successful performance with only moderate degree of modification.

Table 4.5. Schizophrenic Children Achieving Equivocal Success (Score 2) to Total Failure (Score 0) in Finger to Finger Test

Year of treatment	Percent
Admission	40.0
First year	30.0
Second year	40.0
Third year	35.0

Table 4.6. Schizophrenic Children
Achieving Equivocal Success to Total
Failure in Finger to Nose Test

Year of treatment	Percent
Admission	37.5
First year	32.5
Second year	22.5
Third year	7.5

The schizophrenic children showed significant improvement in both Finger to Finger and Finger to Nose Tests between admission and third year of treatment. However, in these tests, in contrast to normal children, instances of total failure (rating 0) were present at all years. For example, at admission 25.0% of the schizophrenic children failed totally in the Finger to Finger Test and 22.5% in the Finger to Nose Test. After three years of treatment the percent of children who failed totally had dropped perceptibly to 7.5% in the Finger to Finger Test and 5.0% in the Finger to Nose Test. A sizeable proportion of schizophrenic children at each year of treatment also showed equivocal success to total failure (Tables 4.5 and 4.6), especially in the Finger to Finger Test (rating 0 to 2).

In summary, the schizophrenic children tended to show no change from low performance in regard to muscle tone during the period of treatment. In all other neurological tests and ratings, however, they demonstrated a significant trend to developmental improvement between admission and third year of treatment. It will be recalled that the children were approximately 7 years of age at admission and 10 years of age after three years of therapeutic management. There are obvious methodologic difficulties in comparing the developmental data of our schizophrenic children with data derived from normal public school children. Most importantly, the former constituted true longitudinal information in that the same schizophrenic children were seen each year, while the latter was based on cross sectional data derived from different and unrelated samples of children each year between 6 and 11. Nevertheless, contrasts between schizophrenic and normal children were impressively large. Unlike normal children, in all the tests and observations a high proportion of the schizophrenic children as individuals showed the most extreme aberrations in functioning. In addition, the mean ratings each year between admission and third year of treatment were below that of the normal children of comparable ages. Indeed, their highest mean ratings—usually after the third year of treatment, when they were 10 years of age—were generally below those for normal 6- and 7-year-olds.

Receptor Behavior

Between the stimulation of the sensory end organ and the attainment of knowledge about oneself in the total situation through cognitive operations (which we term perception and conceptualization), there is a global organismic response embodying reactions such as attention, alertness, self orientation, and self monitoring. When a visual stimulus or scene presents itself, does the child look at it actively? When we speak to a given child, does he listen? In these sensory input experiences, does he give evidence of heightened sensitivity and hyperarousal, or the polar extreme of bland disregard of sensory stimulation (even where the stimulation is abnormally excessive in intensity)? And when he acts, does he monitor his actions on the basis of feedback stimuli set off by the action?

Previous studies of schizophrenic children have demonstrated abnormal patterns of receptor response (Goldfarb & Braunstein, 1958; Goldfarb, 1961). Since sensory thresholds in schizophrenic children have been demonstrated to be normal, their receptor aberrations have been attributed to disturbances in the active integration of sensory impressions and in qualitative organization of receptor behavior. Thus, naturalistic observation has demonstrated extreme hypersensitivity or the antipodal reaction of hyposensitivity. The latter has been more commonly linked, perhaps, to the clinical syndrome of childhood schizophrenia and autism. In the developmental history of schizophrenic children, avoidance or denial of sensory experience has seemed, in the main, to follow and, presumably, to be in protective response to a primary state of uncomfortable hypersensitivity. We have also proposed a related alteration of receptor preferences, in which the distance receptors (vision and audition) are particularly avoided; and the child is more disposed to orient himself by use of the receptors of nearby stimuli (e.g., touch and smell).

Two tests have been employed to observe the child's emotional and behavioral organization and his mode of orienting himself in the course of experiencing sensory input. One test is the auditory startle experiment. Here we evaluate the child's level of auditory awareness and comfort. The other test is the delayed auditory feedback experiment. In this experiment the observer evaluates the extent to which alteration (i.e., delay) in auditory feedback affects the child's speech behavior and consciousness of self.

Auditory Startle

In this experiment, the child hears, through earphones, a sudden, loud (100 decibel), pure, 3000-cycle tone. His spontaneous behavior and verbalizations are observed and categorized (Figure 4.10).

Mean group scores of schizophrenic children did not change in the three years of observation (Tables A variable 24). Since a large number of schizophrenic children have been noted to fall at both extremes, means are not useful as a measure of improvement. Rather, we need to refer to individual changes in categories of response to startle.

Our primary interest is in the proportion of schizophrenic children who showed the most extreme deviations in response— particularly those rated 1 and 6. These most extreme reactions are not seen at any age among any of our normal children, and have undoubted clinical import. On admission, six of the schizophrenic children (17.1%) showed total disregard of the startle stimulus (rating 6)—a response we may term "hyposensitivity"; and one child (2.9%) showed such severe reaction of distress as to be rated

Level of startle	Rating
Awareness and severe discomfort—spontaneous expressions of discomfort such as jumping, yelling, crying, pulling off earphones.	1
Awareness and moderate discomfort—moderate physical signs such as hunching, wincing, blinking, slight jump, squinting, says "It feels funny." or "Sound tickles ears."	2
Awareness and minimal discomfort—slight physical sign such as slight wincing or slight blinking.	3
Manifest awareness without reference to pain—awareness with reference to loudness not pain, signals plus smiles, refers to loudness but no discomfort, no sign of physical tension.	4
Slight or apparent awareness—slight smile, subject looks up at examiner, signals, indirect reference to awareness (such as: "It didn't hurt.")	5
No evidence of awareness—no reaction.	6

FIG. 4.10 Auditory Startle Rating Scale.

1. The latter response is akin to clinical descriptions of "hypersensitivity." A total of seven children, therefore, showed either ratings of 1 or 6. After the third year of treatment, there was no significant change in number with the most extreme ratings, which refer to most dramatic forms of hyper- and hypo-sensitivity. Thus five of the children (14.3%) still showed reactions rated at either 1 or 6 and were still very extremely aberrant.

Delayed Auditory Feedback

The delayed auditory feedback experiment has been employed to evaluate the role of self monitoring in the execution of a skilled act—for example, speech, and in the attainment of clear, unambiguous, consistent self awareness. The smooth, graceful, and harmonious execution of a complex, sequential act (such as speech) requires continuous feedback of regulating and orienting cues stimulated in the child at each phase in the sequence of responses which constitute the active process of speech. Such self monitoring cues are also essential to make one aware of oneself as the responsible agent of intended action. Awareness of the self in action is fundamental to the enhancement and maintenance of the subjective experience of psychological integrity in time and space. As noted, previous studies employing delayed auditory feedback have sharply differentiated schizophrenic and normal children (Goldfarb & Braunstein, 1958; Goldfarb, 1961). Thus, quite unlike normal children, the natural speech and voices of schizophrenic children often were unaffected by artificial delay in feedback of the voice. This finding was interpreted to mean that schizophrenic children were less disposed than normal children to utilize auditory feedback to monitor their speech. In addition, the schizophrenic children showed dramatic confusion in self recognition and associated outbursts of panic. We interpreted this finding to be a manifestation of the schizophrenic child's vulnerability in regard to personal identity and his inadequacies in the utilization of proprioceptive experiences to achieve firm self awareness.

The delayed auditory feedback experiment was administered to the children immediately after evaluation of speech under normal conditions by the same examiner. The subject's voice was returned to him through earphones after a delay of .16 second. Speech was elicited under a variety of standardized conditions—such as reading, singing, and story telling—and tape recorded under normal and then under delayed feedback conditions. Behavior under normal conditions and behavioral changes under delayed feedback conditions were noted. On completion of the test, a semistructured interview to evaluate changes in the child's orientation and emotional comfort under conditions of altered feedback was given to the child. Each child was then rated on experimentally produced differences in speech, language, and in self identity (confusion).

Differences in speech and language resulting from delayed feedback were scored as follows:

(1) No difference   (3) Considerable impairment
(2) Slight impairment   (4) Extreme impairment

In the earlier experimental investigations of the impact of delayed auditory feedback on behavior of schizophrenic children, a single rating of global shifts in voice, speech, and language was employed. In the present longitudinal investigation, alterations in each of the various facets of voice and speech under assay were rated separately and the ratings of change totalled to give a single summed score of change in voice and speech. Similarly, after delay, differences in ratings pertaining to language—as differentiated from voice and speech—were rated separately and summed to give a score of shifts in language. Also, we have considered experimental differences in voice and speech separately from those in language since it has been our general observation in the clinical application of the test to normal children that the delayed auditory feedback experiment caused interference with the sensory monitoring which was of particular relevance in the execution of the mechanical aspects of voice and speech. As will be seen in the discussion of voice and speech to follow, we are referring to the phonative elements of voice and speech (volume, pitch level, voice quality), to the rhythmic elements of voice and speech (rate, phrasing, fluency, stress, intonation), and to articulation. In contrast, language ratings stress the symbolic aspects of language—i.e., the clear, appropriate expression and comprehension of meaning and mood, and the appropriateness of manner and attitude. Language so defined is very much under the primary regulatory influence of the child's general intellectual capacity, his emotional organization, and his social relationships. We have thus proposed that language to a degree is vulnerable to interference with auditory feedback in normals. However, we have further proposed that where the child is intact in his mental capacities and apt in his emotional and social responses, language is less likely than speech and voice to be disrupted by delay in auditory feedback. Introspective reports of normals suggest that the subject with normal adaptive capacities recognizes the disruption of his voice and speech and yet tolerates his powerlessness to correct his errors. In addition, after slight hesitation, he easily mobilizes himself to compensate for the sensory interference and thereby to maintain the clarity and adequacy of his emotional and intellectual responses.

The delayed feedback experiment has also been used to test the impact of interference in self monitoring on self awareness and self recognition. Normal children are ordinarily not confused in self identity by the delay in auditory return (Goldfarb, 1961). Even when their speech is seriously disrupted, they have no difficulty in recognizing their own voices. In contrast, schizophrenic children are more frequently confused and are less inclined to recognize their own voices under conditions of altered feedback.

To evaluate the child's level of self recognition when the delayed auditory feedback condition was introduced, judgments focused on increase in level of confusion after auditory delay. The effect was first evaluated in terms of direction. Did the child become less confused or remain the same? Since improvement in level of self awareness under conditions of delayed feedback never occurred in any child in the longitudinal study, direction of change need not be considered in our longitudinal analysis. In the discussion to follow, disruption and impairment of self recognition and enhancement of confusion when auditory feedback is delayed are scored as follows:

(1) No difference.

(2) Slight impairment in self recognition and increase in confusion.

(3) Considerable impairment in self recognition and increase in confusion.

(4) Extreme impairment in self recognition and increase in confusion.

Data describing the normal children, including group averages each year between 6 and 11 and percentage distributions, are to be found in Tables A variable 25, A variable 26, and A variable 27. Within the age range 7 to 10 years, there were no significant age differences in amount of change (impairment) noted in voice and speech, in language, and in self recognition.

The data may be further interpreted as follows. In voice and speech there was a consistent tendency among normals at each age to show a mild to moderate degree of impairment illustrated in such phenomena as increase in volume, rise in pitch, sound repetition, and a broad variety of disruptions in rate, phrasing, fluency, stress, intonation, and articulation. Only two children attained summed scores between 9 and 11, signifying no impairment or vitually none. On the other hand, summed scores of 27 or above, reflecting considerable impairment or worse, did not ever occur. In others words, the normal children almost always evidenced a degree of disorder in speech and voice when the auditory delay was introduced; but at no time did an extreme state of total lack of control in voice and speech occur. Normals, as noted above, did not shift from year to year in mean language change scores on exposure to delayed feedback, as individuals generally evidenced no change or only slight change in language capacity. Sixty-two of the 65 normal children showed language scores representing no or slight impairment (scores of 6 or less). Finally, normal children tended to show mean scores signifying no impairment in self recognition to only slight impairment under the conditions of delayed auditory feedback. These findings were consistent from year to year. Indeed, the great bulk of the individual children (59 out of 65) showed no experimental increase in confusion in the delayed auditory feedback experiment. In summary, at each age, normal children as individuals almost always showed some degree of impairment in speech and voice as a result of delay in auditory feedback (but the impairment was never the most extreme), maintained their language and communicative aptitude, and with infrequent exception, did not become confused.

In planning the evaluation of longitudinal changes in the complex data derived from the delayed auditory feedback experiment with schizophrenic children, we proposed a set of criteria for changes to be designated as improvement. We have not attempted, in our definitions, to distinguish age determined developmental growth from improvement in clinical status in a precise and exact fashion. On the other hand, therapeutic experience and the normal data we do possess offer gross guides in considerations of such differentiation of developmental change and clinical-therapeutic improvement. Following is a set of propositions regarding longitudinal changes indicative of improvement of growth in the schizophrenic children:

(1) Proficient execution of the speech act requires active self monitoring, so that the individual listens to his voice and speech even as he is talking. In this instance, he monitors himself by responding to an external stimulus, albeit his own voice. In normal children, the interference with self monitoring by delaying the feedback of the individual's own voice almost always causes mild to moderate deterioration in voice and speech. In the case of schizophrenic children, the absence of such deterioration of voice and speech under conditions of delayed feedback has been interpreted as evidence of diminished use of auditory feedback as a self-monitoring tool. Longitudinal improvment in self-monitoring of schizophrenic children for purposes of speech, therefore, will be so interpreted if the speech becomes more impaired under conditions of delayed auditory feedback as the child grows older. (Each year, since higher ratings show more impairment in speech, mean ratings of amount of impairment in speech will rise, if the schizophrenic children manifest increased self-monitoring over time.)

(2) Empirical experience with the delayed auditory feedback experiment in clinical practice as well as systematic study has indicated that language and communication more broadly are less affected in normal children than voice and speech by delay in auditory feedback. In the case of language and communication, the child is presumed to monitor himself largely by the inner stimuli of thought, so that external auditory interference is less of

a hindrance. Both under normal conditions of communication and under the special conditions of delayed feedback, cardinal factors normally influencing any child's language level are primarily the general intactness of his inner capacities for symbolization and thought, his level of relational and interactional response, and the level of appropriateness of his affective response. Improvements over time in intellectual, social, and emotional response, therefore, are likely to reflect themselves in improved language response under conditions of delayed feedback as well as under normal conditions of communication. Such longitudinal improvements in relational and affective response will be manifested in the delayed auditory feedback experiment in a tendency to diminished impairment of language under the standard conditions of the experiment over the three year period of observations. (Each year, since lower ratings show less impairment of language, mean ratings of amount of impairment in language in the delayed feedback will fall, if the schizophrenic children improve in symbolic thought, relationship, and affective responses.)

(3) Longitudinal shifts in stability of self awareness between admission and third year of treatment will be represented in changes over time in level of self recognition (or confusion) under the standardized conditions of auditory feedback. Longitudinal improvement will be shown by lower mean scores for experimentally induced confusion during the test, since the lowest (rating 1) represents no increase in confusion while the highest (rating 4) represents extreme impairment in self recognition and marked increase in confusion.

In summary, we have proposed that improvement between admission and third year of treatment would be demonstrated in three kinds of longitudinal consequences in the delayed auditory feedback experiment:

(1) Improvement in auditory self monitoring will be manifested in increased experimental impairment of *Voice and Speech*. (Mean annual ratings of impairment induced by delay will rise.)

(2) Improvement in cognition, affective organization, and relational behavior will be manifested in diminished disruption of *Language and Communication* under the standardized conditions of the experiment and in spite of feedback interference. (Mean annual ratings of impairment induced by delay will fall.)

(3) Improvement in self awareness in the sense of increased stability, intactness, and predictability will be manifested in diminishing level of confusion induced by the delay in auditory feedback. (Mean annual ratings of extent of experimentally induced confusion will fall.)

We consider first the longitudinal data pertaining to extent of impairment in voice and speech provoked by delayed auditory feedback (Tables A variable 25). The schizophrenic children showed no change between admission and third year of treatment in average level of impairment in voice and speech after auditory delay. We inferred, therefore, that the children did not improve in auditory self monitoring of speech between admission and third year of treatment. We were initially surprised to note, however, that mean ratings of the total group of schizophrenic children in extent of impairment of speech were comparable to mean ratings of normal children at ages between 7 and 10 years, a finding which would at first seem to raise doubts about previous conclusions regarding auditory monitoring of speech by normal and schizophrenic children. On the other hand, the previous conclusions are more strongly sustained when normal children are compared with schizophrenic children with normal levels of IQ (90 or over). As will also be seen, these previous conclusions are supported by further study of the individual children. Such examination of the individual children supplied new and interesting information as well—information not anticipated in the original hypothesis.

In the first place, total absence of impairment in voice and speech (rating 1) among normals on delayed auditory feedback was indeed a rarity, as noted, while instances of such total auditory inattention were found among the schizophrenics at each age between admission and third year. In addition, we reviewed available longitudinal data pertaining to 4 of the 40 schizophrenic children who were not included in the present group summations (always because one or two of the annual ratings could not be obtained from the children). All four, however, had shown no difference in voice and speech ratings under delayed auditory feedback when such ratings had been obtained, so that the mean scores for the schizophrenic children were unduly high and the distribution tables did not sufficiently reflect the high percentage of schizophrenic children who were indeed inattentive to auditory delay. Exclusion of these four children undoubtedly reduced the true difference between normal and schizophrenic children in degree of impairment of voice and speech.

Finally, the present experiment brought to light a phenomenon among schizophrenic children to which we had not been sufficiently alert. At each age, a higher percentage of schizophrenic than normal children showed scores of 24 or higher, indicative of very extreme impairment in voice and speech when exposed to delayed auditory feedback. The most dramatic qualitative examples of extreme impairment in voice and speech among schizophrenic children were never duplicated among the normals. Presence of the two extremes in speech impairment among the schizophrenic children and their relative absence in the normals were hidden in the mean scores. The auditory feedback data remind us of the comparable findings in the auditory startle experiment. As in auditory startle, there were individual instances of children who shifted from the extreme of total auditory inattention (hyposensitivity) to the most extreme disruption and disintegration of voice and speech (hypersensitivity) in the delayed auditory feedback experiment.

Between admission and third year of treatment, the schizophrenic children showed diminishing impairment in language behavior under conditions of delayed auditory feedback (Tables A variable 26)—the most significant improvement occurring during the second year of treatment. As previously noted, this shift in communicative language would suggest that the schizophrenic children improved in thought, emotional organization, and relational behavior in the three year interval of observation. Nevertheless, it should be noted that the median score for the schizophrenic children after three years of treatment showed more language impairment than that of any child in the normal 10-year group, indicating that internal monitoring of language is also relatively impaired at this time. This contrast between the longitudinal curves of speech and language impairment on delay in auditory feedback in schizophrenic children coincided with the qualitative clinical observation that the therapeutic program of the Center has had more impact on self regulative influence of cognitive, social, and emotional behavior as represented in language than on their speech where these factors are less crucial.[8]

Turning now to data pertaining to self awareness, we have proposed that self awareness is a dynamic process which requires a constant flood of inner proprioceptive and outer stimuli. These stimuli link the individual to his own actions and to the world about him. This association between subjective experience of self identity and perceptual input may be demonstrated by shifts in the child's self awareness as a consequence of alterations in sensory information. Thus, for example, confusion in regard to self recognition has been noted in schizophrenic children when their voices are played back to them on tape. Their confused reactions with regard to self recognition are increased when feedback of their voices is delayed (Goldfarb, 1961). Stability of self awareness may thus be gauged by the child's responses on delay in auditory feedback of his voice.

The delayed auditory feedback experiment supported the observation that the schizophrenic children improved in stability of self awareness (Tables A variable 27). Thus the amount of confusion engendered by the delay in auditory feedback diminished significantly between admission and third year of treatment. While

---

[8] Recently we have placed greater emphasis on the enhancement of self monitoring as a key aspect of remedial training of speech itself.

definite improvement was apparent after three years, improvements in smaller, annual intervals were not demonstrable. This group trend is consistent with trends noted in individual schizophrenic children. For example, on admission, nine of the children (25.0%) manifested considerable increase in impairment of self recognition (rating 3) on delay in auditory feedback, while none showed such gross and extreme increase in confusion after three years of treatment. This trend is also reflected in the increased proportion each year of children who showed no rise in confusion at all (rating 1) during the delayed feedback experiment. Thus on admission, 15 (41.7%) showed no evidence of confusion during the experiment on admission, while a larger number—i.e., 25 (69.4%)—were so classified after three years of treatment. It is noteworthy that at age 10, not a single one of the normal children showed any loss in self recognition on delayed auditory feedback.

Study of Mental Functions

In our design for the study of psychological functions, we have found it practical to refer to overlapping categories of response termed sensation, perception, conceptualization, and psychomotor ability. It has been feasible to find and elaborate suitable operational procedures to evaluate each of these purposeful functions. While functions such as sensation, perception, and conceptualization are correlated, it has been productive to differentiate sensation, or the elemental experience of sensory detection, accompanying the discrete stimulation of a sense organ, from conceptualization, or the process of abstracting, generalizing, and categorizing. Thus, a cross sectional comparison (Goldfarb, 1961) has shown that schizophrenic and normal children did not differ in sensory thresholds for vision, audition, and touch. Nor did they differ in color vision. However, the normal children were significantly superior to the schizophrenic children in perceptual tests which assayed a variety of perceptual responses. (The perceptual tests included a test of tactile discrimination, a test of finger location on the basis of touch, an embedded figure test requiring the separation of a visual figure from its background, and the perception of visual form on the basis of closure of discontinuous stimuli.) Schizophrenic children were also inferior to normal in conceptual functions which required the cognitive responses of classification, categorization, orientation, and verbal communication.

Differentiation was thus made between mere sensory stimulation and attainment of meaning and information. Our previous studies showed that the schizophrenic children possessed the peripheral sensory equipment but they had difficulty in categorizing, in experiencing things—as against discrete and unpatterned lights, sounds, and touches—and in giving patterned form to both inner and outer experience. In addition, however, the schizophrenic children were inferior to normal children in global responses to stimulation embodied in descriptive terms such as attention, persistence, and effort. Finally, they were less inclined than normal children to search actively for stimulation necessary in orientative effort and attainment of meaning. They avoided specific modalities of experience, especially looking and listening. Of special significance, they did not employ to a normal degree the monitoring advantages of feedback to assist in the smooth, harmonious execution of adaptive acts. As noted in regard to speech, for instance, the delayed auditory feedback experiment tended to confirm that, unlike the normal child, the schizophrenic often did not sufficiently utilize the return of air conducted sound to monitor his own speech.

Most crucially, impairments of the schizophrenic children in attention, orientation, and the active use of monitoring stimuli augmented deficiencies in self awareness. These deficiencies in self awareness were quantitatively so extreme as to be qualitatively unique to the schizophrenic children. That is to say, while very common in the schizophrenic group, they were never found among the normal children. Thus, for example, as previously noted, schizophrenic children at all ages were more inclined than normals to become confused and not to recognize their voices with slight alteration in auditory feedback. The children lacked those monitoring cues and experiences which they needed to anticipate, to plan, to orient themselves, and to reinforce effective discrimination and clear, unambiguous self perception.

To sum up, it was presumed that the perceptual failures of the schizophrenic child are linked with his deficiencies in active patterning of sensory signals from internal proprioceptive sources and from sources outside his body. At a higher cognitive level, he demonstrates conceptual deficiencies embodying impairments in generalization and categorical response. The child does not possess an unambiguous representation of himself and others. He has great difficulty in orienting himself in space and time; and he cannot comprehend the roles (for example, gender and age) others expect him to play. His world emerges as meaningless, strange, and unpredictable. It is likely, too, that the restrictions in conceptual response are determined by volitional factors as well as primary cognitive failures.

In view of the previous findings that schizophrenic children manifest normal sense organ response when measured by sensory threshold, sensation was not studied longitudinally. Rather, our attention focused on changing capacity to organize, categorize, and utilize adaptively the data of experience. Therefore, the tests and observations to be presented next include assays of perceptual, conceptual, and psychomotor response. They will be grouped in descriptive categories based on key mental operations elicited by the specific task or test at hand. Therefore, we shall refer to tests of perception (which assay the achievement of pattern or form on stimulation of a receptor system), tests of conceptualization (which require the more complex cognitive and symbolic responses of abstraction, generalization, and classification), and psychomotor tests (which feature motor response). Formal tests of general intelligence and evaluations of speech and communication are properly included among the conceptual procedures. As noted previously, the child responds as an organic unit in each test, and labelling a test as conceptual does not imply that perceptual or psychomotor elements do not contribute to the test response. Some tests, such as the Bender Gestalt, elicit behaviors that combine perceptual, conceptual, and motor elements. In actual empirical fact as well, many of the tests of the present battery were highly intercorrelated and the underlying test factors confirm the broad overlapping of perceptual, conceptual, and psychomotor tests (Goldfarb, 1961).

Perceptual Tests

Gottschaldt Embedded Figures Test. The Gottschaldt Embedded Figures Test requires the child to organize a visual configuration by separating a figure from the background in which it is embedded. Fifteen figures were employed and the test was administered with modifications of Thurstone's instructions (Thurstone, 1949). The score was the number of correct responses (maximum score, 15).

The Gottschaldt Test, based on the discrimination of embedded figures, assays a cardinal human function. It probes the child's capacity to select the important from the unimportant in the surrounding world. This capacity is probably linked to the child's attainment of self as differentiated from the non-self. In more exact operational terms, Witkin and his associates (1962) have demonstrated the correlation between ability to differentiate figure from ground on the Gottschaldt Test and degree of independence of the individual from the surrounding field for the orientation of the body in space. In the Gottschaldt Test (as seen in Tables A varibale 28), the schizophrenic children improved significantly each year between admission and third year of treatment (and thus over the three years). Although there was significant improvement each year, the performance level of the schizophrenic children, after three years of treatment at an average age of 10 years, was below the average of the normal children of comparable age. Thirty-five percent of the schizophrenic children showed the very lowest scores (0 to 1) even after three years of treatment, whereas such low scores were seen very rarely (about 2%) above age 7 among our normals.

Street's Gestalt Completion Test. Street's Gestalt Completion Test requires the perception of visual form on the basis of closure of discontinuous line forms. Fifteen figures were used and the score was the number of correct responses (maximum score, 15).

Street's original data, based on application of the Gestalt Completion Test, demonstrated no sex differences. Nor did these data show significant differences among third grade, sixth grade, and high school children (Street, 1931). The schizophrenic children began at a level below that of the six-year-olds in our normal group and improved in a significant fashion between admission and third year of treatment. They also improved each year for three years (Tables A variable 29).

Bender Gestalt Test. The final test of perception, the Bender Gestalt Test, required that the child copy nine geometric forms of increasing complexity. The test was administered and scored in accordance with Bender's instructions and norms (Bender, 1938).

The schizophrenic children improved significantly in their mean scores between admission and third year of treatment, especially in the first two years of observation (Tables A variable 30). Most accelerated improvement occurred during the first year of treatment, with lesser improvement in the second and virtually no change in the third year. At admission and after each year of treatment, mean scores were below the lower range of normal scores provided by Bender. One may interpret that there was continuing and serious impairment in average visuo-motor integration, in spite of the evident developmental improvement in functional level over the three year period of observation.

Conceptual Tests

Longitudinal changes in conceptual behavior were investigated by means of test procedures selected to explore different aspects of categorization and abstraction, including categorization by form and color (Weigl Color Form Sorting Test) and orientation to time, place, and person (Orientation Test).

Weigl Color Form Sorting Test. The Weigl Color Form Sorting Test requires the child to classify objects by form and color. A modification of the Zubin-Thompson directions was employed (Zubin & Thompson, 1941). The score was the sum of credits for number of categories correctly sorted and for number of correctly verbalized generalizations to explain the basis for the sorting (maximum score, 8). The schizophrenic children as a whole (and most of the subgroups) improved significantly in conceptual response between admission and third year of treatment (Tables A variable 31)—the most significant improvement occurring in the second year of treatment. It is also true that the children began at an extremely inferior level of conceptual response and, although they improved regularly, did not attain normal levels at any point in treatment. For example, by third year of treatment, at about 10 years of age, their mean Weigl Test rating was below that of the normal 6-year-old children.

Orientation Test. The Orientation Test consists of 20 questions appraising the child's orientation to time, place, and person. (For example: "How old are you?" "What time is it now?") Some responses to questions were credited for each of several points in the response. For instance, in "When is your birthday?" month, day, and year were each credited one point if correct. Maximum credit was 29. As seen in Tables A variable 32, the schizophrenic children were very retarded, relative to normal children, at admission to treatment (7 years of age). They then improved in orientation each year in a significant fashion for three years. All subgroups improved significantly. At no point in treatment, however, did they attain normal levels for their age; and after three years of treatment, at 10 years of age, they still had not surpassed the normal 7-year-old group in mean performance.

Motor Tests

Lincoln-Oseretsky Motor Development Scales. For purposes of reducing administration time, this scale was abbreviated by administering only 15 of the test items. The latter were scored with the directions of the Lincoln-Oseretsky standardization (Sloan, 1955). The specific tests administered included:

Item	Description
1	Walking backwards.

3	Standing on one foot.
4	Touching nose.
5	Touching fingertips.
6	Tapping rhythmically with feet and fingers.
9	Standing heel to toe.
10	Closing and opening the hands alternately.
12	Catching a ball.
13	Making a ball.
14	Winding a thread.
16	Describing circles in the air.
18	Coins and matchsticks.
22	Throwing a ball.
25	Cutting a circle.
27	Tracing mazes.

It is apparent that the test items covered a very broad range of motor tasks. Because of the abbreviated modification of the test, existing standardization norms are not applicable to our data. However, we had administered the abbreviated form of the test to 13 normal public school schildren at median age 7 years and 13 children at median age 10 years. These data provide normal information to contrast with the Oseretsky test findings of the schizophrenic children when they were admitted to treatment at about 7 years of age and three years later when they were approximately 10 years of age. The normal data are summarized in Table 4.7.

As recorded in Tables A variable 33, the schizophrenic children improved in coordination between admission to treatment and last observation three years later. They also showed improvement

Table 4.7. Lincoln-Oseretsky Test Data for Public School Children

Group	Mean score	Standard deviation
6 to 8 year olds	33.7	8.6
9 to 11 year olds	50.3	6.9

during each of the three years of treatment. However, when they began treatment at 7 years, they were far below the normal 6-to-8-year-olds in motor coordination. Three years later, despite steady improvement and growth, they were still strikingly inferior to the normals in motor ability. For example, their motor performance at about age 10 was below that of the normal 6-to-8-year-old group.

Heath Railwalking Test. The Heath Railwalking Test (Tables A variable 34) has been used extensively as a test of locomotor balance (Heath, 1942). The schizophrenic children showed steady and significant improvement between admission and third year of treatment. They also demonstrated significant improvement in balance during each year of observation. However, they showed striking inferiority, at each age observed, relative to the normal children of equal age. After three years of treatment at about 10 years of age, the mean level of performance of the schizophrenic children was approximately equal to that of the 6-year-old boys and girls in Heath's standardization group.

Dynamometer. In the Dynamometer Test of strength of grip (Tables A variable 35) the children were given three trials with each hand, and the final score was the highest record for either hand. The schizophrenic children showed significant improvement in strength of grip between admission and third year of treatment. All subcategories improved. They also demonstrated significant improvement in strength during each of the three years of observation. Relative to our public school group, however, the schizophrenic children were weaker at each age than normal children of comparable age.

Wechsler Intelligence Scale for Children

The present report of changes in the children's IQ in the Wechsler Intelligence Scale for Children over a three year period while they were in residential treatment replicates a previous study (Goldfarb, Goldfarb & Pollack, 1969). The present investigation was based on testing of a larger number of children and the analysis now refers to Verbal IQ (VIQ) and Performance IQ (PIQ) as well as Full IQ (FIQ) (Tables A variable 36, A variable 37, and A variable 38). The schizophrenic children as a whole showed a significant change in mean FIQ between admission and third year of treatment. The gain in mean FIQ was 7.9 points over the three years. Most of the subgroups improved similarly. Significant improvements occurred in each of the first two years of treatment. The highest increment in mean FIQ occurred in the first year.

Individual children showed a wide range between lowest and highest of their four FIQ scores—69.0% showed fluctuation of of 10 FIQ points or more, 10.0% showed changes of 20 FIQ points or more, and 5.0% showed changes of 30 FIQ points or more. The children at most deficient levels (FIQs of less than 70), who constituted 40.0% of the children at admission, tended not to change. Most of these children, therefore, remained at deficient levels; 35.0% of all the children after their third year still had IQs below 70. At higher levels, there was a tendency to drift to even higher levels. Thus, while 22.5% of the children at admission had FIQs between 70-79, only 7.5% of the group fell at this range after three years of treatment. The change was chiefly accounted for by the movement upward into the 80–89 range, so while 12.5% of the children had FIQs between 80–89 at admission, 25.0% of the children fell at this range after three years of treatment. In a similar fashion, while 10.0% of the children showed FIQs of 110 or over at admission, 27.5% of the group were in this range after three years of treatment.

These changes in FIQ reflected comparable changes in VIQ and in PIQ. Thus, the children improved significantly in VIQ between admission and third year of treatment (8.7 VIQ points). Most significant improvement occurred in first and second years. Sixty-five percent of the children showed variations of 10 VIQ points or more between lowest and highest scores, 25.0% showed individual ranges of 20 VIQ points or more, and 10.0% showed ranges of 30 VIQ points or more. One child actually varied as much as 61 VIQ points.

The children also improved significantly in PIQ between admission and third year of treatment. The three year gain for the whole group was 5.5 PIQ points, somewhat less than that noted in VIQ over the same period. Major improvements occurred in the first year. Variations of more than 10 PIQ points were shown by 67.5% of the children and variations of 20 PIQ points or more were shown by 32.5%. Extremely high variations of 30 PIQ points or more were not demonstrated.

Rutter (1965) has proposed that psychotic children demonstrate segmental deficiency in verbal response relative to their non-verbal performance. His data support this proposition. However, in the present investigation there was no significant difference between VIQ and PIQ at admission to treatment; in addition, the children did not show less improvement in VIQ than PIQ. While individual examples of aphasoid-like disturbances in language behavior have been noted in our own sampling, segmental areas of verbal impairment have not been universal or even typical. We must conclude that differences in sampling may account for the differences between present findings and those of other investigators such as Rutter.

Communication

The diagnosis and treatment of communication and its aberrations in childhood schizophrenia are of crucial importance inasmuch as one or another disability in communication is found in every schizophrenic child. Further, the communication disorders, the detailed processes involved in the disorders, and their historical course explain a large portion of the phenomenology and development of childhood schizophrenia. Certainly, changes in a schizophrenic child's more general clinical course are always paralleled by relevant changes in communication. For example, when a schizophrenic child improves, he, himself, becomes more comprehensible and he shows more understanding of the speech of others. When he declines in clinical status, his speech and language also deteriorate.

Previous studies of speech at the Ittleson Center have demonstrated clear differences between schizophrenic and normal children in speech and language. Schizophrenic children fail to achieve culturally expected patterns of voice and speech including phonation, rhythm, articulation, and gesture (Goldfarb, Braunstein, & Lorge, 1956; Goldfarb, 1961). The general impact is to impair their communication of meaning and mood in a massive fashion and thus, consequently, to increase their social isolation from children and adults.

The Ittleson Center has developed special methods for the appraisal of speech of early school age children. Such appraisals are made by speech pathologists who have extensive experience with the speech of normal and aberrant children. The speech pathologist records the child's speech responses on tape in free and directed speech activities (e.g., reading, singing, story telling.) She then evaluates speech and language with reference to the presumptive normal in phonation (volume, pitch, voice quality), rhythm (rate, phrasing, fluency, stress, intonation) articulation, communication of meaning and mood, and gestural expression. Nine facets of voice and speech and three facets of language are rated between 1 for very poor and 5 for excellent. The scores are then summed to give a voice and speech score (minimum 9, maximum 45) and a language score (minimum 3, maximum 15). In a previous study, the scores have been demonstrated to be highly reliable. Two observers of 20 children correlated .9 or above in summed scores for phonation, rhythm, articulation, and symbolization. In the present longitudinal analysis the two scores (voice and speech, and language) are considered separately, inasmuch as we have recently observed massive defects in level of clarity of communication of some schizophrenic children who, on casual observation, seem to have mastered reasonably the simple elements of voice and speech. In other words the children may manifest pronounced impediments to the communication of mood and meaning; but the delineation of such impediments requires observational techniques other than those employed in the appraisal of voice and speech. Disturbances in mutuality of verbal attention and in clarity of communication are demonstrated even by the brightest and most accomplished of schizophrenic children and require special, highly refined techniques of analysis only recently developed.

Voice and Speech. The schizophrenic children as a whole demonstrated significant improvement in mean voice and speech ratings between admission to the treatment residence and third year (Tables A variable 39). Significant improvement occurred in the first year and, as previously noted, was also clearly evident after three years of treatment.

Language. As a group, too, the children improved in language mean ratings which were based on summed ratings for communication of meaning and mood and for gestural behavior. In contrast to the significant changes noted in voice and speech in the first year, significant improvement in language occurred a year later, in the second year of treatment (Tables A variable 40). Again, however, improvement in language level between admission and third year was unequivocal.

Although the schizophrenic children improved in speech and voice and in communication of meaning and mood, they began below normal levels in these communication skills and continued to be below average after three years of treatment.[9]

[9]Normals understandably showed constant levels between 6 and 11 years of age because the method of the presumptive norm takes age standards into account.

CHAPTER V
Changes in Subgroups

Up to now, changes in behavior and functional capacity in the schizophrenic group as a whole has been emphasized. Although measures of central tendency have been employed, simultaneous study of the children as individuals has revealed dramatic individual differences in capacity levels, behavioral responses and longitudinal patterns of change. The material thus offers powerful empirical support for the conviction that among any group of diagnosed schizophrenic children there are wide variations in personality organization, clinical course, patterns and level of cognitive organization and socio-environmental circumstances affecting adjustment of the children (such as social class). As noted, at any given point in time, the children ranged from near total deficiency to very high levels of social, cognitive, and communicative response. For the group as a whole, change and growth were impressive. However, the children differed among themselves in extent and quality of change. These findings are akin to clinical findings of variations among the children in affectivity, psychodynamic organization, and in protective mechanisms. Some schizophrenic children show complex defenses (including phobic, obsessional, paranoid, and depressed reactions). Others are extremely meagre in emotional response and can only withdraw totally. Some remain unchanged in clinical manifestations as they age. Others attain normal educational, social, and affective levels. Thus, in clinical research as well as in treatment the conviction is strengthened that the primary requirement is the precise study of the growth of individual children.

This observation of individual differences indicates that there would be profit in subdividing the present sample of schizophrenic children, so as to achieve subclusters which are relatively homogeneous. The subclusters are intermediate in homogeneity between the group as a whole and individual children. This chapter, therefore, will consider longitudinal changes of subclusters of the present total sample of schizophrenic children.

The subdivisions are based on a system of subclassification which reflects previous empirical findings in the course of therapeutic, experimental, and follow-up observation, and also theoretic considerations regarding the etiology of childhood schizophrenia (Goldfarb, 1967). We also expected that the present study would demonstrate empirically the meaningfulness and value of the subclassification scheme, since previous comparable subdivisions have been shown to differ from each other in adaptive level, familial and neurological influences and in curves of change and growth.

The children in the present sample of schizophrenic children have thus been subdivided on the basis of five variables:

(1) Sex
(2) Age of admission to residential treatment
(3) Level of neurological integrity

Variables	Subcategories
1. Sex	A. Girls B. Boys
2. Age of admission to residential treatment	A. Children admitted below 8 years of age B. Children admitted at 8 years of age and older
3. Level of neurological integrity	A. Children with positive findings in either examination or history (organic children) B. Children with no positive findings in either examination or history (nonorganic children)
4. Social class	A. Upper class children (Hollingshead-Redlich Class I, II) B. Middle class children (Hollingshead-Redlich Class III) C. Lower class children (Hollingshead-Redlich Class IV, V)
5. Level of intellectual functioning	Children with WISC FIQ A. Below 46 B. 46–69 C. 70–89 D. 90–109 E. Above 109

FIG. 5.1 Basis for Subcategorization.

(4) Social class position

(5) Level of intellectual functioning

Using these dimensions, the subclusters of schizophrenic children, whose longitudinal curves are to be contrasted, are shown in Figure 5.1.

It is clear that these published Ittleson findings should not be generalized to all potential samples of schizophrenic children, and that these curves of change do not permit prediction for other children. Moreover, they may not necessarily have bearing on fundamental issues of etiology. Such clarification of etiologic influences would require controls beyond the capacity of the present study. For example, we shall be noting differences in annual means and in longitudinal curves of change among children from different social classes. However, we shall not be inferring from these data that social class is a causal factor in early childhood psychosis, in view of numerous correlated factors and the contaminative influence of selective sampling. Even so, the delineation of changes in carefully defined subclasses of schizophrenic children does suggest etiological and other productive hypotheses to be studied further with adequate controls.

In a trend study such as this one, it is necessary to note that not all subgroups to be contrasted were comparable in ages at admission (Table 5.1). For example, while the boys and girls did not differ much in mean age at admission from each other and from the total sample of schizophrenic children, it is obvious that the group of children admitted at 8 years and above were older at admission than those children admitted below 8 years. Similarly, children of lower social class had been admitted to treatment 15 months older, on the average, than children from upper social classes. Where significant age differences existed among the subclusters, direct, precise, highly accurate comparisons of these subgroups are impossible, especially when comparisons pertain to behavioral and psychological functions which normally grow and mature in childhood. However, it is still of interest to delineate differences among subclasses as they arose in the present sample of schizophrenic children, particularly if we do so with an alertness to the factor of age. In addition, as noted, some of the subclasses (e.g., boys and girls) did not differ significantly from each other in age at admission. In this event, longitudinal comparison of the subclasses is simpler and more feasible. Methodologically, too, some units of measurement are so defined as to remove the

Table 5.1. Average Age at Admission of Subgroups of Schizophrenic Children*

Subgroup (and size of subgroup)	Average age (months)	Standard deviation (months)
Male (27)	82.0	12.1
Female (13)	82.7	10.9
Admitted below 8 years of age (25)	74.4	6.1
Admitted at 8 years of age or older (15)	95.3	5.3
Organic (14)	80.4	11.4
Nonorganic (26)	85.7	11.5
Upper class (5)	71.0	4.5
Middle class (15)	80.3	11.0
Lower class (20)	86.5	6.7
FIQ less than 46 (6)	72.7	5.6
FIQ of 46–69 (10)	83.3	8.6
FIQ of 70–89 (14)	83.6	10.9
FIQ of 90–109 (6)	78.8	15.0
FIQ greater than 109 (4)	94.3	9.0

*See Figure 5.1 for definitions of subgroups.

importance of age considerations in comparisons of longitudinal curves. This applies particularly to WISC IQ in which the means and variabilities of the standardization data are the same at all ages. (Mean IQ at each age is 100; standard deviation, 15.)

As a general rule of thumb for considering the age factor, therefore, we shall proceed as follows in our discussion of the subgroups. If we accept as comparable in age any divergence of less than six months in either direction, we shall be able to compare boys with girls and organics with nonorganics without special attention to age. On the other hand, age will need to be given consideration in comparisons of children admitted at 8 years of age or older with those admitted below 8 years. Similarly, age will need to be considered in the comparison of various subclasses of children when categorized by IQ and in the comparison of subdivisions by social class position.

In making our longitudinal comparisons of subgroups of schizophrenic children, we shall consider longitudinal changes in the 40 behavioral dimensions we have included in the present study; here we ask, "In what proportion of the 40 curves did the subcategories of children differ significantly from each other?" How did they differ at admission and during treatment up to discharge? Where there were wide age differences, it should nevertheless be feasible to compare subclasses in functional capacity as measured in WISC IQ. Further, as will be seen, we can compare subclasses at comparable ages in the longitudinal curves.

Sex

Samples of schizophrenic children have consistently demonstrated a higher proportion of boys than girls, although the ratio varies in size from study to study (e.g., Bender & Grugett, 1956; Boatman & Szurek, 1960; Kallman & Roth, 1956; Kanner, 1954). The basis for this sex distribution is not known. However, at the Ittleson Center, the boy to girl ratio has varied suggestively among subclusters of schizophrenic children grouped by several independent variables. For example, the proportion of boys to girls is considerably higher among schizophrenic children with evidence of neurological dysfunction than among children free of such evidence (Meyers & Goldfarb, 1962). Indeed, as is evident in the present study as well as in previous studies, the proportion of boys and girls is about equal in schizophrenic children who present no evidence of neurological aberration in their histories or neurological examinations (Table 3.10). Apart from these differences in regard to the contribution of neurological factors, in previous studies girls at the Ittleson Center have tended, as a group, to be lower in adaptive status than boys. Here reference is being made to average status in a variety of measures (such as language, "normality" or proximity to the normal) and in studies of longitudinal curves of school performance and IQ (Goldfarb & Pollack, 1964; Goldfarb, Goldfarb, & Pollack, 1969). Although not of pertinence in the present report, schizophrenic boys and girls have also differed in psychodynamic features as they have emerged in psychoanalytic treatment. While there is probable overlapping between sex of the schizophrenic child and other variables in the study, separate longitudinal studies of boys and girls matched on appropriate characteristics to appraise differing patterns of behavioral growth and change are needed, since studies of combined sex groups will reflect the relative distribution of boys and girls in the sample.

In light of previous experience, two findings were anticipated. First, we expected boys to be superior to girls in general clinical status, in the perceptual, conceptual and psychomotor aspects of cognitive proficiency, and in academic performance. Secondly, we proposed that the girls would be superior to the boys in neurological functioning and in behavior such as startle response which we have previously shown to be linked to level of neurological integrity.

In the evaluation of present data, no correction for age was necessary because the boys and girls were about equal in age. The results tended to be in the predicted direction, although there were fewer significant differences between boys and girls than anticipated. Boys and girls showed significant differences in 11 of the 40 curves. Thus, at admission and throughout residential treatment, boys were superior to girls in general orientation (Tables A variable 32) and in verbal capacity (WISC VIQ) (Tables A variable 36). Supporting the finding of the boys' better verbal functioning was their superiority in language communication as studied by the language and speech specialist (Tables A variable 40). Further, boys were superior in their curves of arithmetic attainment (Tables A variable 3). They were also stronger in the dynamometer test (Tables A variable 35). Girls were superior in only one cognitive test—the Weigl Test (Tables A variable 31), which measures ability to categorize objects on the basis of color and shape. We cannot explain this finding which stands in rather isolated contrast to the others.

In partial confirmation of the proposition of their more normal neurological integrity, girls did show significantly superior curves of growth in the two Romberg Tests—with hands at side and with arms outstretched (Tables A variable 20 and A variable 21). In these tests of body balance, they were superior to boys at each point between admission and third year.

The boys and girls differed significantly in longitudinal response to the startle. Here the boys showed higher mean ratings at each point between admission and third year of treatment—that is to say, they were disposed to respond with greater tendency to hyposensitivity than the girls. This finding reflects the rather surprising observation that all of the most extreme individual cases of hyposensitivity or total auditory imperception at admission (six children) and thereafter were boys.

Age of Admission to Residential Treatment

The Ittleson Center at first restricted admissions to psychotic children between 5 and 7 years of age. Somewhat later it began to accept applications for children above 7. While it was noted that virtually all children in both younger and older groups had manifested developmental aberrations from earliest infancy, it nevertheless soon became impressively clear that the younger children at admission were different from those admitted at an older age. We have already reported that the children in the present study who were admitted to treatment below 8 years of age differed in a number of important attributes from those admitted at 8 years or older. Thus, more of the children who were admitted at 8 years or older came from families of lower social class position than did the children admitted at a younger age, and fewer of the older children came from upper and middle class families. Furthermore, all the children with WISC FIQ scores below 46 (i.e., the unscorable children) had been admitted below 8 years of age. It will be recalled too that the children who were most impaired intellectually, and were thus unscorable in the WISC, tended in the main to be in the organic subcluster, so that very serious cerebral dysfunction influenced admission age, particularly if so severe as to be noted very early in life.

Examination of the longitudinal data also demonstrated strong differences between the two groups of children classified by age of admission in most functions and in curves of change.

Thirty-eight of 40 longitudinal curves significantly differentiated the two subclasses of children classified by age of admission to treatment. With great consistency, children admitted at 8 years or older were superior at admission to those admitted below 8 years at time of admission and at each year of treatment. The differences in age accounted for much of the superiority in ratings of the older cluster of children at each point in treatment, but not entirely so. The older children gave undoubted evidence of basic superiority in adaptive potentiality. Thus, the longitudinal pattern described herein is seen in a comparison of curves of WISC FIQ by duration of treatment (Tables A variable 38). It will be noted that the subcluster of children admitted at 8 years or older showed higher mean FIQs at admission and at each year of treatment for three years.

The adaptive superiority of the children admitted at the older age is also consistently revealed if one compares them with children admitted below 8 years of age when the latter have also reached 8 years of age after about two years of treatment. In this comparison at 8 years of age, the children admitted below eight years of age will have had the advantage of two years of comprehensive treatment which the older admission group will not as yet have been exposed to. This comparison, then, is a conservative test of the presumptive superiority in adaptive capacity of the subclass of children admitted at 8 years and older. In the great majority of ratings, at 8 years of age, the group which had been admitted at 8 years of age was superior to the group of children admitted below 8 years of age.

There were several exceptions to the generalized superiority of the schizophrenic children admitted to residential treatment at the older age of 8 years or more. Thus the children admitted to treatment below 8 years showed slightly higher reading accomplishment, equal arithmetic accomplishment, and total educational attainment at age 8 (Tables A variable 2, A variable 3, and A variable 4). This is of interest in view of their presumptive inferiority in intellectual potentiality. It seems safe to conclude that this reflects the therapeutic and educational opportunities to which the younger group had been exposed in treatment residence in the two years prior to achievement testing at age 8. Of course, at age 8, the group admitted to treatment at an older age had not as yet been offered these same opportunities.

An even more striking exception to our generalization of functional superiority of the group admitted at an older age is the observation that the younger admissions improved more dramatically in social quotient, so that after three years of treatment the group admitted at the earlier age was actually higher in social quotient (Tables A variable 6). In other words, while both groups improved in social age, the group admitted below age 8 showed more dramatic improvement in relative social competence. (The mean social quotients at admission were 69 for the children admitted below 8 years and 75 for the group admitted at eight years. The younger group accelerated consistently, however, so that its mean social quotient after three years was 82; while the group admitted at an older age did not change significantly and continued to show a mean social quotient of 75 three years after admission to treatment).

Level of Neurological Integrity

It is crucial—and feasible as well—to subdivide schizophrenic children into those with and those without evidence of cerebral dysfunction. At the Ittleson Center, a qualified pediatric neurologist, trained in developmental neurology, makes his independent judgment on the basis of neurological history and examination. Of course, he seeks the "hard" unequivocal evidence of neurological impairment, such as alteration in normal reflexes, abnormal reflexes, asymmetrical failures in sensory and motor responses, and EEG abnormalities. Of greater significance, however, in the neurological appraisal of children with psychiatric problems, he bases his judgment of neurological deficit on careful observation of deviation in gait, posture, balance, motor coordination, muscle tone, and integration of multiple and multi-modal stimuli. In previous studies, when schizophrenic children have been divided into those who provide evidence of cerebral impairment (organic schizophrenic children) and those who do not show signs and symptoms of cerebral impairment (nonorganic schizophrenic children), the two classes have shown many differences in functioning and in background. Of pertinence for the present study, nonorganic have been superior to organic schizophrenic children in most adaptive functions. Thus the nonorganic children have been higher in perceptual response, conceptual ability, intellectual functioning, speech and language, and psychomotor ability (Goldfarb, 1961).

As anticipated, there were significant and, oftimes, very large differences between organic and nonorganic children in 37 of the 40 longitudinal curves. In every case of significant difference, too, the nonorganic children were clearly superior. In other words, they were superior to the organic children at admission and continued to be superior at each point of subsequent longitudinal study for three years in most of the functions assayed. This observation applied to appraisals of perceptual and conceptual capacity, psychomotor ability, functional intelligence, orientation, speech and language, social maturity, and educational attainment, and was confirmed by the general psychiatric appraisal of ego status. The two groups were similarly differentiated in longitudinal changes in level of confusion in response to the delayed feedback experiment (Tables A variable 27). While apparently undifferentiated in longitudinal curves of mean response to the startle experiment (Tables A variable 24), it is of interest that five of the six children who showed total unawareness, and the child who showed most extreme hypersensitivity at admission, were in the organic subgroup. This observation supports previous data which tended to link organicity and the most extreme patterns of hyper- and hyposensitive response (Goldfarb, 1961). There was also no difference between longitudinal curves of change in language on delayed feedback, although both groups improved (Tables A variable 26).

The mean age of admission was 85.7 months for nonorganic and 80.3 months for organic children. The nonorganic children were thus approximately 5.4 months older at each point of assay. By our rule of thumb, however, age is not regarded as a consideration in the present discussion, and the differences between organic and nonorganic schizophrenics described above are accepted as significant. In support of this conclusion, the differences are perhaps more sharply illustrated in the WISC IQ data, where it may be presumed that the age factor is not an issue at all (Tables A variable 36, A variable 37, and A variable 38). Here it can be seen that the nonorganic were superior to organic children in mean VIQ, PIQ, and FIQ at admission and at each year thereafter. The nonorganic children were within the normal range in mean IQ (above IQ 90) at every point, and the organic children were consistently below normal (below IQ 90). Both groups showed largest improvement in the first year. The nonorganic children continued to show a significant rise in the last two of the three years, while the organic children did not show such continuing improvement.

These findings are in accord with a previous statement (Goldfarb, Goldfarb, & Pollack, 1969) which noted that there was a pattern of rise in FIQ during the three year period for the entire group of schizophrenic children; but that, after the first year, the pattern of increase resulted chiefly from the effect of rise among the nonorganic children. In the present study, the longitudinal curves suggest that the nonorganic children might be expected to continue to improve after the third year while the organic children had reached their peak before the third year; and we are impressed by the possibilities for sharpest and most dramatic improvement in the organic group during the first year of treatment. Aside from the fact that the group mean trends confirmed that by far the greatest part of the three year cumulative improvement of organic children occurred in the first year, as many as 6 of the 26 organic children showed improvement in FIQ of more than 10 points during the first year. (Only one nonorganic child showed such a large jump in WISC FIQ in the first year.)

Social Class Position

Distribution of the children by social class position (Hollingshead-Redlich Scale) and their average age of admission to treatment are shown in Table 5.1. It is evident that those from upper class families (classes I and II) were admitted to treatment at a younger age than middle class children (class III); and the latter, in turn, were admitted at a younger age than lower class children (classes IV and V). For statistical analysis and in view of the small size of our study sample, classes I and II (upper class), and IV and V (lower class) have been combined. The mean ages of admission to treatment of upper, middle, and lower class subsets were thus in order: 71.0 months, 80.3 months, and 86.5 months respectively.

In view of these differences in average age of admission to treatment (and, thus, in age at each year of treatment), the discussion will begin with a comparison of the three social classes in longitudinal curves of WISC IQ. It will be recalled that we have considered direct IQ comparisons feasible because, by definition, the means and measures of variability of the standardization population have been kept constant at each year of age. The upper, middle, and lower social class children differed significantly in longitudinal curves for VIQ, PIQ, and FIQ. The findings are consistent in all three measures of intelligence, since in each measure of adaptive competence and at each point of measurement at admission and thereafter, upper class children attained the lowest mean scores, middle class children attained intermediate scores, and lower class children attained highest mean scores.

Average age may be kept about the same for the lower and upper class children by comparing the upper class children after one year of treatment (average age, 83 months) with lower class children at admission (average age, 86 months). We can make similar comparisons in subsequent years of treatment. In these comparisons, even though the upper class children have the advantage of a year more of residential treatment at each comparison point, in the case of virtually every measurement except that of social maturity at age 7, lower social class children were superior to upper class children. (In the case of social maturity, upper class children would seem to show the advantageous effect of a year of treatment at age 7 and are superior to the untreated lower class children at that age.) These data support the WISC IQ trends reported herein.

In our population, therefore, social class position would seem to be inversely related to functional capacity of the child. While the basis for this relationship is not clear, the explanation would seem to be in other variables (themselves linked to both IQ and contributing physical and psychosocial factors) and in selective influences. It may be presumed that all social classes contain schizophrenic children at all levels of functional capacity. To understand our specific findings, therefore, it would be necessary to discover why upper class families are perhaps more prone to bring their more impaired children at an earlier age for residential treatment than lower class families.

Level of Intellectual Functioning

All follow-up studies have demonstrated the association between degree of early adaptive impairment and later progress of the psychotic child. Eisenberg (1956), for example, first reported that virtually all children lacking in speech by 5 years of age were extremely impaired in clinical and general social status in adolescence. In contrast, the majority of psychotic children with language by 5 years of age were adapting to school and community in adolescence. In this study, nonspeaking children with IQs above 50 showed more improvement than those with IQs below 50. In the longitudinal studies at the Ittleson Center, children with WISC IQs below 46 were extremely restricted in potentialities for educational and therapeutic response (Goldfarb & Pollack, 1964; Goldfarb, Goldfarb, & Pollack, 1969; Goldfarb, 1970). It is obviously necessary to categorize schizophrenic children by level of adaptive ability at the beginning of any therapeutic program and in any prospective evaluation of treatment.

In the present study, children were classified by WISC FIQ on admission. For purposes of analyzing their longitudinal curves, they were placed into one of five FIQ categories, as follows:

below 46
46–69
70–89

Table 5.2. Age and Grade Equivalents* in Reading Attainments of Schizophrenic Children at Varying IQ Levels by Chronological Age at each Year of Treatment

Average chronological age	Full Intelligence Quotient									
	Below 46 equivalent*		46–69 equivalent*		70–89 equivalent*		90–109 equivalent*		Above 109 equivalent*	
	Age	Grade	Age	Grade	Age	Grade	Age	Grade	Age	Grade
6	†	†	†	†	6.5	1.4	6.8	1.5		
7	†	†	6.7	1.4	7.3	1.9	7.8	2.3		
8	6.3	1.3	7.7	2.3	7.9	2.5	8.8	3.4	10.2	4.8
9	6.6	1.4	8.1	2.7	8.1	2.9	9.9	4.6	11.3	5.9
10									13.6	8.2
11									14.4	9.0

*Age equivalents are based on median scores of a large and unselected group of children at successive age levels regardless of school grade. Grade equivalents are based on the median scores of a large and unselected group of children at successive grade levels regardless of age.
†Below normal.

Note.—The admission age differs among the IQ groups for age 6 for the lowest IQ groups to age 8 for the highest IQ groups. Also each row presents scores for IQ groups at the same chronological age.

121

Table 5.3. Age and Grade Equivalents* in Arithmetic Attainments of Schizophrenic Children at Varying IQ Levels by Chronological Age at Each Year of Treatment

Average chronological age	Full Intelligence Quotient									
	Below 46 equivalent*		46–69 equivalent*		70–89 equivalent*		90–109 equivalent*		Above 109 equivalent*	
	Age	Grade	Age	Grade	Age	Grade	Age	Grade	Age	Grade
6	†	†								
7	†	†	†	†	†	†	7.5	2.2		
8	†	†	†	†	7.3	2.0	8.7	3.6	10.2	4.8
9	†	†	6.9	1.5	8.2	3.1	9.7	4.4	10.8	5.4
10			8.0	2.9	8.0	3.6	10.8	5.4	11.7	6.2
11									12.5	7.1

*Age equivalents are based on median scores of a large and unselected group of children at successive age levels regardless of school grade. Grade equivalents are based on the median scores of a large and unselected group of children at successive grade levels regardless of age.
†Below normal.

Note.—The admission age differs among the IQ groups for age 6 for the lowest IQ groups to age 8 for the highest IQ groups. Also each row presents scores for IQ groups at the same chronological age.

90–109

110 and above

The number and mean age of children in each of these FIQ categories is presented in Table 5.1. The range in mean age among the subdivisions is approximately 2 years, so that comparisons of these IQ groups with regard to other tests are hazardous for most of the tests. However, it is feasible to compare the five subclusters of children in their longitudinal curves of IQ. In all the IQ subgroups, except children with FIQ below 46, the means improved over the three years. The five subdivisions of children by initial FIQ (who were different by definition at admission) continued to show similar differences in longitudinal curves over the next three years. In other words, they maintained their relative positions.

It is also reasonable and pertinent to comment especially on the relationship between IQ level and educational curves of the schizophrenic children. Educational expectancy is always very much determined by each child's intellectual potentiality, best reflected in IQ. Indeed, a previous investigation (Goldfarb & Pollack, 1964) confirmed large differences among groups of schizophrenic children when classified by IQ. Since the schizophrenic children with lowest IQs were admitted to treatment at lowest mean age and children with highest IQ were admitted to treatment at highest mean age (Table 5.1), care must be taken to compare the various subdivisions by IQ at comparable ages. In doing so, however, it should be noted that the children with lower IQs will, therefore, have had generally more residential psychiatric treatment at each specified age than those with higher IQs. Our present data may thus be regarded as a conservative test of our experimental proposition of the high correlation between IQ and educational attainment, since the expected differences between low and high IQ children were diminished by the differences in amount of psychiatric treatment.

Tables 5.2 and 5.3 present educational response of schizophrenic children in terms of age and grade equivalents in reading and arithmetic and by IQ levels at varying ages and years of treatment. As in the previous study of the response of schizophrenic children to schooling (Goldfarb & Pollack, 1964), the hierarchical ordering of the children by level of intellectual functioning is in consistent agreement with the hierarchical ordering of the children by level of educational attainments. Thus the longitudinal group curves of reading and arithmetic may be arranged from most superior to most inferior in the following order: Children with IQs above 109, those with IQs between 90 and 109, those with IQs between 70 and 89, those with IQs between 46 and 69, and finally the unscorable children with IQs below 46. Again, as in the previous study (Goldfarb & Pollack, 1964), it is striking that the children with IQs above 90 achieved substantially as well or even better than those in the normal standardization population at each point of study. Schizophrenic children below IQ 90 showed reading and arithmetic curves below that of the normal population, and the schizophrenic children with IQs below 46 showed extremely meagre response to learning over the three years of treatment. It also needs to be mentioned that, as in the previous study, some children showed better than average rates of increment in their educational curves over time.

CHAPTER VI
Conclusion

There is little question that the concept of childhood schizo-phrenia as a diagnostic entity has been a useful one. It has permitted the delineation of a group of children with a common cluster of diagnostic symptoms, although their aberrations have been broadly defined. As a consequence, comprehensive programs of treatment for these most severely disordered children have been elaborated with increasing sophistication; and research directed toward the clarification of the nature and cause of the disorders embodied in the classification has increased. On the other hand, diagnostic labeling of schizophrenic children may have the unfortunate consequence of encouraging the conviction that they are highly homogeneous in fundamental characteristics, unalter-able in their aberrations, and permanently inaccessible to social and therapeutic influence. Yet, intimate therapeutic experiences with a large group of schizophrenic children in which attention is actively directed toward an understanding of their inner experiential existence, and observation of the children in real life interaction with others, have contradicted this notion. Thus, schizophrenic children have been noted to be clearly diversified in capacities and motivational attributes, in level of neurological integrity, and in the kind of psychosocial influences to which they have been exposed. In addition, it has been possible in clinical work to elaborate the unique and adaptational significance of each schizophrenic child's symptomatic expression. Finally, the psychodynamic and adaptational point of view has helped to bring into relief individual variations in extent and patterns of growth of schizophrenic children.

Such observations of individual variation in attributes and the multiplicity of factors contributing to these trait variations indicate the primary need in research for detailed descriptive study of individual schizophrenic children before meaningful experimental and etiologic investigation can be designed. Among these descriptive studies, longitudinal observation of development is the most useful tool for establishing characteristic patterns of stability and change among schizophrenic children. Just as it is still necessary to establish the range and diversity of characteristics among schizophrenic children at any given age, so it is necessary to record the breadth of change and growth among these children. Even presuming that every schizophrenic child suffers from chronic limitations and restrictions in adaptive integrity, it is clear that his potentialities and the bounds of his behavior and capacity in the entire course of his life and in relation to definable environmental changes are still not known. We do not know yet how much success is possible in his educational and therapeutic management. Descriptive longitudinal study of individual schizophrenic children is thus our best tool for the delineation of the boundaries of change in behavior and performance to be expected among schizophrenic children and also within the children as individuals. Following such descriptive longitudinal studies, we shall be in a better position to appraise by analytic, etiologic, and experimental study what influences may be brought to bear on the growth of schizophrenic children.

As stated previously, data of the present investigation were derived from longitudinal observations of schizophrenic children in which the same children were studied annually over a three year period. The information permits a quantitative description of growth and change in key attributes and adaptive functions in individual schizophrenic children and in groups. As already stressed, this is a study of a particular group of children in a particular setting.

In the design of the longitudinal study, characteristics and purposeful responses being observed annually for each child were represented quantitatively on scales ranging from high to low, or many to few—so that the children could be compared and ranked with each other in terms of quantity of the characteristics. The judgments and ratings referred either to qualities which were usually observable in standard tests or to broader, less standardized observations. Thus, evaluation of intelligence by standardized testing represents the ranking of a child in a quality by inference from direct test observation. The ego status scale requires ranking of a child on the basis of inference from real life observations. Both varieties of observation do not include judgments of some qualities which were excluded from the present study—not because they are unimportant, but rather because they do not permit quantitative representation. Examples of this kind of important assay—crucial yet only qualitatively apparent—are the key clinical and therapeutic observations of traits such as emotional attachment and conscience. Psychodynamic and motivational factors (as seen in psychotherapy) are most important for explaining inter-individual variations in schizophrenic children. Even so, the variables which were assayed quantitatively in the present study are meaningful and important indeed. In the analysis, we have tended to consider inferences and ratings of single dimensions, easily definable in terms of observable operations. Yet it is true that some of the ratings, such as ego status or social competence, referred to global or multi-dimensional characteristics.

The 40 characteristics selected for longitudinal assay fall into the following two categories:

(1) *Characteristics which, on the face of it, represent capacity levels in which normal children may be expected to improve solely on the basis of maturation as they get older.* Just as normal children grow in height and weight, so do they improve in early childhood in level of response in areas such as perception, conceptualization, psychomotor performance, integration of multiple sensory stimuli, balance and postural adjustment. It is true that in some of these responses, peak development may be expected on a maturational basis alone in the preschool period or even infancy, [for example, visual following behavior (Gesell, 1945)] or in elementary school age [for example, the control of overflow response (Cohen et al., 1967)], or the integration and discrimination of multiple, simultaneous stimulation (Fink & Bender (1952), or in prepubescence or pubescence [for example, the successful attainment of capacity for abstraction or, in Piagetian terms, formal operations (Inhelder & Piaget, 1958)].

(2) *Characteristics which reflect with strong certainty the primary influences of social and educational experience.* An obvious example of this kind of characteristic is the level of educational attainment. It may be presumed with little hesitation that for most children the learning of the essentials of reading, writing, and arithmetic presupposes exposure to formal schooling. Serious educational progress was not observed among these children till after admission to the comprehensive therapeutic and educational program of the Ittleson Center. A less obvious example of this kind of characteristic is social competence. One may expect some degree of growth in social competence merely because the children grow older. However, in our residential management of the children we have had the repeated experience of teaching the children the elements of self care which had not been learned prior to arrival at the Center. Finally, several of the

measures in the present investigation represent the child's rank with reference to his own age group (for example, the WISC Intelligence Quotient and Vineland Social Quotient). Although definitive evidence of the influence of the therapeutic program will require longitudinal study of an untreated group of schizophrenic children, the conviction that psychiatric treatment and the total impact of the treatment milieu affects these measures has received a degree of support from careful studies of individual schizophrenic children. We have thus presumed that significant improvements in these quotient scores may strongly reflect the therapeutic, socializing, and educational influences of the comprehensive program of the Ittleson Center.

Overall, the most impressive findings of the present investigation are the many definite evidences of growth and change (in both of the above noted types of variables) which were demonstrated by the schizophrenic children during the three year period of observation. They showed significant improvements in most functions which normally mature in childhood. They grew in level of perceptual response, conceptual behavior, orientation, ability to communicate, psychomotor ability, motor strength, and a variety of neurological functions embodying locomotor balance, inhibition of motor overflow, integration of multiple stimuli, and motor coordination. They also improved in educational achievement and social competence. Change and improvement, rather than fixity and arrest in these functional capacities, were thus typical of schizophrenic children. Indeed, individual declines in any of the variables were rare.

In most instances, while the schizophrenic children improved in functions which develop in normal childhood and also those which reflect educational and social influence, they tended to remain below normal levels in group averages in these functions at each of the ages studied between admission at age 7 and final observation three years later at age 10. It should be noted again that, in general, we did not attempt to evaluate precise rates of change in the self regulative functions studied. In spite of below normal group competence in most attributes at each age, the schizo-phrenic children seemed to show better than normal rates of improvement in competence level in some of the functions. An example was the accelerated rate of improvement in mental level, implied in the rise in mean WISC IQ scores over the three year treatment period. Many of the children also showed better than average rate of growth in educational achievement and social competence. In addition, the below normal mean intellectual functioning of the schizophrenic children as a group needs to be considered in appraising the significance of the inferior average levels of competence of these children in most functions. This consideration is particularly applicable in the longitudinal study of attainment levels in areas where active schooling and learning ability were unequivocal factors affecting outcome. Thus the schizophrenic children with initial IQs above 90 showed normal or even superior longitudinal curves of attainment in reading and arithmetic; and children with IQs above 109 were dramatically superior to the average normal child in level of educational attainment during the three years of observation.

It is also crucial to grasp the very broad range of individual differences in all of the characteristics appraised. In most of the assays, the individual children ranged from below scale to average or even superior for a given age. In each of the functions, too, the children varied individually in curves of change over time. Some of the individual curves were inflexibly unchanging. The remainder varied in amount and pattern of change over the three years. Some improved early, others late, and still others throughout the period of observation.

The present investigation demonstrates how schizophrenic children may improve significantly—even dramatically—in many attributes and adaptive functions and still remain globally deviant relative to normal children. In psychiatric observation, the bulk of the children showed growth in many factors of ego and yet were still considered quite aberrant by ordinary clinical criteria after three years of treatment. It will be recalled, for example, that the children improved in all but a few of the characteristics which were assayed. Nevertheless, most of the children remained below acceptable normal levels in the significant shifts in many specific functions tested. The longitudinal data offer explanation for the continued classification of the children as globally deviant. As a whole, the schizophrenic children did not improve sufficiently, in most of the functions observed, to bring them to normal levels over the three years of observation. So, while they improved in group averages in 35 of the 40 characteristics appraised, they did not in most instances attain normal levels in these tests and observations by the third year. Some individual children, it is true, attained normal or even superior levels of capacity in a few of the attributes measured but remained impaired in other functions—so that they remained quite deviant overall. The most obvious example of this pattern of improvement were those children who were able to attain normal or superior levels of educational attainment while remaining quite deviant in social and affective response, and in some aspects of cognition, communication, and motility. After three years of apparent improvement under therapeutic management, these children were still classified as schizophrenic although intellectually bright and educated. At this time, it would seem we are better able to school these children successfully than to alleviate the more total maladaptive process described as childhood schizophrenia.

Even so, it is of interest that the children as a whole improved in the individual functions studied. Not surprisingly, too, the bulk of the children as individuals improved in a multidimensional fashion in the numerous functions assayed. Like normal children, they evidenced development in pertinent psychological function just as they grew in height and weight. They also gave evidence of responsiveness to therapeutic, educational, and socializing influences. We find our attention drawn, therefore, to that group of schizophrenic children who showed such little change in ego status and level of adaptive capacity that they might be regarded as essentially unaltered in clinical status. These are the children with most capacities so low that they were untestable in most of our tests when they entered treatment (about 7 years of age) and were still untestable three years later. In less formal but practical therapeutic work with these children, it has been feasible to alter specific aspects of their behavior by suitable educational techniques. To illustrate, they have been assisted somewhat to grow in self care, to achieve a small vocabulary, and to develop some human attachments. However, the noted changes have evidently not been large enough and possibly have not been effected in a sufficient number of key functions to alter the level of total organization significantly during the three years of observation. These children have remained very low in mental level, largely mute, totally dependent on others for physical care, extremely restricted in human response and awareness. In the statistical analysis of the experimental and observational data, it was most useful to separate the untestable children from the testable children because the two groups represented two disparate populations in the clusters of data they offered. More importantly, they presented differing patterns of longitudinal change. Globally speaking, the untestable children tended to be individually unchanging in absolute level of adaptive capacity as measured by our data. They had stopped growing significantly at extremely early levels of ego organization. In contrast, the testable children continued to manifest growth and responsiveness to educational or socializing influence throughout the period of observation. The two groups of children also differed in contributory influence of neurological and psychosocial factors and in the kinds of therapeutic and educational influences they have needed.[10] The untestable children, who descriptively were also relatively unchanging, contributed a small proportion of the 40 schizophrenic children in the longitudinal study. If we define as untestable those children who fell below scale in the WISC (FIQ below 46), then they constituted only 15.0% of the entire group studied. The

[10] Apart from the methodologic implications of these findings in research, therefore, it would seem highly profitable to plan for separate, different kinds of therapeutic programs for the two general classes of high and low order (testable and untestable) children. The proportion of testable and non-testable children in the total population of schizophrenic children is not known.

testable children (85.0% of the sample) showed significant growth in most behavioral attributes. There was thus a major trend in most of the children to ego improvement.

It will also be recalled that, as an undifferentiated group, the children improved significantly in most of the characteristics (35 of 40) evaluated over the three year period of observation. They did not improve in these five variables:

1. Muscle Tone.
2. Activity Level.
3. Auditory Startle.
4. Delayed Auditory Feedback, extent of change in speech and voice.
5. Double Simultaneous Stimulation (DSS), Homologous Stimuli with eyes open.

Results in the DSS Test, using homologous stimuli with eyes open, are of little significance because the test was too easy to demonstrate improvement. Average results in this test were high from the beginning, and little change was possible. The remaining dimensions, however, are of more interest for the children functioned in a very deviant fashion in them on admission to treatment and then remained markedly aberrant in these capacities throughout treatment. Deviant muscle tone (hyper- and hypo-tonia) and deviant activity (hyper- and hypoactivity) probably represented the motor aspect of impaired neurological integrity in many of the schizophrenic children. Our attention is also called to the children's responses in the tests of receptor behavior (auditory startle, delayed auditory feedback) of the schizophrenic children. These tests assayed their disposition to pay heed to sensory stimuli and to utilize these stimuli to guide response execution. Here the evidence points to unchanging aberrations between admission and third year of treatment. The schizophrenic children were thus persistently aberrant throughout the three year period in receptor and efferent behavior traits. However, we have been most impressed with the continuing deviations in receptor input behavior.

As noted, receptor behavior was sampled in two experiments utilizing the auditory modality, i.e., the auditory startle experiment and the delayed auditory feedback experiment. In the auditory startle experiment, the schizophrenic children showed no change in mean annual results. Of even more significance, they did not show significant change in incidence of the most deviant responses of hypersensitivity and hyposensitivity.

Similar tendencies were evidenced in the delayed auditory feedback experiment. In this experiment, impact of the delayed auditory feedback on speech and voice remained relatively unchanged over the three year period of treatment. In contrast to normal children, whose speech and voices were typically slightly to moderately affected, the schizophrenic children at admission to treatment and for three years of treatment were more prone to include individuals who manifested extreme deviations. More than normal children, their speech and voices were either totally unaffected, which we interpreted to be evidence for auditory inattention, or their speech and voice as well as their behavior and affective responses were often extremely disorganized by the delayed auditory feedback. We interpreted the latter finding to indicate a kind of hypersensitive response, very much as noted in the startle experiment, in which the children could not cope comfortably with sensory input. Certainly the feedback of auditory information was not used by them in an effective fashion to monitor a graceful and harmonious pattern of voice and speech. The longitudinal study of schizophrenic children gave the additional information that their three years of treatment did not improve significantly the children's inclination to monitor their own voice and speech by auditory feedback or the proficiency with which they utilized auditory perception to achieve an integrated vocal response when they did open the auditory channel.

This finding of persistent deficiency in auditory self monitoring of speech by the schizophrenic children is of considerable interest since it coincides with clinical and therapeutic observation. The schizophrenic child's restrictions on auditory information limits his potentiality for attaining normal levels and patterns of communication and verbal-symbolic response. He lacks an essential instrument for fitting his cognitive and communicative behavior to standard expectation. Less obviously, perhaps, it would also seem that the deficiency in self monitoring more broadly is a primary factor contributing to his failures in perceiving and thus constructing reality and in attaining well articulated self awareness. Erratic attention to proprioceptive cues precludes effective orientation and efficient self direction. Lacking a continuous awareness of perceptual information, the schizophrenic child is inclined to show attenuated or excessively trial and error response rather than reflective, purposeful, and smooth accommodation to the shifting demands of inner and outer experience.

Our attention is thus on the self monitoring, self orienting impairments which result from sensory imperception in schizophrenic children. This study has featured auditory receptor behavior in the schizophrenic children, and has stressed the unique and serious disorientative consequences of specific auditory imperception. However, it has been our conviction that there is actually a more pervasive, sensory insulation involving other sensory modalities as well—for example, visual and vestibular—which may in fact contribute to the spatial disorientation and postural imbalance of the children.

The unchanging abnormalities in motor behavior (muscle tone, activity level) and receptor response (auditory startle, delayed auditory feedback) may be hypothetically related to the level of integrity of the schizophrenic child's nervous system. This idea is supported, to a degree, by the apparent unalterability of these findings as the schizophrenic children grew older. However, recent observations of the children in the course of psychiatric treatment and special educational remediation by the Center speech pathologists have confirmed the individual alterability of monitoring functions, provided suitable and focused therapeutic procedures are employed.

In short, the present report represents a rather ambitious effort to delineate longitudinal changes in behavior of schizophrenic children. The focus of the investigation has been on self regulative aspects of behavior. Its data are 40 measures of different aspects of integrative conduct, carefully selected in terms of a central hypothesis that the schizophrenic child suffers from large deficits in all major self regulative functions including receptive, integrative and executive functions. Our findings obviously are limited by the specific measures employed, and it is quite possible we have omitted variables of more crucial significance in childhood psychosis than those employed in the study. Human behavior is certainly too complex to fit into 40 variables. Nor have we evaluated sufficiently interactions among the variables, although a total explanation of the children's behavior would require reference to such dynamic interplay. Nevertheless, even though the range of characteristics under investigation have obvious restrictions, there is sufficient evidence of the changing, growing character of schizophrenic children.

The present longitudinal findings have reminded us very forcefully that the schizophrenic child is above all else a "child." Like other children observed in life process, he can grow, his functions stabilize, and he gradually improves his interactions with people and his total environment. Perhaps, comprehensive treatment is helpful in persuading him to accept the goals of maturation. Like other children, too, each schizophrenic child is distinctive in his behavior and life course.

That he is a child is reflected in the evidence of change and growth. In our data, even over a brief period of three years, we see him typically moving slowly but consistently in the direction of more mature behavior. In this process his physiological and psychological capacities evolve and we are able to see him accommodating to new and more complex environmental challenges. In short, like all children, he responds to stimulation and he matures.

We believe that we have some evidence (for example, his responses to education and social training) that the treatment environment has helped the child to adapt to his world. What is not so apparent at this time is the direct influence of a treatment climate on the pace of physiological and psychological growth which the study indicates has occurred in most of the children under care.

It is true that we did not demonstrate so much acceleration of growth that the schizophrenic children could be called totally normal after three years of treatment. We are saying, however, that in their growth pattern the schizophrenic children showed in an essential way that they are quite definitely a subgroup of the total universe of children which characteristically grows and develops responsively in a stimulating environment. Like all children, the great bulk of the adaptive capacities of the schizophrenic children unfolded.

We seem to have little difficulty in enhancing functions which are obviously related to social experience. Some functions, in which biological factors would seem to play a more primary role, appear to be less affected. However, even here, we are impressed with the possibilities for improving the children by a comprehensive program embodying the very broad range of psychotherapeutic procedures available to us.

References

Behrens, M. and Goldfarb, W. A study of patterns of interaction of families of schizophrenic children in residential treatment. *American Journal of Orthopsychiatry,* 1958, **28**, 300.

Bender, L. *A visual motor Gestalt test and its clinical use.* New York: American Orthopsychiatric Association, 1938.

Bender, L., & Grugett, A. A study of certain epidemiological factors in a group of children with childhood schizophrenia. *American Journal of Orthopsychiatry,* 1956, **26**, 131.

Bender, M. B. *Disorders in perception.* Springfield, Ill.: Charles C Thomas, 1952.

Bloom, B. S. *Stability and change in human characteristics.* New York: John Wiley & Sons, 1966.

Boatman, M. J., & Szurek, S. A. A clinical study of childhood schizophrenia. In D. D. Jackson (Ed.), *The etiology of schizophrenia.* New York: Basic Books, 1960.

Cohen, H. J., Taft, L. T., Mahadevia, M. S., & Birch, H. G. Developmental changes in overflow in normal and aberrantly functioning children. *Journal of Pediatrics,* 1967, **71**(1), 39.

Creak, M. Schizophrenic syndrome in childhood. *Cerebral Palsy Bulletin,* 1961, 3, 501.

Doll, E. A. *The measurement of social competence.* U.S.A.: Educational Test Bureau, Educational Publishers, 1953.

Eisenberg, L. The autistic child in adolescence. *American Journal of Psychiatry,* 1956, 112, 607.

Fink, M., & Bender, M. B. Perception of simultaneous tactile stimuli in normal children. *Neurology,* 1952, 3, 27.

Fink, M., Green, M. A., & Bender, M. B. Perception of simultaneous tactile stimuli by mentally defective subjects. *Journal of Nervous and Mental Disease,* 1953, 117, 43.

Gesell, A. L. *The embryology of behavior.* New York: Harper & Bros., 1945.

Goldfarb, W. *Childhood schizophrenia.* Cambridge, Mass.: Harvard University Press, 1961.

Goldfarb, W. Families of schizophrenic children. In L. C. Kolb, R. L. Masland, & R. E. Cooke (Eds.), *Mental retardation.* Baltimore: Williams & Wilkins, 1962.

Goldfarb, W. Corrective socialization: A rationale for the treatment of schizophrenic children. *Canadian Psychiatric Association Journal,* 1965, 10, 481.

Goldfarb, W. Factors in the development of schizophrenic children: An approach to subclassification. In J. Romano (Ed.), *Excerpta Medica International.* Congress Series, No. 151, 1967.

Goldfarb, W. The subclassification of psychotic children: Application to a study of longitudinal change. *Journal of Psychiatric Research,* 1968, 6(1), 333.

Goldfarb, W. A follow-up investigation of schizophrenic children treated in residence. *Psychosocial Process,* 1970, 1(1), 9.

Goldfarb, W., & Braunstein, P. Reactions to delayed auditory feedback among a group of schizophrenic children. In P. Hoch & J. Zubin (Eds.), *Psychopathology of communication.* New York: Grune & Stratton, 1958.

Goldfarb, W., Braunstein, P., & Lorge, I. A study of speech patterns in a group of schizophrenic children. *American Journal of Orthopsychiatry,* 1956, 26, 544.

Goldfarb, W., Goldfarb, N., & Pollack, R. Treatment of childhood schizophrenia: A three-year comparison of day and residential treatment of schizophrenic children. *Archives of General Psychiatry,* 1966, 14, 119.

Goldfarb, W., Goldfarb, N., & Pollack, R. Changes in IQ of schizophrenic children during residential treatment. *Archives of General Psychiatry,* 1969, 21, 673.

Goldfarb, W., Levy, D. M., & Meyers, D. I. The verbal encounter between the schizophrenic child and his mother. In G. S. Goldman & D. Shapiro (Eds.), *Developments in psychoanalysis at Columbia University.* New York: Hafner, 1966.

Goldfarb, W., Levy, D. M., & Meyers, D. I. The mother speaks to her schizophrenic child: Language in childhood schizophrenia. *Psychiatry,* 1972, 35(3), 217.

Goldfarb, W., Mintz, I., & Stroock, K. W. *A time to heal.* New York: International Universities Press, 1969.

Goldfarb, W., & Pollack, R. C. The childhood schizophrenic's response to schooling in a residential treatment center. In P. 'H. Hoch & J. Zubin (Eds.), *The evaluation of psychiatric treatment.* New York: Grune & Stratton, 1964.

Goldfarb, W., Sibulkin, L., Behrens, M., & Jahoda, H. Parental perplexity and childhood confusion. In A. H. Esman (Ed.), *New frontiers in child guidance.* New York: International Universities Press, 1958.

Heath, S. R. Railwalking performances as related to mental age and ethological type among the mentally retarded. *American Journal of Psychology,* 1942, 55, 240.

Hollingshead, A. B., & Redlich, F. C. *Social class and mental illness.* New York: John Wiley & Sons, 1958.

Inhelder, B., & Piaget, J. *The growth of logical reasoning.* New York: Basic Books, 1958.

Kallman, F. J., & Roth, B. Genetic aspects of preadolescent schizophrenia. *American Journal of Psychiatry,* 1956, 112, 599.

Kanner, L. To what extent is early infantile autism determined by constitutional inadequacies? In D. Hooker & C. C. Hare (Eds.), *Genetics and the inheritance of integrated neurological and psychiatric patterns.* Baltimore, Md.: Williams & Wilkins, 1954.

Metropolitan Achievement Tests Manual. New York: World Book, 1948.

Meyers, D. I., & Goldfarb, W. Studies of perplexity in mothers of schizophrenic children. *American Journal of Orthopsychiatry,* 1961, 31, 551.

Meyers, D. I., & Goldfarb, W. Psychiatric appraisals of parents and siblings of schizophrenic children. *American Journal of Psychiatry,* 1962, 118, 902.

Newman, H. H., Freeman, F. N., & Holzinger, K. T. *Twins: A study of heredity and environment.* Chicago: University of Chicago Press, 1937.

Rutter, M. The influence of organic and emotional factors on the origins, nature and outcome of childhood psychosis. *Developmental Medicine and Child Neurology,* 1965, 7, 518.

Sloan, W. The Lincoln-Oseretsky motor development scale. *Genetic Psychology Monographs,* 1955, **51**, 183.

Street, R. F. Gestalt completion test: A study of a cross section of intellect. *Contributions to Education,* No. 481. New York: Teachers College, 1931.

Thurstone, L. L. A factorial study of perception. *Psychiatric Mongraphs,* No. 4. Chicago: University of Chicago Press, 1949.

Witkins, H. et al. *Psychological differentiation.* New York: John Wiley & Sons, 1962.

Zubin, J., & Thompson, J. *Sorting tests in relation to drug therapy in schizophrenia.* New York: State Psychiatric Hospital, 1941.

Appendix

The Appendix which follows contains 40 sets of tables—a set of tables for each of the 40 variables in the study, in the following order:

Set Number	Variable
10	Muscle Tone
11	Double Simultaneous Stimuli—Homologous—Eyes Open
12	Double Simultaneous Stimuli—Heterologous—Eyes Open
13	Double Simultaneous Stimuli—Homologous—Eyes Closed
14	Double Simultaneous Stimuli—Heterologous—Eyes Closed
15	Double Simultaneous Stimuli—Total
16	Oculomotor Functioning—Eye Movement
17	Oculomotor Functioning—Dissociation of Head and Eye Movement
18	Whirling—Arms at Side
19	Whirling—Arms Outstretched and Parallel
20	Romberg—Arms at Side
21	Romberg—Arms Outstretched and Parallel
22	Finger to Finger Test
23	Finger to Nose Test
24	Auditory Startle
25	Delayed Auditory Feedback—Voice and Speech
26	Delayed Auditory Feedback—Language
27	Delayed Auditory Feedback—Self Awareness
28	Gottschaldt Embedded Figures Test
29	Street's Gestalt Completion Test
30	Bender Gestalt Test
31	Weigl Color Form Sorting Test
32	Orientation Test
33	Lincoln-Oseretsky Motor Development Scales
34	Railwalking
35	Dynamometer
36	Wechsler Intelligence Scale for Children—Verbal
37	Wechsler Intelligence Scale for Children—Performance
38	Wechsler Intelligence Scale for Children—Full
39	Communication—Voice and Speech
40	Communication—Language

It should be noted that the 40 sets of tables in the Appendix are so identified in the table numbers by the prefix A. In each of the 40 sets there are three tables based on schizophrenic children which are identified by intermediate codes, 1, 2, and 3 in the table number. Where data are also available for normal children, there are two more tables with intermediate codes 4 and 5. The third component in the table number represents the variable under consideration and has values 1 to 40. These three components of the table numbers thus contain a sequence of three codes—the prefix A; the numbers 1 to 5 indicating the tables 1 to 5 in each of the 40 sets; and the numbers 1 to 40 representing the 40 variables. The three components are separated by hyphens as can be seen, for example, in the following set of tables for Muscle Tone which is variable number 10:

A-1-10	Means, Trends (and other data) by Year of Treatment for Specific Strata of Schizophrenic Children
A-2-10	Probability of No Annual Change for Schizophrenic Children
A-3-10	Percentage Distribution by Average Age for Schizophrenic Children
A-4-10	Annual Means and Standard Deviations by Age for Normal Children
A-5-10	Percentage Distribution by Age for Normal Children

In the text, references to each variable in the Appendix will be noted as in the following example—the 5 tables for muscle tone is referred to as Tables A variable 10.

Appendix Tables coded with the intermediate code, A-1. The 15 data columns of this group of appendix tables relate to the 15 groupings of the schizophrenic children in the study and thereby distinguish between the total group, and 14 sub-groups which are used to stratify the children. It will be noted that there are two sub-groupings by Sex, Admission Age, and Neurological Status, while Social Position calls for three sub-groupings and IQ has five sub-groupings, thus providing the 14 sub-groupings of the children. It should also be noted that for each of the five variables of stratification, the same total group of children is involved.

Section A— The row designation in the stub indicates that Section A contains the number of children under each specified column designation.

Section B— Contains the Mean and Standard Deviations at admission and at each subsequent year for each column designation.

Section C— Provides, in each column, a linear trend equation with the computed score at admission in the first row and the average annual change in the second row. The third row gives the probability that the trend arises by chance alone.

Section D— For each column, this section compares the sub-groups within each of the five types of stratification—Sex, Age at Admission, Neurological Status, Social Position and Full Intelligence Quotient at Admission. Within each of these stratifications, the probabilities are shown that the slopes of the related sub-groups (within each of these stratifications) show only chance differences; and the next row gives the probabilities that the overall regression equations show only chance differences.

Section E— Using the Friedman One-way Analysis of Variance Test, there is shown the probability that individual changes for the individual children in each specified sub-grouping, linear or otherwise, arise by chance alone.

Appendix Tables coded with the intermediate code, A-2. The second table in each of the 40 sets is also based on the schizophrenic children in the study. It provides the probabilities that the recorded individual changes for the specified time intervals of each of the 40 variables may be due to chance alone. These probabilities are based on computations using the Wilcoxon Matched Pairs Signed Ranks Test and are shown for the total group of children and for each of the same 14 sub-groups (which are specified in the first table of each set).

Appendix Tables coded with the intermediate code, A-3. The third table in each of the 40 sets provides percentage distributions of the schizophrenic children by average score at each age, 7 to 10 years. The age is the average age for the children at admission and in each subsequent year of treatment. Thus, for example, scores at admission appear under the age of seven years, and scores for the first year of treatment appear under age of 8 years.

Appendix Tables coded with the intermediate code, A-4. Where data is available for normal children, means and standard deviations are provided by age, 6 to 11 years. For the normal children, the age is the actual age of the normal children.

Appendix Tables coded with the intermediate code, A-5. Where data is available for normal children, this table provides percentage distributions of scores for these children by age. In this table, the age is based upon the actual age of the children.

TABLES A-1

Means, Trends (and other data)
by Year of Treatment for Specific Strata
of Schizophrenic Children
(for Variables 1–40)

Table A-1-1. Ego Status

Variable	Total all children (1)	I Sex Males (2)	I Sex Females (3)	II Admission age less than 8 years (4)	II Admission age 8 years or more (5)	III Neurological status Non organics (6)	III Neurological status Organics (7)	IV Social position 1 or 2 (8)	IV Social position 3 (9)	IV Social position 4 or 5 (10)	V WISC Full IQ at admission Below 46 (11)	V WISC 46-69 (12)	V WISC 70-89 (13)	V WISC 90-109 (14)	V WISC Above 109 (15)
A. No. of children	40.	27.	13.	25.	15.	14.	26.	5.	15.	20.	6.	10.	14.	6.	4.
B. Annual scores															
Admission															
Mean	2.05	2.11	1.92	1.88	2.33	2.28	1.92	1.60	2.00	2.20	1.16	1.90	2.07	2.50	3.00
Std. Dev.	0.67	0.69	0.64	0.72	0.48	0.61	0.68	0.54	0.75	0.61	0.40	0.31	0.61	0.54	0.00
First year															
Mean	2.32	2.33	2.30	2.20	2.53	2.42	2.26	1.80	2.33	2.45	1.16	2.40	2.42	2.66	3.00
Std. Dev.	0.69	0.73	0.63	0.76	0.51	0.64	0.72	0.83	0.61	0.68	0.40	0.51	0.51	0.51	0.00
Second year															
Mean	2.45	2.40	2.53	2.32	2.66	2.71	2.30	2.00	2.33	2.65	1.16	2.60	2.42	3.00	3.25
Std. Dev.	0.74	0.74	0.77	0.80	0.61	0.72	0.73	1.00	0.61	0.74	0.40	0.51	0.51	0.00	0.50
Third year															
Mean	2.55	2.48	2.69	2.40	2.80	2.92	2.34	2.00	2.53	2.70	1.33	2.70	2.57	3.00	3.25
Std. Dev.	0.71	0.70	0.75	0.76	0.56	0.47	0.74	1.00	0.63	0.65	0.51	0.48	0.51	0.00	0.50
C. Linear trend equation															
Admission score	2.10	2.15	1.98	1.94	2.35	2.25	2.01	1.64	2.05	2.24	1.13	2.00	2.15	2.51	2.97
Annual change	0.16	0.11	0.25	0.16	0.15	0.22	0.13	0.14	0.16	0.17	0.05	0.26	0.15	0.18	0.10
Probability	0.0017	0.0534	0.0048	0.0143	0.0158	0.0039	0.0388	0.5918	0.0356	0.0127	0.5278	0.0005	0.0217	0.0114	0.1981
D. Sub groups within I to V															
Prob. equal slopes		*** 0.2039 ***		*** 0.8784 ***		*** 0.6229 ***		*****	0.9808	*****	*****	*****	0.3510	*****	*****
Prob. equal trends		*** 0.7852 ***		*** 0.0011 ***		*** 0.0014 ***		*****	0.0010	*****	*****	*****	0.0000	*****	*****
E. Friedman Anova															
Probability	0.0000	0.0038	0.0000	0.0000	0.0053	0.0000	0.0003	0.2647	0.0033	0.0001	0.8273	0.0000	0.0075	0.0430	0.6191

Table A-1-2. Metropolitan Achievement Test—Reading

Variable	Total all children (1)	I Sex — Males (2)	I Sex — Females (3)	II Admission age — less than 8 years (4)	II Admission age — 8 years or more (5)	III Neurological status — Non organics (6)	III Neurological status — Organics (7)	IV Social position — 1 or 2 (8)	IV Social position — 3 (9)	IV Social position — 4 or 5 (10)	V WISC Full IQ at admission — Below 46 (11)	V — 46-69 (12)	V — 70-89 (13)	V — 90-109 (14)	V — Above 109 (15)
A. No. of children	38.	25.	13.	24.	14.	14.	24.	5.	15.	18.	6.	9.	13.	6.	4.
B. Annual scores															
Admission															
Mean	86.31	87.48	84.07	72.41	110.14	104.21	75.87	65.00	85.53	92.88	65.00	65.00	82.46	89.50	174.00
Std. Dev.	37.84	40.50	33.57	19.23	49.53	51.07	22.83	0.00	40.88	39.50	0.00	0.00	28.44	23.28	30.29
First year															
Mean	105.65	108.96	99.30	96.00	122.21	125.71	93.95	83.00	102.60	114.50	65.00	86.00	106.46	117.83	190.00
Std. Dev.	40.31	44.00	32.76	31.18	49.37	47.97	30.43	24.64	43.72	39.73	0.00	25.60	29.78	12.40	15.66
Second year															
Mean	126.81	130.40	119.92	119.50	139.35	157.00	109.20	101.20	123.33	136.83	76.00	116.88	121.07	145.50	216.00
Std. Dev.	42.89	43.50	42.53	36.28	51.37	42.30	32.72	33.64	47.47	39.65	17.04	25.83	26.75	16.87	13.71
Third year															
Mean	140.13	143.44	133.76	134.50	149.78	171.35	121.91	113.40	136.73	150.38	83.16	129.00	134.69	169.83	223.75
Std. Dev.	45.59	47.98	41.68	42.66	50.36	38.34	39.65	45.46	48.39	42.15	28.18	31.81	27.81	15.13	7.63
C. Linear trend equation															
Admission score	87.33	89.17	83.81	74.14	109.96	104.66	77.23	66.14	85.89	94.42	62.46	65.78	85.47	90.36	174.65
Annual change	18.26	18.93	16.96	20.97	13.60	23.27	15.33	16.34	17.43	19.48	6.55	22.28	17.13	26.86	17.52
Probability	0.0000	0.0000	0.0008	0.0000	0.0232	0.0001	0.0000	0.0113	0.0016	0.0000	0.0325	0.0000	0.0000	0.0000	0.0008
D. Sub groups within I to V															
Prob. equal slopes		*** 0.7562 ***		*** 0.2180 ***		*** 0.1507 ***		*****	0.9186	*****	*****	*****	0.0103	*****	*****
Prob. equal trends		*** 0.2419 ***		*** 0.0005 ***		*** 0.0000 ***		*****	0.0054	*****	*****	*****	0.0000	*****	*****
E. Friedman Anova															
Probability	0.0000	0.0000	0.0000	0.0000	0.0000	0.0000	0.0000	0.0019	0.0000	0.0000	0.1432	0.0000	0.0000	0.0000	0.0000

Table A-1-3. Metropolitan Achievement Test—Arithmetic

Variable	Total all children (1)	I Sex		II Admission age		III Neurological status		IV Social position			V WISC Full IQ at admission				
		Males (2)	Females (3)	less than 8 years (4)	8 years or more (5)	Non organics (6)	Organics (7)	1 or 2 (8)	3 (9)	4 or 5 (10)	Below 46 (11)	46-69 (12)	70-89 (13)	90-109 (14)	Above 109 (15)
A. No. of children	38.	25.	13.	24.	14.	14.	24.	5.	15.	18.	6.	9.	13.	6.	4.
B. Annual scores															
Admission															
Mean	117.92	119.44	115.00	110.12	131.28	131.64	109.91	105.00	115.93	123.16	105.00	105.00	112.38	129.83	166.50
Std. Dev.	22.22	24.40	17.80	12.91	28.38	30.00	10.19	0.00	23.84	22.90	0.00	0.00	12.17	20.92	19.20
First year															
Mean	129.02	131.68	123.92	122.20	140.71	141.92	121.50	113.40	126.86	135.16	105.00	114.44	127.53	144.83	179.00
Std. Dev.	24.76	27.77	17.46	18.54	30.07	31.55	16.23	11.52	25.22	25.76	0.00	11.66	13.53	15.98	20.31
Second year															
Mean	139.44	142.60	133.38	131.70	152.71	159.57	127.70	124.60	136.00	146.44	108.83	124.44	137.23	158.33	198.00
Std. Dev.	28.41	31.22	21.87	20.32	35.58	33.80	16.20	18.46	29.05	29.23	6.01	11.40	10.28	20.81	23.45
Third year															
Mean	150.26	154.92	141.30	140.66	166.71	173.92	136.45	126.40	144.93	161.33	112.00	135.55	143.53	178.00	221.00
Std. Dev.	36.17	40.34	25.46	28.22	43.06	41.94	23.90	20.61	35.72	37.08	11.48	20.47	15.68	28.78	21.40
C. Linear trend equation															
Admission score	118.04	119.55	115.14	111.00	130.11	130.09	111.02	106.03	116.51	122.66	103.98	104.61	114.69	129.05	163.75
Annual change	10.74	11.73	8.83	10.11	11.82	14.45	8.58	7.54	9.61	12.57	2.48	10.16	10.31	15.80	18.25
Probability	0.0000	0.0001	0.0014	0.0000	0.0055	0.0011	0.0000	0.0160	0.0049	0.0002	0.0386	0.0000	0.0000	0.0007	0.0013
D. Sub groups within I to V															
Prob. equal slopes		*** 0.5072 ***		*** 0.6692 ***		*** 0.1123 ***		*****	·0.6500	*****	*****	*****	0.0017	*****	*****
Prob. equal trends		*** 0.6656 ***		*** 0.0000 ***		*** 0.0000 ***		*****	0.0017	*****	*****	*****	0.0000	*****	*****
E. Friedman Anova															
Probability	0.0000	0.0000	0.0000	0.0000	0.0000	0.0000	0.0000	0.0037	0.0000	0.0000	0.1432	0.0000	0.0000	0.0000	0.0000

Table A-1-4. Metropolitan Achievement Test—Total Achievement

Variable	Total all children (1)	I Sex — Males (2)	I Sex — Females (3)	II Admission age — less than 8 years (4)	II Admission age — 8 years or more (5)	III Neurological status — Non organics (6)	III Neurological status — Organics (7)	IV Social position — 1 or 2 (8)	IV Social position — 3 (9)	IV Social position — 4 or 5 (10)	V WISC — Below 46 (11)	V WISC — 46-69 (12)	V WISC — 70-89 (13)	V WISC — 90-109 (14)	V WISC — Above 109 (15)
A. No. of children	38.	25.	13.	24.	14.	14.	24.	5.	15.	18.	6.	9.	13.	6.	4.
B. Annual scores															
Admission															
Mean	94.00	95.32	91.46	82.62	113.50	110.28	84.50	75.00	93.20	99.94	75.00	75.00	90.07	103.16	164.25
Std. Dev.	32.00	34.27	28.24	18.10	41.06	42.09	19.75	0.00	36.56	31.36	0.00	0.00	24.43	23.10	27.10
First year															
Mean	112.07	115.08	106.30	103.45	126.85	130.14	101.54	90.60	109.00	120.61	75.00	93.22	112.92	127.50	184.25
Std. Dev.	35.92	39.11	29.38	28.47	43.20	42.36	27.33	21.36	38.64	35.36	0.00	22.22	26.26	14.74	15.37
Second year															
Mean	131.63	135.92	123.38	124.20	144.35	160.71	114.66	108.80	126.20	142.50	88.50	119.55	125.92	152.33	211.00
Std. Dev.	38.79	39.96	36.55	31.30	47.69	36.71	29.06	31.81	41.79	35.99	22.35	21.52	23.40	17.40	15.70
Third year															
Mean	144.57	148.52	137.00	136.83	157.85	174.00	127.41	118.00	139.60	156.11	91.00	132.77	139.69	172.50	225.50
Std. Dev.	43.23	46.29	37.17	37.94	49.71	39.43	35.96	40.42	45.50	40.10	24.98	29.13	24.12	18.21	17.71
C. Linear trend equation															
Admission score	94.87	96.64	91.48	84.27	113.05	110.52	85.75	76.02	93.54	101.23	73.15	75.18	92.87	103.95	164.67
Annual change	17.12	18.04	15.36	18.33	15.05	22.17	14.18	14.72	15.64	19.03	6.15	19.96	16.18	23.28	21.05
Probability	0.0000	0.0000	0.0006	0.0000	0.0067	0.0000	0.0000	0.0115	0.0016	0.0000	0.0476	0.0000	0.0000	0.0000	0.0003
D. Sub groups within I to V															
Prob. equal slopes		*** 0.6464 ***		*** 0.5510 ***		*** 0.1047 ***		*****	*****	*****	*****	*****	0.0158	*****	*****
Prob. equal trends		*** 0.1493 ***		*** 0.0002 ***		*** 0.0000 ***		*****	*****	*****	*****	*****	0.0000	*****	*****
E. Friedman Anova															
Probability	0.0000	0.0000	0.0000	0.0000	0.0000	0.0000	0.0000	0.0019	0.0000	0.0000	0.1855	0.0000	0.0000	0.0000	0.0000

Table A-1-5. Vineland Social Maturity Scale—Social Age

Variable	Total all children (1)	I Sex — Males (2)	Females (3)	II Admission age — less than 8 years (4)	8 years or more (5)	III Neurological status — Non organics (6)	Organics (7)	IV Social position — 1 or 2 (8)	3 (9)	4 or 5 (10)	V WISC Full IQ at admission — Below 46 (11)	46-69 (12)	70-89 (13)	90-109 (14)	Above 109 (15)
A. No. of children	37.	26.	11.	24.	13.	13.	24.	5.	13.	19.	6.	10.	12.	5.	4.
B. Annual scores															
Admission															
Mean	60.32	59.65	61.90	56.37	75.00	67.61	56.37	52.20	58.07	64.00	39.00	48.50	68.08	69.80	86.75
Std. Dev.	19.98	18.70	23.64	15.21	19.85	20.16	19.14	11.30	22.96	19.55	10.15	12.30	16.24	16.43	11.81
First year															
Mean	74.75	73.46	77.81	69.16	85.07	84.23	69.62	66.60	70.46	79.84	52.50	62.40	78.83	95.40	101.00
Std. Dev.	22.30	20.84	26.26	20.97	21.70	23.24	20.45	29.88	23.70	19.03	18.84	15.63	15.61	15.24	15.64
Second year															
Mean	86.02	83.92	91.00	82.20	93.07	101.00	77.91	67.80	85.69	91.05	62.33	72.00	90.58	106.40	117.50
Std. Dev.	24.69	23.96	26.85	25.50	22.35	21.70	22.65	24.78	26.74	22.07	15.88	16.76	20.05	17.09	17.78
Third year															
Mean	92.89	92.65	93.45	90.12	98.00	99.30	89.41	84.00	88.92	97.94	64.50	86.20	100.91	104.40	113.75
Std. Dev.	24.13	21.81	30.10	24.64	23.23	21.76	25.07	27.54	19.18	26.28	21.05	19.95	18.41	19.03	22.57
C. Linear trend equation															
Admission score	62.15	61.00	64.87	54.52	76.23	71.26	57.22	53.15	59.62	66.25	41.63	48.87	68.06	76.78	90.12
Annual change	10.89	10.94	10.78	12.62	7.70	11.18	10.74	9.66	10.77	11.30	8.63	12.27	11.02	11.48	9.75
Probability	0.0000	0.0000	0.0044	0.0000	0.0056	0.0003	0.0000	0.0503	0.0007	0.0000	0.0087	0.0000	0.0000	0.0045	0.0215
D. Sub groups within I to V															
Prob. equal slopes		*** 0.9632 ***		*** 0.1384 ***		*** 0.8904 ***		*****	0.9464	*****	*****	*****	0.9079	*****	*****
Prob. equal trends		*** 0.6179 ***		*** 0.0004 ***		*** 0.0003 ***		*****	0.0130	*****	*****	*****	0.0000	*****	*****
E. Friedman Anova															
Probability	0.0000	0.0000	0.0000	0.0000	0.0000	0.0000	0.0000	0.0287	0.0000	0.0000	0.0013	0.0000	0.0000	0.0000	0.0002

Table A-1-6. Vineland Social Maturity Scale–Social Quotient

Variable	Total all children (1)	I. Sex Males (2)	Females (3)	II. Admission age less than 8 years (4)	8 years or more (5)	III. Neurological status Non organics (6)	Organics (7)	IV. Social position 1 or 2 (8)	3 (9)	4 or 5 (10)	V. WISC Full IQ at admission Below 46 (11)	46-69 (12)	70-89 (13)	90-109 (14)	Above 109 (15)
A. No. of children	37.	26.	11.	24.	13.	13.	24.	5.	13.	19.	6.	10.	12.	5.	4.
B. Annual scores															
Admission															
Mean	70.86	70.61	71.45	68.66	74.92	77.00	67.54	72.60	68.92	71.73	53.00	54.90	77.83	93.00	89.00
Std. Dev.	21.00	20.55	23.05	20.95	21.32	16.39	22.75	18.39	26.93	17.87	17.01	15.43	14.95	15.87	2.16
First year															
Mean	79.32	79.38	79.18	79.83	78.38	86.92	75.20	77.20	76.07	82.10	63.00	65.30	81.08	111.40	93.50
Std. Dev.	21.74	21.56	23.20	24.14	17.28	18.53	22.58	29.75	23.59	18.98	21.79	12.72	16.94	9.78	5.50
Second year															
Mean	81.86	81.15	83.54	83.87	78.15	92.00	76.37	77.40	82.53	82.57	61.83	71.80	83.83	107.60	99.00
Std. Dev.	21.14	21.50	21.19	23.79	15.26	14.75	22.29	19.64	22.80	21.33	14.13	12.14	20.81	13.27	10.73
Third year															
Mean	79.29	79.84	78.00	81.62	75.00	83.30	77.12	77.20	78.46	80.42	59.66	72.80	84.25	96.60	88.50
Std. Dev.	19.75	18.59	23.19	21.27	16.51	16.34	21.39	24.59	18.36	20.45	17.99	19.28	15.87	10.40	18.43
C. Linear trend equation															
Admission score	73.66	73.33	74.44	72.06	76.61	81.20	69.57	74.00	71.23	75.23	56.55	57.16	78.45	101.10	91.90
Annual change	2.78	2.94	2.40	4.29	0.00	2.40	2.99	1.40	3.50	2.65	1.88	6.02	2.20	0.70	0.40
Probability	0.0693	0.1012	0.5628	0.0378	1.0000	0.2576	0.1376	0.7541	0.2197	0.1907	0.5667	0.0070	0.3205	0.8039	0.8695
D. Sub groups within I to V															
Prob. equal slopes		*** 0.8668 ***		*** 0.1826 ***		*** 0.8455 ***		*****	0.9107	*****	*****	*****	0.5246	*****	*****
Prob. equal trends		*** 0.9359 ***		*** 0.6098 ***		*** 0.0030 ***		*****	0.7213	*****	*****	*****	0.0000	*****	*****
E. Friedman Anova															
Probability	0.0000	0.0006	0.0000	0.0000	0.1663	0.0000	0.0104	0.1130	0.0001	0.0001	0.0460	0.0000	0.5708	0.0000	0.1065

Table A-1-7. Activity Level

Variable	Total all children (1)	I Sex		II Admission age		III Neurological status		IV Social position			V WISC Full IQ at admission				
		Males (2)	Females (3)	less than 8 years (4)	8 years or more (5)	Non organics (6)	Organics (7)	1 or 2 (8)	3 (9)	4 or 5 (10)	Below 46 (11)	46-69 (12)	70-89 (13)	90-109 (14)	Above 109 (15)
A. No. of children	40.	27.	13.	25.	15.	14.	26.	5.	15.	20.	6.	10.	14.	6.	4.
B. Annual scores															
Admission															
Mean	1.92	1.88	2.00	1.80	2.13	2.00	1.88	2.00	1.60	2.15	1.50	2.00	1.85	2.16	2.25
Std. Dev.	0.69	0.69	0.70	0.70	0.63	0.78	0.65	0.70	0.63	0.67	0.54	0.66	0.66	0.75	0.95
First year															
Mean	1.97	1.88	2.15	1.92	2.06	2.28	1.80	2.00	2.00	1.95	1.33	2.00	2.00	2.33	2.25
Std. Dev.	0.65	0.64	0.68	0.64	0.70	0.61	0.63	0.70	0.53	0.75	0.51	0.66	0.67	0.51	0.50
Second year															
Mean	1.95	1.88	2.07	1.92	2.00	2.21	1.80	2.00	1.86	2.00	1.83	1.70	1.78	2.33	2.75
Std. Dev.	0.71	0.69	0.75	0.64	0.84	0.89	0.56	0.70	0.83	0.64	0.75	0.67	0.57	0.51	0.95
Third year															
Mean	2.02	2.00	2.07	2.00	2.06	2.28	1.88	1.60	1.93	2.20	1.83	1.70	2.07	2.33	2.50
Std. Dev.	0.65	0.73	0.49	0.57	0.79	0.61	0.65	0.89	0.45	0.69	0.40	0.67	0.61	0.81	0.57
C. Linear trend equation															
Admission score	1.92	1.86	2.05	1.81	2.10	2.07	1.84	2.07	1.72	2.04	1.40	2.03	1.86	2.21	2.25
Annual change	0.02	0.03	0.01	0.06	-0.02	0.07	0.00	-0.12	0.08	0.02	0.15	-0.12	0.04	0.05	0.12
Probability	0.5742	0.5813	0.8455	0.2949	0.7539	0.6279	1.0000	0.5768	0.2372	0.7709	0.1547	0.2014	0.5797	0.6738	0.5327
D. Sub groups within I to V															
Prob. equal slopes		*** 0.8553 ***		*** 0.6142 ***		*** 0.5711 ***		*****	*****		*****	*****			
Prob. equal trends		*** 0.1585 ***		*** 0.1541 ***		*** 0.0020 ***		*****	*****		*****	*****			
E. Friedman Anova															
Probability	0.7058	0.7021	0.8435	0.5575	0.6071	0.3894	0.7377	0.2275	0.0822	0.1199	0.1341	0.0890	0.2167	0.8273	0.8273

Table A-1-8. Attentiveness

Variable	Total all children (1)	I Sex Males (2)	I Sex Females (3)	II Admission age less than 8 years (4)	II Admission age 8 years or more (5)	III Neurological status Non organics (6)	III Neurological status Organics (7)	IV Social position 1 or 2 (8)	IV Social position 3 (9)	IV Social position 4 or 5 (10)	V WISC Full IQ at admission Below 46 (11)	V 46-69 (12)	V 70-89 (13)	V 90-109 (14)	V Above 109 (15)
A. No. of children	40.	27.	13.	25.	15.	14.	26.	5.	15.	20.	6.	10.	14.	6.	4.
B. Annual scores															
Admission															
Mean	2.82	2.92	2.61	2.52	3.33	3.00	2.73	2.00	2.40	3.35	1.16	2.40	3.21	3.83	3.50
Std. Dev.	1.17	1.23	1.04	1.15	1.04	1.03	1.25	1.22	0.98	1.08	0.40	0.84	1.05	0.40	1.00
First year															
Mean	2.75	2.62	3.00	2.48	3.20	3.28	2.46	2.40	2.60	2.95	1.33	3.10	2.78	3.16	3.25
Std. Dev.	1.12	1.04	1.29	1.04	1.14	0.99	1.10	1.14	0.98	1.23	0.51	1.37	0.80	0.98	0.95
Second year															
Mean	3.05	2.92	3.30	2.84	3.40	3.57	2.76	2.80	2.93	3.20	1.83	2.60	3.28	3.66	4.25
Std. Dev.	1.13	1.10	1.18	1.10	1.12	1.15	1.03	1.64	1.16	1.00	0.40	0.84	1.06	1.03	0.95
Third year															
Mean	3.20	3.40	2.76	3.00	3.53	3.64	2.96	2.20	2.93	3.65	2.16	2.80	3.28	4.00	4.25
Std. Dev.	1.30	1.33	1.16	1.25	1.35	1.21	1.31	1.09	1.09	1.34	1.16	1.22	1.06	1.54	0.95
C. Linear trend equation															
Admission score	2.74	2.71	2.80	2.44	3.24	3.04	2.58	2.20	2.42	3.11	1.10	2.62	3.03	3.51	3.32
Annual change	0.14	0.17	0.07	0.18	0.08	0.22	0.10	0.10	0.19	0.11	0.35	0.07	0.07	0.10	0.32
Probability	0.0861	0.0890	0.6069	0.0759	0.5581	0.0900	0.6637	0.6964	0.1107	0.6647	0.0090	0.6586	0.5613	0.6182	0.1407
D. Sub groups within I to V															
Prob. equal slopes		*** 0.5955 ***		*** 0.5574 ***		*** 0.5171 ***		*****	0.8862	*****	*****	*****	0.6181	*****	*****
Prob. equal trends		*** 0.8016 ***		*** 0.0008 ***		*** 0.0012 ***		*****	0.0010	*****	*****	*****	0.0000	*****	*****
E. Friedman Anova Probability	0.0011	0.0000	0.0125	0.0039	0.1395	0.0021	0.0362	0.0890	0.0822	0.0001	0.0018	0.2364	0.2167	0.0205	0.0212

157

Table A-1-9. Sustained Effort

Variable	Total all children	I Sex		II Admission age		III Neurological status		IV Social position			V WISC Full IQ at admission				
		Males	Females	less than 8 years	8 years or more	Non organics	Organics	1 or 2	3	4 or 5	Below 46	46-69	70-89	90-109	Above 109
	(1)	(2)	(3)	(4)	(5)	(6)	(7)	(8)	(9)	(10)	(11)	(12)	(13)	(14)	(15)
A. No. of children	40.	27.	13.	25.	15.	14.	26.	5.	15.	20.	6.	10.	14.	6.	4.
B. Annual scores															
Admission															
Mean	2.60	2.70	2.38	2.36	3.00	2.92	2.42	2.00	2.33	2.95	1.00	2.10	2.78	3.83	3.75
Std. Dev.	1.12	1.20	0.96	1.11	1.06	1.14	1.10	1.00	0.97	1.19	0.00	0.99	0.69	0.40	0.50
First year															
Mean	2.75	2.74	2.76	2.40	3.33	3.28	2.46	2.40	2.46	3.05	1.50	2.90	2.64	3.33	3.75
Std. Dev.	1.14	1.05	1.36	1.11	0.97	1.06	1.10	1.14	0.91	1.27	0.54	1.52	0.84	0.81	0.50
Second year															
Mean	2.87	2.77	3.07	2.60	3.33	3.21	2.69	2.60	2.60	3.15	2.00	2.30	3.14	3.66	3.50
Std. Dev.	1.01	1.01	1.03	0.91	1.04	0.97	1.01	1.14	1.05	0.93	0.89	0.94	0.77	0.81	1.00
Third year															
Mean	3.10	3.25	2.76	3.04	3.20	3.64	2.80	2.40	3.00	3.35	2.16	2.70	3.35	3.50	4.00
Std. Dev.	1.10	0.98	1.30	1.17	1.01	0.92	1.09	1.14	1.13	1.03	1.16	1.15	0.84	1.22	0.00
C. Linear trend equation															
Admission score	2.58	2.61	2.53	2.26	3.12	2.95	2.38	2.14	2.28	2.93	1.06	2.32	2.65	3.68	3.67
Annual change	0.16	0.17	0.14	0.22	0.06	0.20	0.13	0.14	0.21	0.13	0.40	0.12	0.22	-0.06	0.05
Probability	0.0350	0.0624	0.3196	0.0208	0.6171	0.0907	0.1389	0.5220	0.0686	0.2408	0.0081	0.5152	0.0211	0.6729	0.7128
D. Sub groups within I to V															
Prob. equal slopes		*** 0.8789 ***	*****	*** 0.2887 ***	*****	*** 0.6644 ***	*****	*****	0.8713	*****	*****	*****	0.3108	*****	*****
Prob. equal trends		*** 0.5234 ***	*****	*** 0.0007 ***	*****	*** 0.0003 ***	*****	*****	0.0021	*****	*****	*****	0.0000	*****	*****
E. Friedman Anova															
Probability	0.0000	0.0004	0.0006	0.0000	0.1256	0.0023	0.0055	0.1808	0.0026	0.0203	0.0009	0.0208	0.0008	0.3075	0.6695

Table A-1-10. Muscle Tone

Variable	Total all children (1)	I Sex		II Admission age		III Neurological status		IV Social position			V WISC Full IQ at admission				
		Males (2)	Females (3)	less than 8 years (4)	8 years or more (5)	Non organics (6)	Organics (7)	1 or 2 (8)	3 (9)	4 or 5 (10)	Below 46 (11)	46-69 (12)	70-89 (13)	90-109 (14)	Above 109 (15)
A. No. of children	38.	25.	13.	23.	15.	13.	25.	5.	14.	19.	6.	10.	14.	4.	4.
B. Annual scores															
Admission															
Mean	2.23	2.28	2.15	2.08	2.46	2.69	2.00	2.20	2.07	2.36	1.83	1.90	2.21	3.00	3.00
Std. Dev.	0.67	0.67	0.68	0.66	0.63	0.48	0.64	0.44	0.82	0.59	0.75	0.31	0.69	0.00	0.00
First year															
Mean	2.28	2.20	2.46	2.17	2.46	2.53	2.16	2.20	2.21	2.36	2.00	2.20	2.14	3.00	2.75
Std. Dev.	0.51	0.50	0.51	0.49	0.51	0.51	0.47	0.44	0.42	0.59	0.00	0.42	0.53	0.00	0.50
Second year															
Mean	2.28	2.20	2.46	2.21	2.40	2.61	2.12	2.40	2.07	2.42	2.16	2.10	2.21	2.75	2.75
Std. Dev.	0.65	0.64	0.66	0.67	0.63	0.50	0.66	0.54	0.82	0.50	0.75	0.56	0.69	0.50	0.50
Third year															
Mean	2.15	2.08	2.30	2.13	2.20	2.30	2.08	2.40	1.92	2.26	2.00	2.20	2.00	2.25	2.75
Std. Dev.	0.59	0.64	0.48	0.62	0.56	0.63	0.57	0.54	0.73	0.45	0.63	0.63	0.55	0.50	0.50
C. Linear trend equation															
Admission score	2.27	2.27	2.27	2.12	2.51	2.69	2.05	2.17	2.15	2.39	1.90	1.98	2.22	3.12	2.92
Annual change	-0.02	-0.06	0.04	0.01	-0.08	-0.10	0.02	0.08	-0.05	-0.02	0.06	0.08	-0.05	-0.25	-0.07
Probability	0.6002	0.2767	0.5407	0.7595	0.1992	0.1053	0.7072	0.5857	0.5126	0.6396	0.5542	0.2584	0.5512	0.0069	0.5707
D. Sub groups within I to V															
Prob. equal slopes		*** 0.2534 ***		*** 0.2436 ***		*** 0.1420 ***		******	0.6254	******	******	******	0.1653	******	******
Prob. equal trends		*** 0.1310 ***		*** 0.0207 ***		*** 0.0000 ***		******	0.0259	******	******	******	0.0000	******	******
E. Friedman Anova Probability	0.5894	0.6053	0.2821	0.7812	0.1589	0.0907	0.7257	0.7005	0.5685	0.5489	0.7920	0.2275	0.3894	0.0128	0.7214

Table A-1-11. Double Simultaneous Stimuli–Homologous—Eyes Open

Variable	Total all children (1)	I Sex Males (2)	I Sex Females (3)	II Admission age less than 8 years (4)	II Admission age 8 years or more (5)	III Neurological status Non organics (6)	III Neurological status Organics (7)	IV Social position 1 or 2 (8)	IV Social position 3 (9)	IV Social position 4 or 5 (10)	V WISC Below 46 (11)	V WISC 46-69 (12)	V WISC 70-89 (13)	V WISC 90-109 (14)	V WISC Above 109 (15)
A. No. of children	38.	25.	13.	24.	14.	12.	26.	5.	14.	19.	5.	10.	14.	6.	3.
B. Annual scores															
Admission															
Mean	3.21	3.24	3.15	2.87	3.78	3.83	2.92	2.40	3.07	3.52	0.00	3.40	3.71	4.00	4.00
Std. Dev.	1.52	1.56	1.51	1.75	0.80	0.57	1.74	2.19	1.68	1.17	0.00	1.07	1.06	0.00	0.00
First year															
Mean	3.13	3.16	3.07	2.79	3.71	3.66	2.88	2.40	3.00	3.42	0.00	2.80	4.00	3.83	4.00
Std. Dev.	1.57	1.51	1.75	1.84	0.72	1.15	1.70	2.19	1.70	1.30	0.00	1.68	0.00	0.40	0.00
Second year															
Mean	3.50	3.56	3.38	3.37	3.71	4.00	3.26	3.20	3.35	3.68	1.80	3.50	3.78	4.00	4.00
Std. Dev.	1.08	1.04	1.19	1.27	0.61	0.00	1.25	1.78	1.00	0.94	2.04	0.84	0.42	0.00	0.00
Third year															
Mean	3.57	3.60	3.53	3.50	3.71	4.00	3.38	3.20	3.57	3.68	2.20	3.40	4.00	3.83	4.00
Std. Dev.	1.05	1.00	1.19	1.17	0.82	0.00	1.23	1.78	0.93	0.94	2.04	1.07	0.00	0.40	0.00
C. Linear trend equation															
Admission score	3.13	3.16	3.06	2.76	3.76	3.75	2.85	2.32	2.97	3.46	-0.25	3.17	3.77	3.96	4.00
Annual change	0.14	0.14	0.14	0.24	-0.02	0.08	0.17	0.32	0.18	0.07	0.84	0.07	0.06	-0.03	0.00
Probability	0.1242	0.2025	0.5580	0.0778	0.8027	0.3195	0.1755	0.5857	0.2576	0.5193	0.0083	0.6876	0.6440	0.5364	1.0000
D. Sub groups within I to V															
Prob. equal slopes		*** 0.9889 ***		*** 0.1691 ***		*** 0.6472 ***		*****	0.6808	*****	*****		0.0023		*****
Prob. equal trends		*** 0.6608 ***		*** 0.0071 ***		*** 0.0012 ***		*****	0.0472	*****	*****		0.0000		*****
E. Friedman Anova Probability	0.5932	0.5056	0.7295	0.1768	0.9952	0.8795	0.5052	0.7005	0.7214	0.7939	0.0047	0.3697	0.5462	0.7566	0.9999

Table A-1-12. Double Simultaneous Stimuli--Heterologous--Eyes Open

Variable	Total all children (1)	I Sex		II Admission age		III Neurological status		IV Social position			V WISC Full IQ at admission				
		Males (2)	Females (3)	less than 8 years (4)	8 years or more (5)	Non organics (6)	Organics (7)	1 or 2 (8)	3 (9)	4 or 5 (10)	Below 46 (11)	46-69 (12)	70-89 (13)	90-109 (14)	Above 109 (15)
A. No. of children	38.	25.	13.	24.	14.	12.	26.	5.	14.	19.	5.	10.	14.	6.	3.
B. Annual scores															
Admission															
Mean	4.50	4.36	4.76	3.08	6.92	6.16	3.73	2.20	4.07	5.42	0.00	1.90	6.00	6.33	10.00
Std. Dev.	4.13	4.13	4.30	3.57	4.00	4.26	3.92	2.68	4.28	4.22	0.00	2.84	4.01	2.80	0.00
First year															
Mean	5.78	5.48	6.38	4.75	7.57	7.58	4.96	2.60	5.71	6.68	0.00	3.30	7.50	8.66	10.00
Std. Dev.	4.15	4.25	4.05	4.15	3.63	3.77	4.12	3.20	4.42	3.91	0.00	3.68	3.03	2.16	0.00
Second year															
Mean	7.21	6.84	7.92	6.70	8.07	9.75	6.03	4.40	6.64	8.36	0.40	5.70	9.14	9.50	10.00
Std. Dev.	3.96	4.11	3.70	4.18	3.54	0.62	4.31	4.33	4.49	3.11	0.89	4.57	1.29	1.22	0.00
Third year															
Mean	7.89	7.64	8.38	7.33	8.85	10.00	6.92	4.80	7.28	9.15	0.80	6.80	9.92	9.83	10.00
Std. Dev.	3.82	3.92	3.73	4.18	3.00	0.00	4.30	5.01	4.25	2.60	1.78	4.34	0.26	0.40	0.00
C. Linear trend equation															
Admission score	4.60	4.40	5.00	3.26	6.91	6.32	3.81	2.06	4.34	5.47	-0.12	1.85	6.12	6.88	10.00
Annual change	1.16	1.12	1.23	1.47	0.62	1.36	1.06	0.96	1.05	1.28	0.28	1.71	1.34	1.13	0.00
Probability	0.0002	0.0030	0.0127	0.0002	0.1349	0.0008	0.0043	0.2101	0.0416	0.0008	0.1547	0.0033	0.0001	0.0034	1.0000
D. Sub groups within I to V															
Prob. equal slopes IV V		*** 0.8413 ***		*** 0.1415 ***		*** 0.6161 ***		*****	0.8923	*****	*****	*****	0.0941	*****	*****
Prob. equal trends		*** 0.2507 ***		*** 0.0005 ***		*** 0.0000 ***		*****	0.0004	*****	*****	*****	0.0000	*****	*****
E. Friedman Anova Probabiliy	0.0000	0.0000	0.0000	0.0000	0.0005	0.0000	0.0000	0.0008	0.0000	0.0000	0.7005	0.0000	0.0000	0.0002	0.9999

161

Table A-1-13. Double Simultaneous Stimuli—Homologous—Eyes Closed

Variable	Total all children (1)	I Sex Males (2)	I Sex Females (3)	II Admission age less than 8 years (4)	II Admission age 8 years or more (5)	III Neurological status Non organics (6)	III Neurological status Organics (7)	IV Social position 1 or 2 (8)	IV Social position 3 (9)	IV Social position 4 or 5 (10)	V Below 46 (11)	V 46-69 (12)	V 70-89 (13)	V 90-109 (14)	V Above 109 (15)
A. No. of children	38.	25.	13.	24.	14.	12.	26.	5.	14.	19.	5.	10.	14.	6.	3.
B. Annual scores															
Admission															
Mean	3.00	3.12	2.76	2.58	3.71	3.58	2.73	2.20	2.78	3.36	0.00	2.80	3.64	3.83	4.00
Std. Dev.	1.62	1.48	1.92	1.88	0.61	1.16	1.75	2.04	1.84	1.30	0.00	1.61	1.08	0.40	0.00
First year															
Mean	2.97	3.04	2.84	2.62	3.57	3.50	2.73	2.00	2.71	3.42	0.20	2.50	3.78	3.66	4.00
Std. Dev.	1.55	1.56	1.57	1.76	0.85	1.24	1.63	2.00	1.72	1.16	0.44	1.64	0.57	0.81	0.00
Second year															
Mean	3.55	3.56	3.53	3.29	4.00	4.00	3.34	3.00	3.50	3.73	1.40	3.70	3.92	4.00	4.00
Std. Dev.	1.13	1.12	1.19	1.36	0.00	0.00	1.32	1.73	1.16	0.93	1.94	0.67	0.26	0.00	0.00
Third year															
Mean	3.65	3.72	3.53	3.50	3.92	4.00	3.50	3.20	3.64	3.78	2.00	3.70	4.00	4.00	4.00
Std. Dev.	0.99	0.89	1.19	1.21	0.26	0.00	1.17	1.78	0.74	0.91	2.00	0.67	0.00	0.00	0.00
C. Linear trend equation															
Admission score	2.91	3.01	2.72	2.48	3.64	3.50	2.63	2.00	2.65	3.34	-0.17	2.59	3.65	3.75	4.00
Annual change	0.25	0.23	0.30	0.34	0.10	0.17	0.29	0.40	0.33	0.15	0.72	0.39	0.12	0.08	0.00
Probability	0.0098	0.0438	0.1047	0.0181	0.1019	0.1106	0.0251	0.2829	0.0509	0.1543	0.0150	0.0326	0.1013	0.3206	1.0000
D. Sub groups within I to V															
Prob. equal slopes		*** 0.7424 ***		*** 0.2281 ***		*** 0.5762 ***			0.5904		*****	*****	0.0262	*****	*****
Prob. equal trends		*** 0.5747 ***		*** 0.0005 ***		*** 0.0032 ***			0.0092		*****	*****	0.0000	*****	*****
E. Friedman Anova															
Probability	0.0007	0.0103	0.0753	0.0043	0.1111	0.5173	0.0012	0.1548	0.0071	0.2843	0.0430	0.0004	0.6916	0.7214	0.9999

Table A-1-14. Double Simultaneous Stimuli–Heterologous–Eyes Closed

Variable	Total all children (1)	I Sex — Males (2)	I Sex — Females (3)	II Admission age — less than 8 years (4)	II Admission age — 8 years or more (5)	III Neurological status — Non organics (6)	III Neurological status — Organics (7)	IV Social position — 1 or 2 (8)	IV Social position — 3 (9)	IV Social position — 4 or 5 (10)	V WISC Full IQ at admission — Below 46 (11)	V — 46-69 (12)	V — 70-89 (13)	V — 90-109 (14)	V — Above 109 (15)
A. No. of children	38.	25.	13.	24.	14.	12.	26.	5.	14.	19.	5.	10.	14.	6.	3.
B. Annual scores															
Admission															
Mean	3.63	3.24	4.38	2.62	5.35	6.16	2.46	3.60	3.14	4.00	0.00	1.50	4.35	5.33	10.00
Std. Dev.	4.27	4.13	4.59	3.68	4.78	4.64	3.60	4.97	4.05	4.44	0.00	3.24	4.12	4.50	0.00
First year															
Mean	5.02	4.60	5.84	3.87	7.00	6.66	4.26	3.60	5.07	5.36	0.00	2.70	6.64	6.83	10.00
Std. Dev.	4.46	4.40	4.63	4.48	3.80	4.59	4.27	4.92	4.68	4.36	0.00	4.05	3.89	4.02	0.00
Second year															
Mean	6.97	6.68	7.53	6.37	8.00	9.00	6.03	4.20	7.00	7.68	0.20	4.80	9.28	9.33	10.00
Std. Dev.	3.79	3.93	3.59	3.96	3.37	1.85	4.11	4.49	4.31	3.00	0.44	3.29	1.13	1.03	0.00
Third year															
Mean	7.78	7.56	8.23	7.25	8.71	9.83	6.84	4.80	7.35	8.89	0.80	6.70	9.78	9.66	10.00
Std. Dev.	3.71	3.78	3.67	4.09	2.84	0.38	4.17	4.76	4.28	2.46	1.78	4.00	0.57	0.51	0.00
C. Linear trend equation															
Admission score	3.69	3.26	4.51	2.57	5.60	5.91	2.66	3.41	3.45	3.93	-0.14	1.26	4.67	5.46	10.00
Annual change	1.44	1.50	1.32	1.63	1.10	1.33	1.49	0.42	1.45	1.70	0.26	1.77	1.89	1.55	0.00
Probability	0.0000	0.0002	0.0113	0.0001	0.0147	0.0037	0.0001	0.6522	0.0063	0.0000	0.1555	0.0015	0.0000	0.0089	1.0000
D. Sub groups within I to V															
Prob. equal slopes		*** 0.7680 ***		*** 0.6268 ***		*** 0.7865 ***		*****	0.3661	*****	*****	*****	0.0346	*****	*****
Prob. equal trends		*** 0.1542 ***		*** 0.0012 ***		*** 0.0000 ***		*****	0.0481	*****	*****	*****	0.0000	*****	*****
E. Friedman Anova															
Probability	0.0000	0.0000	0.0000	0.0000	0.0001	0.0001	0.0000	0.2108	0.0000	0.0000	0.7005	0.0000	0.0000	0.0014	0.9999

163

Table A-1-15. Double Simultaneous Stimuli—Total

Variable	Total all children (1)	I Sex		II Admission age		III Neurological status		IV Social position			V WISC Full IQ at admission				
		Males (2)	Females (3)	less than 8 years (4)	8 years or more (5)	Non organics (6)	Organics (7)	1 or 2 (8)	3 (9)	4 or 5 (10)	Below 46 (11)	46-69 (12)	70-89 (13)	90-109 (14)	Above 109 (15)
A. No. of children	38.	25.	13.	24.	14.	12.	26.	5.	14.	19.	5.	10.	14.	6.	3.
B. Annual scores															
Admission															
Mean	14.34	13.96	15.07	11.16	19.78	19.75	11.84	10.40	13.07	16.31	0.00	9.60	17.71	19.50	28.00
Std. Dev.	10.13	9.76	11.19	9.45	9.15	9.69	9.49	11.17	10.41	9.76	0.00	7.10	8.64	7.00	0.00
First year															
Mean	17.00	16.40	18.15	14.12	21.92	21.41	14.96	11.00	16.50	18.94	0.20	11.60	21.92	23.00	28.00
Std. Dev.	10.79	10.64	11.40	11.13	8.40	9.46	10.91	12.20	11.83	9.53	0.44	10.07	6.86	5.62	0.00
Second year															
Mean	21.26	20.68	22.38	19.79	23.78	26.75	18.73	15.00	20.50	23.47	3.80	17.80	26.14	26.83	28.00
Std. Dev.	9.25	9.37	9.28	10.09	7.26	2.37	10.16	11.18	10.42	7.31	4.96	8.76	2.14	2.04	0.00
Third year															
Mean	22.94	22.52	23.76	21.66	25.14	27.83	20.69	16.00	22.00	25.47	5.80	20.70	27.71	27.33	28.00
Std. Dev.	9.02	9.03	9.31	9.98	6.85	0.38	10.18	12.10	9.73	6.75	6.64	9.41	0.61	0.81	0.00
C. Linear trend equation															
Admission score	14.37	13.89	15.30	11.11	19.97	19.50	12.01	9.97	13.40	16.25	-0.70	9.00	18.24	20.06	28.00
Annual change	3.00	2.99	3.03	3.71	1.79	2.95	3.03	2.08	3.07	3.20	2.10	3.95	3.42	2.73	0.00
Probability	0.0001	0.0011	0.0188	0.0002	0.0575	0.0018	0.0012	0.6390	0.0160	0.0006	0.0161	0.0030	0.0000	0.0033	1.0000
D. Sub groups within I to V															
Prob. equal slopes		*** 0.9794 ***		*** 0.1694 ***		*** 0.9586 ***		******	0.8697	******	******	******	0.2227	******	******
Prob. equal trends		*** 0.6104 ***		*** 0.0004 ***		*** 0.0000 ****		******	0.0036	******	******	******	0.0000	******	******
E. Friedman Anova															
Probability	0.0000	0.0000	0.0000	0.0000	0.0000	0.0000	0.0000	0.0006	0.0000	0.0000	0.0191	0.0000	0.0000	0.0000	0.9999

Table A-1-16. Oculomotor Functioning—Eye Movement

Variable	Total all children (1)	I Sex		II Admission age		III Neurological status		IV Social position			V WISC Full IQ at admission				
		Males (2)	Females (3)	less than 8 years (4)	8 years or more (5)	Non organics (6)	Organics (7)	1 or 2 (8)	3 (9)	4 or 5 (10)	Below 46 (11)	46-69 (12)	70-89 (13)	90-109 (14)	Above 109 (15)
A. No. of children	40.	27.	13.	25.	15.	14.	26.	5.	15.	20.	6.	10.	14.	6.	4.
B. Annual scores															
Admission															
Mean	7.47	7.55	7.30	6.76	8.66	8.21	7.07	7.00	7.13	7.85	5.00	7.60	7.71	8.16	9.00
Std. Dev.	2.01	1.90	2.28	1.87	1.67	1.76	2.05	2.82	1.72	2.03	1.54	2.27	1.43	1.94	1.15
First year															
Mean	7.47	7.40	7.61	6.92	8.40	8.21	7.07	7.40	6.86	7.95	4.83	7.70	7.50	8.16	9.75
Std. Dev.	1.94	1.88	2.14	2.08	1.29	1.92	1.87	2.30	2.09	1.70	0.40	1.49	1.65	2.22	0.50
Second year															
Mean	7.37	7.48	7.15	7.04	7.93	8.14	6.96	7.20	7.06	7.65	5.00	7.10	7.71	8.16	9.25
Std. Dev.	2.02	1.98	2.15	2.00	1.98	1.87	2.00	2.68	2.15	1.81	1.09	2.13	1.58	1.94	1.50
Third year															
Mean	7.95	8.03	7.76	7.48	8.73	8.57	7.61	6.60	7.73	8.45	6.00	7.10	8.28	9.33	9.75
Std. Dev.	1.83	1.80	1.96	1.98	1.27	1.60	1.89	1.94	1.86	1.66	1.26	1.28	1.89	1.03	0.50
C. Linear trend equation															
Admission score	7.36	7.39	7.32	6.70	8.47	8.13	6.95	7.25	6.90	7.75	4.73	7.69	7.51	7.93	9.17
Annual change	0.13	0.15	0.09	0.22	-0.02	0.10	0.15	-0.14	0.20	0.15	0.31	-0.21	0.19	0.35	0.17
Probability	0.6598	0.6450	0.7258	0.1957	0.8798	0.6430	0.6130	0.7651	0.6181	0.5868	0.1414	0.5802	0.6710	0.2953	0.5588
D. Sub groups within I to V															
Prob. equal slopes		*** 0.8352 ***		*** 0.6537 ***		*** 0.8528 ***		*****	0.7459	*****	*****	*****	0.5011	*****	*****
Prob. equal trends		*** 0.6367 ***		*** 0.0000 ***		*** 0.0008 ***		*****	0.0279	*****	*****	*****	0.0000	*****	*****
E. Friedman Anova															
Probability	0.0006	0.0012	0.2513	0.0009	0.0467	0.5509	0.0006	0.2108	0.0125	0.0142	0.0067	0.6391	0.0469	0.0527	0.3373

Table A-1-17. Oculomotor Functioning—Dissociation of Head and Eye Movement

Variable	Total all children (1)	I Sex Males (2)	Females (3)	II Admission age less than 8 years (4)	8 years or more (5)	III Neurological status Non organics (6)	Organics (7)	IV Social position 1 or 2 (8)	3 (9)	4 or 5 (10)	V WISC Full IQ at admission Below 46 (11)	46-69 (12)	70-89 (13)	90-109 (14)	Above 109 (15)
A. No. of children	40.	27.	13.	25.	15.	14.	26.	5.	15.	20.	6.	10.	14.	6.	4.
B. Annual scores															
Admission															
Mean	0.62	0.66	0.53	0.16	1.40	0.92	0.46	0.00	0.46	0.90	0.00	0.10	0.78	0.66	2.25
Std. Dev.	1.12	1.20	0.96	0.47	1.45	1.38	0.94	0.00	0.91	1.33	0.00	0.31	1.18	1.21	1.50
First year															
Mean	0.85	0.77	1.00	0.44	1.53	1.50	0.50	0.40	0.80	1.00	0.00	0.20	0.92	1.16	3.00
Std. Dev.	1.12	1.18	1.00	0.82	1.24	1.28	0.86	0.89	1.08	1.21	0.00	0.42	1.07	0.98	0.00
Second year															
Mean	1.22	1.11	1.46	1.12	1.40	1.71	0.96	1.40	1.26	1.15	0.00	0.90	1.14	2.50	2.25
Std. Dev.	1.31	1.31	1.33	1.33	1.29	1.32	1.24	1.51	1.33	1.30	0.00	1.28	1.16	0.83	1.50
Third year															
Mean	1.55	1.74	1.15	1.24	2.06	2.00	1.30	0.80	1.06	2.10	0.00	0.80	1.78	2.83	3.00
Std. Dev.	1.37	1.37	1.34	1.39	1.22	1.41	1.31	1.30	1.33	1.25	0.00	1.03	1.36	0.40	0.00
C. Linear trend equation															
Admission score	0.59	0.54	0.69	0.15	1.32	1.02	0.35	0.14	0.56	0.72	0.00	0.08	0.67	0.61	2.40
Annual change	0.31	0.35	0.23	0.39	0.18	0.34	0.30	0.34	0.22	0.37	0.00	0.28	0.32	0.78	0.15
Probability	0.0006	0.0018	0.1143	0.0002	0.2157	0.0335	0.0028	0.1354	0.0952	0.0047	1.0000	0.0252	0.0261	0.0002	0.5375
D. Sub groups within I to V															
Prob. equal slopes		*** 0.5122 ***		*** 0.2250 ***		*** 0.8033 ***		*****	0.7297	*****	*****	*****	0.0285	*****	*****
Prob. equal trends		*** 0.8588 ***		*** 0.0000 ***		*** 0.0005 ***		*****	0.0483	*****	*****	*****	0.0000	*****	*****
E. Friedman Anova															
Probability	0.0000	0.0000	0.0231	0.0000	0.1017	0.0228	0.0003	0.0191	0.0311	0.0000	0.9999	0.0170	0.0543	0.0000	0.6191

Table A-1-18. Whirling—Arms at Side

Variable	Total all children (1)	I Sex		II Admission age		III Neurological status		IV Social position			V WISC Full IQ at admission				
		Males (2)	Females (3)	less than 8 years (4)	8 years or more (5)	Non organics (6)	Organics (7)	1 or 2 (8)	3 (9)	4 or 5 (10)	Below 46 (11)	46-69 (12)	70-89 (13)	90-109 (14)	Above 109 (15)
A. No. of children	40.	27.	13.	25.	15.	14.	26.	5.	15.	20.	6.	10.	14.	6.	4.
B. Annual scores															
Admission															
Mean	15.92	15.44	16.92	14.96	17.53	17.00	15.34	12.40	15.40	17.20	15.16	13.00	17.85	15.33	18.50
Std. Dev.	5.16	5.07	5.42	5.05	5.11	4.70	5.39	5.68	5.56	4.46	3.65	7.05	3.61	4.41	5.44
First year															
Mean	16.45	16.66	16.00	15.00	18.86	17.07	16.11	14.20	17.00	16.60	13.00	14.00	18.57	17.16	19.25
Std. Dev.	4.48	3.59	6.08	4.71	2.79	4.53	4.51	3.70	4.88	4.38	4.60	5.94	2.27	2.63	3.09
Second year															
Mean	16.57	16.33	17.07	15.52	18.33	18.57	15.50	14.00	15.33	18.15	11.83	15.40	17.64	18.66	19.75
Std. Dev.	4.62	4.55	4.90	4.86	3.69	2.53	5.15	7.14	5.19	2.77	4.11	5.23	3.83	3.66	2.06
Third year															
Mean	18.05	18.51	17.07	17.20	19.46	20.57	16.69	16.60	16.86	19.30	11.33	17.20	19.57	20.16	21.75
Std. Dev.	4.60	3.90	5.86	5.34	2.58	1.55	5.13	4.27	5.33	3.93	5.00	4.96	2.53	0.75	0.95
C. Linear trend equation															
Admission score	15.77	15.40	16.53	14.58	17.76	16.47	15.39	12.44	15.73	16.63	14.73	12.80	17.77	15.43	18.27
Annual change	0.65	0.88	0.15	0.72	0.52	1.22	0.34	1.24	0.27	0.78	-1.26	1.40	0.42	1.60	1.02
Probability	0.0496	0.0173	0.8169	0.1024	0.2132	0.0059	0.5547	0.2381	0.6558	0.0466	0.1089	0.0870	0.2650	0.0083	0.1598
D. Sub groups within I to V															
Prob. equal slopes		*** 0.3046 ***		*** 0.7631 ***		*** 0.1933 ***		0.6122		*****	*****				
Prob. equal trends		*** 0.9701 ***		*** 0.0003 ***		*** 0.0023 ***		0.0050		*****	*****				
E. Friedman Anova Probability	0.0017	0.0000	0.8435	0.0051	0.1191	0.0007	0.1025	0.5078	0.0039	0.0004	0.2549	0.1739	0.0456	0.0008	0.0964

167

Table A-1-19. Whirling—Arms Outstretched and Parallel

Variable	Total all children (1)	I Sex		II Admission age		III Neurological status		IV Social position			V WISC Full IQ at admission				
		Males (2)	Females (3)	less than 8 years (4)	8 years or more (5)	Non organics (6)	Organics (7)	1 or 2 (8)	3 (9)	4 or 5 (10)	Below 46 (11)	46-69 (12)	70-89 (13)	90-109 (14)	Above 109 (15)
A. No. of children	40.	27.	13.	25.	15.	14.	26.	5.	15.	20.	6.	10.	14.	6.	4.
B. Annual scores															
Admission															
Mean	6.92	6.74	7.30	5.72	8.93	8.28	6.19	4.80	6.73	7.60	3.50	5.80	7.57	8.00	11.00
Std. Dev.	3.18	3.12	3.40	2.35	3.43	3.40	2.85	1.09	3.08	3.43	0.83	2.85	2.50	3.22	2.70
First year															
Mean	7.47	7.11	8.23	6.60	8.93	8.78	6.76	6.60	7.13	7.95	4.00	6.80	8.07	8.33	11.00
Std. Dev.	3.08	3.01	3.19	2.66	3.26	3.14	2.86	2.19	3.04	3.33	2.00	3.01	2.52	2.94	1.41
Second year															
Mean	7.92	7.92	7.92	7.12	9.26	9.07	7.30	8.00	7.46	8.25	5.00	7.20	8.21	9.50	10.75
Std. Dev.	3.13	3.14	3.22	3.09	2.78	2.89	3.13	3.39	2.99	3.29	3.16	3.58	2.45	2.58	0.50
Third year															
Mean	9.40	9.48	9.23	8.76	10.46	11.21	8.42	8.60	9.00	9.90	5.83	9.30	9.50	10.66	12.75
Std. Dev.	3.01	3.05	3.03	3.24	2.29	1.96	3.04	4.03	3.09	2.75	3.18	2.90	2.34	2.16	0.50
C. Linear trend equation															
Admission score	6.75	6.45	7.35	5.60	8.65	7.97	6.08	5.08	6.51	7.34	3.38	5.64	7.44	7.75	10.62
Annual change	0.78	0.90	0.54	0.96	0.49	0.90	0.72	1.28	0.71	0.72	0.80	1.09	0.59	0.91	0.50
Probability	0.0007	0.0012	0.1674	0.0005	0.1482	0.0108	0.0063	0.0306	0.0426	0.0253	0.0759	0.0149	0.0432	0.0674	0.1751
D. Sub groups within I to V															
Prob. equal slopes		*** 0.5471 ***		*** 0.2640 ***		**** 0.6760 ***		******	0.7000	******	******	******	0.8392	******	******
Prob. equal trends		*** 0.5015 ***		*** 0.0000 ***		**** 0.0000 ***		******	0.0972	******	******	******	0.0000	******	******
E. Friedman Anova															
Probability	0.0000	0.0000	0.0077	0.0000	0.0001	0.0000	0.0001	0.0001	0.0063	0.0000	0.5252	0.0000	0.0166	0.0287	0.0002

Table A-1-20. Romberg–Arms at Side

Variable	Total all children (1)	I Sex		II Admission age		III Neurological status		IV Social position			V WISC Full IQ at admission				
		Males (2)	Females (3)	less than 8 years (4)	8 years or more (5)	Non organics (6)	Organics (7)	1 or 2 (8)	3 (9)	4 or 5 (10)	Below 46 (11)	46-69 (12)	70-89 (13)	90-109 (14)	Above 109 (15)
A. No. of children	40.	27.	13.	25.	15.	14.	26.	5.	15.	20.	6.	10.	14.	6.	4.
B. Annual scores															
Admission															
Mean	17.12	16.29	18.84	15.20	20.33	19.71	15.73	12.60	18.00	17.60	11.83	13.30	19.50	19.83	22.25
Std. Dev.	6.20	6.29	5.85	5.56	6.03	5.68	6.11	5.72	6.48	5.90	6.21	5.96	5.15	2.40	4.85
First year															
Mean	18.15	16.81	20.92	16.32	21.20	20.57	16.84	13.40	19.20	18.55	13.83	14.70	20.07	21.16	22.00
Std. Dev.	6.75	6.46	6.73	6.39	6.41	5.86	6.94	6.38	7.55	6.01	6.17	7.90	5.39	5.74	5.41
Second year															
Mean	19.70	19.07	21.00	17.84	22.80	23.35	17.73	14.40	18.86	21.65	14.66	14.70	21.07	25.16	26.75
Std. Dev.	6.50	6.46	6.67	6.30	5.78	5.52	6.21	8.73	6.93	4.84	5.46	5.96	5.15	2.48	0.50
Third year															
Mean	20.37	19.85	21.46	19.20	22.33	23.21	18.84	12.80	20.13	22.45	12.83	17.60	22.07	24.83	26.00
Std. Dev.	6.42	6.78	5.69	6.88	5.20	4.82	6.73	7.46	6.04	5.13	5.84	7.56	3.79	2.13	1.82
C. Linear trend equation															
Admission score	17.14	16.07	19.36	15.11	20.52	19.72	15.75	13.05	18.14	17.41	12.71	13.13	19.37	19.90	21.85
Annual change	1.13	1.29	0.79	1.35	0.76	1.32	1.02	0.16	0.60	1.76	0.38	1.29	0.87	1.90	1.60
Probability	0.0134	0.0206	0.3046	0.0163	0.2594	0.0426	0.0698	0.9034	0.5601	0.0021	0.7186	0.1815	0.1328	0.0067	0.0709
D. Sub groups within I to V															
Prob. equal slopes		*** 0.6095 ***		*** 0.5130 ***		*** 0.7361 ***		0.3245			*****	*****	0.8078	*****	*****
Prob. equal trends		*** 0.0175 ***		*** 0.0000 ***		*** 0.0001 ***		0.0002			*****	*****	0.0000	*****	*****
E. Friedman Anova															
Probability	0.0000	0.0000	0.0006	0.0000	0.0000	0.0000	0.0002	0.5431	0.1630	0.0000	0.2549	0.0036	0.0028	0.0000	0.0002

Table A-1-21. Romberg—Arms Outstretched and Parallel

Variable	Total all children (1)	I Sex		II Admission age		III Neurological status		IV Social position			V WISC Full IQ at admission				
		Males (2)	Females (3)	less than 8 years (4)	8 years or more (5)	Non organics (6)	Organics (7)	1 or 2 (8)	3 (9)	4 or 5 (10)	Below 46 (11)	46-69 (12)	70-89 (13)	90-109 (14)	Above 109 (15)
A. No. of children	40.	27.	13.	25.	15.	14.	26.	5.	15.	20.	6.	10.	14.	6.	4.
B. Annual scores															
Admission															
Mean	7.40	6.88	8.46	6.00	9.73	9.64	6.19	5.40	6.73	8.40	4.66	7.10	7.50	7.83	11.25
Std. Dev.	3.62	3.28	4.17	2.44	4.11	3.62	3.04	1.34	3.51	3.87	1.21	4.22	3.10	3.81	3.59
First year															
Mean	8.07	7.37	9.53	6.68	10.40	10.64	6.69	6.20	7.86	8.70	4.83	7.30	8.28	8.83	13.00
Std. Dev.	3.68	3.76	3.17	2.77	3.92	3.65	2.93	2.28	3.46	4.07	1.32	2.98	3.60	4.21	2.16
Second year															
Mean	8.40	7.85	9.53	6.96	10.80	11.28	6.84	6.60	8.53	8.75	5.66	6.00	8.28	12.00	13.50
Std. Dev.	3.97	3.76	4.29	3.29	3.93	3.62	3.25	3.43	4.18	3.99	1.86	2.62	3.72	3.52	1.73
Third year															
Mean	9.20	8.66	10.30	7.84	11.46	11.85	7.76	6.40	8.73	10.25	6.16	7.10	9.28	11.66	15.00
Std. Dev.	3.89	3.79	4.02	3.47	3.58	3.43	3.38	4.33	3.78	3.64	2.04	2.99	3.68	2.73	1.41
C. Linear trend equation															
Admission score	7.40	6.82	8.63	6.00	9.76	9.76	6.14	5.64	6.96	8.18	4.53	7.07	7.53	7.88	11.42
Annual change	0.57	0.58	0.55	0.58	0.56	0.72	0.48	0.34	0.66	0.56	0.53	-0.13	0.53	1.46	1.17
Probability	0.0314	0.0617	0.2528	0.0310	0.2074	0.0854	0.0749	0.5716	0.1194	0.1478	0.0744	0.7734	0.2007	0.0309	0.0310
D. Sub groups within I to V															
Prob. equal slopes		*** 0.9594 ***		*** 0.9660 ***		*** 0.6274 ***		*****	0.9280	*****	*****	*****	0.2176	*****	*****
Prob. equal trends		*** 0.0053 ***		*** 0.0000 ***		*** 0.0000 ***		*****	0.0066	*****	*****	*****	0.0000	*****	*****
E. Friedman Anova															
Probability	0.0004	0.0097	0.0368	0.0126	0.0320	0.0040	0.0047	0.8273	0.0030	0.0035	0.1030	0.0013	0.0056	0.0000	0.0065

Table A-1-22. Finger to Finger Test

Variable	Total all children (1)	I Sex — Males (2)	Females (3)	II Admission age — less than 8 years (4)	8 years or more (5)	III Neurological status — Non organics (6)	Organics (7)	IV Social position — 1 or 2 (8)	3 (9)	4 or 5 (10)	V WISC Full IQ at admission — Below 46 (11)	46-69 (12)	70-89 (13)	90-109 (14)	Above 109 (15)
A. No. of children	40.	27.	13.	25.	15.	14.	26.	5.	15.	20.	6.	10.	14.	6.	4.
B. Annual scores															
Admission															
Mean	2.25	2.00	2.76	2.04	2.60	3.21	1.73	1.60	2.20	2.45	0.83	1.80	2.35	3.00	4.00
Std. Dev.	1.56	1.56	1.48	1.56	1.54	1.12	1.53	1.51	1.65	1.53	1.32	1.75	1.44	0.63	0.00
First year															
Mean	2.67	2.44	3.15	2.24	3.40	3.14	2.42	1.20	2.66	3.05	1.00	2.00	3.14	3.66	3.75
Std. Dev.	1.50	1.50	1.46	1.56	1.12	1.46	1.50	1.64	1.44	1.35	1.26	1.76	1.09	0.51	0.50
Second year															
Mean	2.62	2.59	2.69	2.48	2.86	3.28	2.26	1.60	2.66	2.85	1.16	1.90	3.00	3.50	4.00
Std. Dev.	1.42	1.44	1.43	1.41	1.45	0.99	1.51	1.67	1.44	1.30	1.32	1.28	1.30	0.54	0.00
Third year															
Mean	2.90	3.03	2.61	2.60	3.40	3.14	2.76	2.60	2.46	3.30	1.33	3.00	3.00	3.83	3.25
Std. Dev.	1.25	1.19	1.38	1.38	0.82	1.16	1.30	1.94	1.12	1.08	1.50	0.94	1.17	0.40	0.95
C. Linear trend equation															
Admission score	2.32	2.02	2.94	2.05	2.78	3.20	1.85	1.24	2.38	2.55	0.83	1.64	2.60	3.15	4.05
Annual change	0.19	0.32	-0.09	0.19	0.18	-0.00	0.29	0.34	0.08	0.23	0.16	0.35	0.17	0.23	-0.20
Probability	0.0601	0.0088	0.6099	0.1436	0.2093	0.9586	0.0216	0.3168	0.6323	0.0762	0.5045	0.0958	0.2396	0.0252	0.1217
D. Sub groups within I to V															
Prob. equal slopes		*** 0.0504 ***		*** 0.9772 ***		*** 0.1336 ***		******	0.6596	******	******	******	0.5500	******	******
Prob. equal trends		*** 0.2327 ***		*** 0.0021 ***		*** 0.0003 ***		******	0.0038	******	******	******	0.0000	******	******
E. Friedman Anova															
Probability	0.0017	0.0000	0.0488	0.0332	0.0107	0.9291	0.0002	0.1130	0.1072	0.0024	0.6191	0.0009	0.1472	0.0049	0.1739

Table A-1-23. Finger to Nose Test

		I Sex		II Admission age		III Neurological status		IV Social position			V WISC Full IQ at admission				
Variable	Total all children (1)	Males (2)	Females (3)	less than 8 years (4)	8 years or more (5)	Non organics (6)	Organics (7)	1 or 2 (8)	3 (9)	4 or 5 (10)	Below 46 (11)	46-69 (12)	70-89 (13)	90-109 (14)	Above 109 (15)
A. No. of children	40.	27.	13.	25.	15.	14.	26.	5.	15.	20.	6.	10.	14.	6.	4.
B. Annual scores															
Admission															
Mean	2.52	2.51	2.53	1.92	3.53	2.78	2.38	1.40	2.66	2.70	0.66	2.00	3.14	2.83	4.00
Std. Dev.	1.53	1.52	1.61	1.60	0.63	1.62	1.49	1.94	1.58	1.34	1.03	1.49	1.16	1.47	0.00
First year															
Mean	3.02	3.03	3.00	2.68	3.60	3.64	2.69	1.60	2.93	3.45	1.66	2.60	3.28	3.83	4.00
Std. Dev.	1.31	1.22	1.52	1.43	0.82	0.63	1.46	1.67	1.43	0.82	0.81	1.57	1.20	0.40	0.00
Second year															
Mean	3.12	3.00	3.38	2.92	3.46	3.42	2.96	2.40	3.40	3.10	1.50	2.90	3.57	3.83	3.50
Std. Dev.	1.20	1.20	1.19	1.32	0.91	1.22	1.18	1.51	0.82	1.33	1.76	0.99	0.64	0.40	1.00
Third year															
Mean	3.37	3.51	3.07	3.24	3.60	3.78	3.15	2.80	3.33	3.55	2.33	3.40	3.42	3.83	4.00
Std. Dev.	0.95	0.84	1.11	1.12	0.50	0.42	1.08	1.64	0.61	0.94	1.86	0.69	0.51	0.40	0.00
C. Linear trend equation															
Admission score	2.61	2.57	2.70	2.05	3.53	2.99	2.41	1.29	2.71	2.86	0.81	2.05	3.18	3.13	3.95
Annual change	0.26	0.29	0.20	0.42	0.00	0.27	0.25	0.50	0.24	0.22	0.48	0.45	0.11	0.30	-0.05
Probability	0.0037	0.0058	0.2420	0.0012	0.9350	0.0348	0.0250	0.1348	0.0706	0.0548	0.0682	0.0119	0.3051	0.0573	0.6730
D. Sub groups within I to V															
Prob. equal slopes		*** 0.6222 ***		*** 0.0164 ***		*** 0.9054 ***		******		******	******	******		******		
Prob. equal trends		*** 0.9286 ***		*** 0.0001 ***		*** 0.0034 ***		******		******	******	******		******		
E. Friedman Anova															
Probability	0.0001	0.0001	0.0077	0.0000	0.7708	0.0313	0.0020	0.0366	0.0822	0.0005	0.0071	0.0011	0.5348	0.0179	0.7214

Table A-1-24. Auditory Startle

Variable	Total all children (1)	I Sex — Males (2)	Females (3)	II Admission age — less than 8 years (4)	8 years or more (5)	III Neurological status — Non organics (6)	Organics (7)	IV Social position — 1 or 2 (8)	3 (9)	4 or 5 (10)	V WISC Full IQ at admission — Below 46 (11)	46-69 (12)	70-89 (13)	90-109 (14)	Above 109 (15)
A. No. of children	35.	24.	11.	23.	12.	13.	22.	5.	14.	16.	4.	8.	13.	6.	4.
B. Annual scores															
Admission															
Mean	3.85	4.20	3.09	3.78	4.00	3.76	3.90	3.40	3.50	4.31	5.00	4.00	3.46	3.83	3.75
Std. Dev.	1.43	1.28	1.51	1.65	0.95	1.36	1.50	1.67	1.78	0.87	1.41	2.07	1.45	0.40	0.50
First year															
Mean	3.54	3.95	2.63	3.60	3.41	3.38	3.63	4.60	3.00	3.68	5.75	3.00	3.46	3.16	3.25
Std. Dev.	1.37	1.23	1.28	1.43	1.31	1.19	1.49	1.34	1.51	1.07	0.50	1.41	1.12	0.98	1.50
Second year															
Mean	3.42	3.70	2.81	3.69	2.91	3.07	3.63	5.00	3.21	3.12	4.50	3.12	3.46	3.50	2.75
Std. Dev.	1.37	1.33	1.32	1.36	1.31	1.32	1.39	1.00	1.47	1.08	2.38	1.45	1.12	0.83	1.50
Third year															
Mean	3.54	3.70	3.18	3.86	2.91	3.30	3.68	5.00	3.28	3.31	4.00	3.50	3.61	3.50	3.00
Std. Dev.	1.31	1.33	1.25	1.28	1.16	1.37	1.28	0.70	1.48	1.01	2.16	1.60	1.26	0.83	0.81
C. Linear trend equation															
Admission score	3.75	4.15	2.86	3.68	3.87	3.63	3.81	3.72	3.31	4.14	5.45	3.61	3.43	3.60	3.60
Annual change	-0.10	-0.17	0.04	0.03	-0.37	-0.16	-0.06	0.52	-0.04	-0.35	-0.42	-0.13	0.04	-0.06	-0.27
Probability	0.3107	0.1352	0.7971	0.7905	0.0166	0.2992	0.6198	0.0428	0.8132	0.0031	0.2843	0.6065	0.7600	0.6542	0.2820
D. Sub groups within I to V															
Prob. equal slopes		*** 0.3000 ***		*** 0.0553 ***		*** 0.6437 ***		******	0.0120	******	******	******	0.6667	******	******
Prob. equal trends		*** 0.0002 ***		*** 0.0769 ***		*** 0.1647 ***		******	0.0021	******	******	******	0.0040	******	******
E. Friedman Anova															
Probability	0.2202	0.1885	0.0865	0.2570	0.0017	0.2821	0.7024	0.0311	0.6333	0.0001	0.0173	0.0334	0.8273	0.2715	0.5952

Table A-1-25. Delayed Auditory Feedback—Voice and Speech

Variable	Total all children (1)	I Sex		II Admission age		III Neurological status		IV Social position			V WISC Full IQ at admission				
		Males (2)	Females (3)	less than 8 years (4)	8 years or more (5)	Non organics (6)	Organics (7)	1 or 2 (8)	3 (9)	4 or 5 (10)	Below 46 (11)	46-69 (12)	70-89 (13)	90-109 (14)	Above 109 (15)
A. No. of children	36.	26.	10.	22.	14.	12.	24.	4.	14.	18.	4.	10.	13.	5.	4.
B. Annual scores															
Admission															
Mean	19.02	19.84	16.90	19.50	18.28	18.08	19.50	23.75	18.92	18.05	17.00	20.00	20.38	17.60	16.00
Std. Dev.	6.18	6.42	5.23	6.55	5.71	6.21	6.25	7.71	6.17	5.74	7.48	6.53	5.96	5.98	6.37
First year															
Mean	18.94	20.00	16.20	20.27	16.85	17.58	19.62	21.75	18.21	18.88	19.50	21.10	19.00	18.40	13.50
Std. Dev.	5.76	5.55	5.65	5.40	5.88	6.22	5.53	3.77	6.57	5.52	6.80	4.93	5.59	5.85	6.45
Second year															
Mean	19.33	20.46	16.40	20.86	16.92	18.08	19.95	23.50	19.14	18.55	25.25	18.40	19.30	20.60	14.25
Std. Dev.	5.48	5.27	5.14	5.29	5.06	5.31	5.57	4.04	5.36	5.69	1.70	5.68	5.70	3.78	3.94
Third year															
Mean	19.16	19.92	17.20	19.45	18.71	16.83	20.33	19.50	20.35	18.16	21.75	20.00	18.69	20.20	14.75
Std. Dev.	4.80	4.55	5.13	3.93	6.06	3.92	4.85	3.10	5.01	4.93	1.25	5.84	4.47	3.96	4.92
C. Linear trend equation															
Admission score	18.99	19.95	16.51	19.95	17.49	18.13	19.42	23.77	18.37	18.41	17.87	20.28	20.06	17.70	15.07
Annual change	0.08	0.06	0.11	0.04	0.13	-0.32	0.28	-1.10	0.52	0.00	2.00	-0.27	-0.47	1.00	-0.30
Probability	0.8400	0.8798	0.8758	0.9265	0.8356	0.6478	0.5819	0.3233	0.5439	1.0000	0.1082	0.7386	0.5159	0.3071	0.7951
D. Sub groups within I to V															
Prob. equal slopes		*** 0.9624 ***		*** 0.9105 ***		*** 0.5093 ***		*****		*****	*****		*****		
Prob. equal trends		*** 0.0012 ***		*** 0.0130 ***		*** 0.0223 ***		*****		*****	*****		*****		
E. Friedman Anova															
Probability	0.9238	0.8913	0.9924	0.1286	0.2690	0.6525	0.7478	0.0116	0.6051	0.5553	0.0037	0.1377	0.1819	0.8273	0.1065

Table A-1-26. Delayed Auditory Feedback—Language

Variable	Total all children (1)	I Sex		II Admission age		III Neurological status		IV Social position			V WISC Full IQ at admission				
		Males (2)	Females (3)	less than 8 years (4)	8 years or more (5)	Non organics (6)	Organics (7)	1 or 2 (8)	3 (9)	4 or 5 (10)	Below 46 (11)	46-69 (12)	70-89 (13)	90-109 (14)	Above 109 (15)
A. No. of children	36.	26.	10.	22.	14.	12.	24.	4.	14.	18.	4.	10.	13.	5.	4.
B. Annual scores															
Admission															
Mean	7.41	7.34	7.60	7.68	7.00	7.91	7.16	10.25	6.35	7.61	8.25	9.30	6.23	7.00	6.25
Std. Dev.	2.54	2.62	2.45	2.41	2.77	2.46	2.59	2.06	2.23	2.42	3.30	2.31	1.58	1.87	3.59
First year															
Mean	7.25	7.61	6.30	7.54	6.78	7.58	7.08	8.25	6.71	7.44	8.00	8.60	6.38	7.60	5.50
Std. Dev.	2.40	2.43	2.16	2.01	2.93	3.14	1.99	0.50	2.72	2.38	2.44	1.64	1.80	2.30	4.35
Second year															
Mean	6.58	7.07	5.30	7.13	5.71	6.91	6.41	8.25	6.35	6.38	7.75	7.40	5.92	7.00	5.00
Std. Dev.	2.38	2.41	1.82	2.12	2.58	2.71	2.24	0.50	2.84	2.17	2.36	2.27	2.36	1.22	3.36
Third year															
Mean	6.27	6.61	5.40	6.86	5.35	6.83	6.00	7.50	6.21	6.05	7.50	7.80	5.00	6.40	5.25
Std. Dev.	2.57	2.53	2.59	2.31	2.76	2.88	2.41	1.00	3.26	2.20	1.29	1.98	2.67	1.14	3.86
C. Linear trend equation															
Admission score	7.49	7.57	7.28	7.73	7.11	7.90	7.29	9.80	6.52	7.73	8.25	9.13	6.50	7.36	6.02
Annual change	-0.40	-0.27	-0.76	-0.28	-0.60	-0.39	-0.41	-0.82	-0.07	-0.57	-0.25	-0.57	-0.41	-0.24	-0.35
Probability	0.0259	0.2107	0.0207	0.1720	0.0672	0.2760	0.0475	0.0083	0.8067	0.0186	0.6353	0.0537	0.1177	0.5192	0.6682
D. Sub groups within I to V															
Prob. equal slopes		*** 0.2273 ***		*** 0.5984 ***		*** 0.9473 ***		******			******				
Prob. equal trends		*** 0.0248 ***		*** 0.0088 ***		*** 0.1344 ***		******			******				
E. Friedman Anova Probability	0.0005	0.0386	0.0007	0.0365	0.0089	0.0583	0.0084	0.0023	0.8424	0.0001	0.9291	0.0004	0.0204	0.5803	0.6695

Table A-1-27. Delayed Auditory Feedback--Self Awareness

Variable	Total all children (1)	I Sex		II Admission age		III Neurological status		IV Social position			V WISC Full IQ at admission				
		Males (2)	Females (3)	less than 8 years (4)	8 years or more (5)	Non organics (6)	Organics (7)	1 or 2 (8)	3 (9)	4 or 5 (10)	Below 46 (11)	46-69 (12)	70-89 (13)	90-109 (14)	Above 109 (15)
A. No. of children	36.	26.	10.	22.	14.	12.	24.	5.	13.	18.	5.	10.	13.	4.	4.
B. Annual scores															
Admission															
Mean	1.83	1.76	2.00	1.90	1.71	2.00	1.75	2.00	1.76	1.83	1.40	2.20	1.76	1.75	1.75
Std. Dev.	0.81	0.81	0.81	0.81	0.82	0.85	0.79	0.70	0.83	0.85	0.89	0.63	0.83	0.95	0.95
First year															
Mean	1.69	1.73	1.60	1.86	1.42	1.66	1.70	1.80	1.46	1.83	1.80	2.10	1.53	1.75	1.00
Std. Dev.	0.82	0.87	0.69	0.83	0.75	0.77	0.85	0.44	0.87	0.85	1.30	0.73	0.77	0.50	0.00
Second year															
Mean	1.50	1.53	1.40	1.59	1.35	1.33	1.58	2.00	1.30	1.50	2.00	1.70	1.30	1.50	1.00
Std. Dev.	0.69	0.76	0.51	0.73	0.63	0.49	0.77	1.00	0.63	0.61	1.00	0.82	0.48	0.57	0.00
Third year															
Mean	1.30	1.38	1.10	1.31	1.28	1.08	1.41	1.40	1.30	1.27	1.80	1.40	1.15	1.25	1.00
Std. Dev.	0.46	0.49	0.31	0.47	0.46	0.28	0.50	0.54	0.48	0.46	0.44	0.51	0.37	0.50	0.00
C. Linear trend equation															
Admission score	1.85	1.80	1.96	1.97	1.65	1.98	1.78	2.03	1.69	1.91	1.54	2.26	1.75	1.82	1.52
Annual change	-0.17	-0.13	-0.29	-0.20	-0.13	-0.30	-0.11	-0.16	-0.15	-0.20	0.14	-0.28	-0.20	-0.17	-0.22
Probability	0.0013	0.0391	0.0019	0.0041	0.0941	0.0007	0.0944	0.2603	0.0841	0.0093	0.5370	0.0056	0.0105	0.2234	0.0587
D. Sub groups within I to V															
Prob. equal slopes		*** 0.1864 ***		*** 0.5307 ***		*** 0.0771 ***		*****	0.9144	*****	*****	*****	0.1472	*****	*****
Prob. equal trends		*** 0.5491 ***		*** 0.0608 ***		*** 0.5371 ***		*****	0.1708	*****	*****	*****	0.0067	*****	*****
E. Friedman Anova															
Probability	0.0005	0.0579	0.0020	0.0007	0.2690	0.0002	0.1946	0.0822	0.0777	0.0187	0.5879	0.0021	0.0552	0.5952	0.1432

176

Table A-1-28. Gottschaldt Embedded Figures Test

Variable	Total all children (1)	I Sex Males (2)	I Sex Females (3)	II Admission age less than 8 years (4)	II Admission age 8 years or more (5)	III Neurological status Non organics (6)	III Neurological status Organics (7)	IV Social position 1 or 2 (8)	IV Social position 3 (9)	IV Social position 4 or 5 (10)	V WISC Below 46 (11)	V WISC 46-69 (12)	V WISC 70-89 (13)	V WISC 90-109 (14)	V WISC Above 109 (15)
A. No. of children	40.	27.	13.	25.	15.	14.	26.	5.	15.	20.	6.	10.	14.	6.	4.
B. Annual scores															
Admission															
Mean	2.25	2.33	2.07	0.72	4.80	5.14	0.69	1.00	1.53	3.10	0.00	0.30	1.07	4.66	11.00
Std. Dev.	4.02	4.27	3.59	1.86	5.29	5.48	1.54	2.23	3.56	4.61	0.00	0.67	1.97	4.84	3.16
First year															
Mean	3.65	3.22	4.53	1.64	7.00	6.78	1.96	2.00	2.80	4.70	0.00	1.20	2.92	7.00	12.75
Std. Dev.	5.03	4.79	5.57	2.58	6.31	6.01	3.49	4.47	4.93	5.23	0.00	1.87	4.35	4.85	3.86
Second year															
Mean	4.62	4.03	5.84	2.92	7.46	8.35	2.61	3.20	3.86	5.55	0.00	2.00	4.21	9.33	12.50
Std. Dev.	5.06	4.46	6.13	3.82	5.69	5.71	3.31	6.61	4.67	5.04	0.00	2.74	3.80	5.35	2.51
Third year															
Mean	5.85	5.92	5.69	4.48	8.13	9.07	4.11	4.40	4.13	7.50	0.50	3.00	6.00	9.83	14.50
Std. Dev.	5.52	5.34	6.11	4.44	6.50	6.06	4.42	6.10	5.12	5.45	0.54	3.33	4.83	5.19	1.00
C. Linear trend equation															
Admission score	2.32	2.14	2.71	0.55	5.27	5.33	0.70	0.93	1.75	3.10	-0.09	0.29	1.14	5.03	11.15
Annual change	1.17	1.15	1.21	1.25	1.04	1.33	1.09	1.14	0.88	1.40	0.15	0.89	1.60	1.78	1.02
Probability	0.0012	0.0052	0.0714	0.0001	0.1249	0.1531	0.0005	0.2545	0.0923	0.0066	0.0110	0.0096	0.0012	0.0541	0.1059
D. Sub groups within I to V															
Prob. equal slopes		*** 0.9380 ***		*** 0.7463 ***		*** 0.7056 ***		***** 0.7843 *****			***** 0.2368 *****				
Prob. equal trends		*** 0.5657 ***		*** 0.0000 ***		*** 0.0000 ***		***** 0.0137 *****			***** 0.0000 *****				
E. Friedman Anova															
Probability	0.0000	0.0000	0.0000	0.0000	0.0000	0.0000	0.0000	0.0191	0.0000	0.0000	0.0430	0.0002	0.0000	0.0000	0.0053

177

Table A-1-29. Street's Gestalt Completion Test

Variable	Total all children (1)	I Sex		II Admission age		III Neurological status		IV Social position			V WISC Full IQ at admission				
		Males (2)	Females (3)	less than 8 years (4)	8 years or more (5)	Non organics (6)	Organics (7)	1 or 2 (8)	3 (9)	4 or 5 (10)	Below 46 (11)	46-69 (12)	70-89 (13)	90-109 (14)	Above 109 (15)
A. No. of children	40.	27.	13.	25.	15.	14.	26.	5.	15.	20.	6.	10.	14.	6.	4.
B. Annual scores															
Admission															
Mean	4.47	4.59	4.23	3.92	5.40	5.28	4.03	2.60	4.86	4.65	2.83	4.00	4.78	4.33	7.25
Std. Dev.	2.06	2.11	2.00	2.19	1.45	2.12	1.92	1.94	1.92	2.03	2.40	1.88	1.36	2.25	1.25
First year															
Mean	5.57	5.59	5.53	4.80	6.86	6.92	4.84	3.00	5.60	6.20	3.66	4.90	5.92	5.66	8.75
Std. Dev.	2.34	2.37	2.36	2.10	2.19	2.20	2.11	2.44	1.99	2.21	3.01	2.07	1.54	2.33	0.95
Second year															
Mean	6.42	6.62	6.00	6.12	6.93	7.28	5.96	4.00	6.73	6.80	5.00	5.30	7.00	6.83	8.75
Std. Dev.	2.39	2.37	2.48	2.47	2.25	2.39	2.30	2.12	2.28	2.28	2.96	2.31	1.61	2.48	2.21
Third year															
Mean	7.12	7.00	7.38	6.60	8.00	8.21	6.53	5.00	6.93	7.80	6.33	6.20	7.57	6.83	9.50
Std. Dev.	2.19	2.01	2.59	1.89	2.44	2.15	2.02	1.00	2.37	1.96	2.06	2.65	1.82	1.83	1.29
C. Linear trend equation															
Admission score	4.57	4.71	4.30	3.95	5.61	5.55	4.05	2.42	4.93	4.85	2.68	4.05	4.90	4.61	7.55
Annual change	0.88	0.82	0.99	0.93	0.78	0.91	0.86	0.82	0.73	1.00	1.18	0.70	0.94	0.86	0.67
Probability	0.0000	0.0001	0.0015	0.0000	0.0023	0.0013	0.0000	0.0379	0.0043	0.0000	0.0166	0.0282	0.0000	0.0372	0.0516
D. Sub groups within I to V															
Prob. equal slopes		*** 0.6310 ***	******	*** 0.6390 ***	******	*** 0.8613 ***	******	******	0.6935	******	******	******	0.8444	******	******
Prob. equal trends		*** 0.6677 ***	******	*** 0.0001 ***	******	*** 0.0000 ***	******	******	0.0000	******	******	******	0.0000	******	******
E. Friedman Anova															
Probability	0.0000	0.0000	0.0000	0.0000	0.0000	0.0000	0.0000	0.0000	0.0000	0.0000	0.0000	0.0000	0.0000	0.0000	0.0025

Table A-1-30. Bender Gestalt Test

Variable	Total all children (1)	I Sex		II Admission age		III Neurological status		IV Social position			V WISC Full IQ at admission				
		Males (2)	Females (3)	less than 8 years (4)	8 years or more (5)	Non organics (6)	Organics (7)	1 or 2 (8)	3 (9)	4 or 5 (10)	Below 46 (11)	46-69 (12)	70-89 (13)	90-109 (14)	Above 109 (15)
A. No. of children	32.	22.	10.	21.	11.	13.	19.	4.	13.	15.	5.	6.	12.	5.	4.
B. Annual scores															
Admission															
Mean	25.90	25.04	27.80	20.57	36.09	31.61	22.00	12.25	23.84	31.33	9.60	19.16	29.33	27.80	43.75
Std. Dev.	11.82	12.26	11.16	10.02	7.64	9.77	11.71	4.92	13.55	7.61	3.57	7.35	6.97	10.20	2.87
First year															
Mean	31.65	31.36	32.30	26.23	42.00	35.53	29.00	18.50	31.15	35.60	16.60	24.00	34.16	38.40	46.00
Std. Dev.	11.36	11.47	11.71	9.62	6.00	11.82	10.53	8.81	10.75	10.19	9.15	8.80	6.36	7.05	2.94
Second year															
Mean	35.31	35.27	35.40	32.00	41.63	39.84	32.21	23.75	34.15	39.40	19.80	33.33	36.83	41.40	45.50
Std. Dev.	10.23	11.43	7.47	10.29	6.78	7.02	11.07	12.81	10.15	7.14	10.77	7.50	6.40	6.69	2.38
Third year															
Mean	35.93	36.59	34.50	32.85	41.81	39.53	33.47	23.75	34.76	40.20	21.80	31.50	39.08	40.80	44.75
Std. Dev.	9.83	11.28	5.72	9.97	6.56	6.51	11.07	11.78	10.06	5.87	11.71	6.71	5.51	7.25	2.21
C. Linear trend equation															
Admission score	27.14	26.28	29.02	21.52	37.86	32.42	23.52	13.60	25.61	32.07	10.97	20.05	30.06	30.79	44.62
Annual change	3.37	3.85	2.32	4.26	1.68	2.80	3.76	3.97	3.57	3.04	3.98	4.63	3.19	4.20	0.25
Probability	0.0003	0.0010	0.0797	0.0001	0.0710	0.0139	0.0017	0.0788	0.0120	0.0016	0.0367	0.0035	0.0004	0.0169	0.6734
D. Sub groups within I to V															
Prob. equal slopes		*** 0.5844 ***		*** 0.0840 ***		*** 0.5708 ***		*****	0.9030	*****	*****	*****	0.2435	*****	*****
Prob. equal trends		*** 0.8298 ***		*** 0.0000 ***		*** 0.0002 ***		*****	0.0000	*****	*****	*****	0.0000	*****	*****
E. Friedman Anova															
Probability	0.0000	0.0000	0.0000	0.0000	0.0003	0.0000	0.0000	0.0016	0.0000	0.0000	0.0000	0.0000	0.0000	0.0000	0.0212

Table A-1-31. Weigl Color Form Sorting Test

Variable	Total all children (1)	I Sex		II Admission age		III Neurological status		IV Social position			V WISC Full IQ at admission				
		Males (2)	Females (3)	less than 8 years (4)	8 years or more (5)	Non organics (6)	Organics (7)	1 or 2 (8)	3 (9)	4 or 5 (10)	Below 46 (11)	46-69 (12)	70-89 (13)	90-109 (14)	Above 109 (15)
A. No. of children	38.	27.	11.	23.	15.	13.	25.	5.	14.	19.	5.	10.	13.	6.	4.
B. Annual scores															
Admission															
Mean	2.36	2.00	3.27	2.08	2.80	3.92	1.56	2.20	2.07	2.63	0.60	0.90	2.23	5.16	4.50
Std. Dev.	2.82	2.54	3.37	2.67	3.07	3.54	2.00	3.49	2.92	2.71	0.89	1.44	2.35	3.25	4.12
First year															
Mean	3.26	3.14	3.54	2.39	4.60	5.07	2.32	2.20	2.28	4.26	1.40	2.30	3.23	3.33	8.00
Std. Dev.	2.86	2.91	2.84	2.67	2.69	2.69	2.51	2.04	2.92	2.76	1.51	2.62	2.94	1.50	0.00
Second year															
Mean	3.97	3.88	4.18	2.95	5.53	4.92	3.48	2.60	2.07	5.73	1.40	4.30	4.07	3.66	6.50
Std. Dev.	2.91	3.01	2.78	2.56	2.79	2.69	2.95	1.94	2.23	2.53	1.67	3.05	2.95	2.33	3.00
Third year															
Mean	4.18	3.66	5.45	3.47	5.26	5.53	3.48	2.40	3.28	5.31	1.00	3.50	4.69	5.00	7.00
Std. Dev.	3.22	3.15	3.17	3.05	3.26	3.38	2.95	3.28	3.04	3.05	1.00	3.47	3.03	3.28	2.00
C. Linear trend equation															
Admission score	2.52	2.31	3.03	2.01	3.29	4.16	1.67	2.20	1.91	3.05	0.91	1.28	2.32	4.31	5.60
Annual change	0.61	0.57	0.71	0.47	0.83	0.46	0.69	0.10	0.34	0.95	0.12	0.98	0.82	-0.01	0.60
Probability	0.0047	0.0224	0.0787	0.0616	0.0169	0.2186	0.0042	0.8452	0.3051	0.0017	0.6488	0.0159	0.0197	0.9720	0.6457
D. Sub groups within I to V															
Prob. equal slopes		*** 0.7572 ***		*** 0.6041 ***		*** 0.6070 ***		*****	0.2287	*****	*****	*****	0.4099	*****	*****
Prob. equal trends		*** 0.0713 ***		*** 0.0003 ***		*** 0.0000 ***		*****	0.0001	*****	*****	*****	0.0000	*****	*****
E. Friedman Anova															
Probability	0.0000	0.0002	0.0081	0.0228	0.0001	0.1025	0.0000	0.1808	0.2351	0.0000	0.5078	0.0000	0.0092	0.0603	0.0964

Table A-1-32. Orientation Test

Variable	Total all children (1)	I Sex Males (2)	I Sex Females (3)	II Admission age less than 8 years (4)	II Admission age 8 years or more (5)	III Neurological status Non organics (6)	III Neurological status Organics (7)	IV Social position 1 or 2 (8)	IV Social position 3 (9)	IV Social position 4 or 5 (10)	V WISC Below 46 (11)	V WISC 46-69 (12)	V WISC 70-89 (13)	V WISC 90-109 (14)	V WISC Above 109 (15)
A. No. of children	40.	27.	13.	25.	15.	14.	26.	5.	15.	20.	6.	10.	14.	6.	4.
B. Annual scores															
Admission Mean	12.07	13.00	10.15	9.44	16.46	15.00	10.50	3.60	11.86	14.35	0.83	8.90	15.07	14.16	23.25
Std. Dev.	7.40	7.85	6.21	7.15	5.64	8.26	6.53	3.36	7.11	6.96	0.98	3.47	4.41	7.05	2.06
First year Mean	15.07	16.25	12.61	12.68	19.06	18.14	13.42	4.40	14.60	18.10	2.66	9.50	18.14	21.00	28.00
Std. Dev.	9.08	9.74	7.25	9.03	7.90	9.70	8.46	4.97	7.34	9.19	2.16	6.09	5.58	6.41	0.81
Second year Mean	18.77	19.66	16.92	16.92	21.86	21.07	17.53	12.00	18.13	20.95	4.00	16.00	21.57	25.50	28.00
Std. Dev.	8.61	9.01	7.72	9.18	6.78	7.91	8.87	10.17	7.45	8.50	4.69	6.83	4.10	2.73	0.81
Third year Mean	20.42	21.51	18.15	18.80	23.13	22.71	19.19	14.60	18.80	23.10	6.16	18.90	23.57	24.50	28.50
Std. Dev.	8.76	8.80	8.58	9.88	5.82	6.39	9.70	10.94	9.10	7.27	5.84	9.24	4.78	1.76	1.00
C. Linear trend equation															
Admission score	12.27	13.26	10.21	9.61	16.71	15.32	10.63	2.56	12.20	14.76	0.81	7.85	15.24	15.96	24.57
Annual change	2.87	2.89	2.83	3.23	2.28	2.60	3.01	4.06	2.43	2.91	1.73	3.65	2.89	3.55	1.57
Probability	0.0000	0.0004	0.0035	0.0002	0.0038	0.0085	0.0002	0.0163	0.0080	0.0007	0.0181	0.0006	0.0000	0.0015	0.0015
D. Sub groups within I to V															
Prob. equal slopes		*** 0.9574 ***		*** 0.5769 ***		*** 0.7368 ***		******	0.6719	******	******	******	0.3386	******	******
Prob. equal trends		*** 0.0251 ***		*** 0.0001 ***		*** 0.0037 ***		******	0.0000	******	******	******	0.0000	******	******
E. Friedman Anova Probability	0.0000	0.0000	0.0000	0.0000	0.0000	0.0000	0.0000	0.0000	0.0000	0.0000	0.0006	0.0000	0.0000	0.0000	0.0001

181

Table A-1-33. Lincoln-Oseretsky Motor Development Scale

Variable	Total all children (1)	I Sex		II Admission age		III Neurological status		IV Social position			V WISC Full IQ at admission				
		Males (2)	Females (3)	less than 8 years (4)	8 years or more (5)	Non organics (6)	Organics (7)	1 or 2 (8)	3 (9)	4 or 5 (10)	Below 46 (11)	46-69 (12)	70-89 (13)	90-109 (14)	Above 109 (15)
A. No. of children	40.	27.	13.	25.	15.	14.	26.	5.	15.	20.	6.	10.	14.	6.	4.
B. Annual scores															
Admission															
Mean	10.15	10.07	10.30	5.40	18.06	17.21	6.34	6.20	7.93	12.80	0.66	3.20	10.57	16.00	31.50
Std. Dev.	12.49	12.62	12.73	7.36	15.31	15.67	8.54	12.25	10.70	13.75	1.63	4.39	9.62	14.39	14.27
First year															
Mean	15.80	15.25	16.92	9.96	25.53	24.14	11.30	9.80	14.60	18.20	1.00	8.90	16.85	24.83	38.00
Std. Dev.	13.85	14.65	12.53	10.61	13.39	16.29	10.07	15.33	15.63	12.16	1.26	6.77	11.21	13.21	9.93
Second year															
Mean	18.85	17.66	21.30	13.00	28.60	28.00	13.92	14.00	18.13	20.60	2.16	13.50	18.21	32.16	39.50
Std. Dev.	15.41	15.28	16.00	12.65	14.98	16.89	12.25	19.58	15.82	14.58	2.40	12.77	10.81	16.31	7.93
Third year															
Mean	24.75	24.22	25.84	19.12	34.13	36.85	18.23	15.00	23.13	28.40	3.33	15.40	27.78	38.66	48.75
Std. Dev.	17.09	17.32	17.24	15.08	16.53	14.82	14.67	19.37	18.63	14.96	3.88	12.40	12.79	8.89	8.01
C. Linear trend equation															
Admission score	10.35	10.07	10.94	5.24	18.89	17.13	6.71	6.66	8.57	12.62	0.41	4.07	10.40	16.61	31.45
Annual change	4.68	4.48	5.10	4.42	5.12	6.27	3.82	3.06	4.91	4.92	0.91	4.12	5.30	7.53	5.32
Probability	0.0000	0.0010	0.0065	0.0001	0.0043	0.0018	0.0005	0.6471	0.0069	0.0009	0.0457	0.0044	0.0004	0.0042	0.0269
D. Sub groups within I to V															
Prob. equal slopes		*** 0.7801 ***		*** 0.7106 ***		**** 0.2061 ***		0.8390			*****				
Prob. equal trends		*** 0.5196 ***		*** 0.0000 ***		**** 0.0000 ***		0.0355			*****				
E. Friedman Anova															
Probability	0.0000	0.0000	0.0000	0.0000	0.0000	0.0000	0.0000	0.0595	0.0000	0.0000	0.0234	0.0000	0.0000	0.0000	0.0000

Table A-1-34. Railwalking

Variable	Total all children (1)	I Sex		II Admission age		III Neurological status		IV Social position			V WISC Full IQ at admission				
		Males (2)	Females (3)	less than 8 years (4)	8 years or more (5)	Non organics (6)	Organics (7)	1 or 2 (8)	3 (9)	4 or 5 (10)	Below 46 (11)	46-69 (12)	70-89 (13)	90-109 (14)	Above 109 (15)
A. No. of children	40.	27.	13.	25.	15.	14.	26.	5.	15.	20.	6.	10.	14.	6.	4.
B. Annual scores															
Admission															
Mean	19.95	17.11	25.84	11.08	34.73	34.78	11.96	9.40	19.00	23.30	0.16	11.10	20.42	33.33	50.00
Std. Dev.	22.06	22.09	21.63	14.43	24.97	27.37	13.41	21.01	22.90	21.85	0.40	18.87	13.92	24.44	28.54
First year															
Mean	25.20	21.70	32.46	16.36	39.93	41.07	16.65	13.20	21.40	31.05	0.66	10.20	31.64	40.83	53.50
Std. Dev.	24.43	22.37	27.75	20.07	24.49	26.89	18.38	27.86	20.35	25.90	1.21	14.84	18.51	25.00	29.41
Second year															
Mean	33.12	34.33	30.61	26.44	44.26	42.50	28.07	18.20	32.86	37.05	2.66	9.30	43.71	61.66	58.50
Std. Dev.	31.29	33.77	26.44	31.54	28.43	26.14	33.10	34.12	33.01	29.77	3.07	10.28	34.48	16.21	6.60
Third year															
Mean	42.10	43.33	39.53	28.84	64.20	65.78	29.34	29.40	30.93	53.65	9.33	23.40	43.28	60.50	106.25
Std. Dev.	37.37	39.25	34.52	30.82	37.75	38.42	30.46	47.58	34.38	35.19	17.42	21.18	33.41	29.57	23.02
C. Linear trend equation															
Admission score	18.93	15.42	26.23	11.17	31.87	31.87	11.97	7.80	18.96	21.70	-1.21	8.10	22.67	33.73	41.00
Annual change	7.43	9.12	3.92	6.33	9.27	9.44	6.35	6.50	4.72	9.70	2.95	3.60	8.06	10.23	17.37
Probability	0.0007	0.0009	0.2544	0.0058	0.0078	0.0107	0.0048	0.3276	0.1451	0.0013	0.0709	0.1366	0.0128	0.0254	0.0084
D. Sub groups within I to V															
Prob. equal slopes		*** 0.2385 ***		*** 0.5413 ***		*** 0.5537 ***		*****			*****				
Prob. equal trends		*** 0.5528 ***		*** 0.0000 ***		*** 0.0000 ***		*****			*****				
E. Friedman Anova															
Probability	0.0000	0.0000	0.0061	0.0000	0.0000	0.0000	0.0000	0.0063	0.0004	0.0000	0.0043	0.0000	0.0000	0.0000	0.0005

Table A-1-35. Dynamometer

Variable	Total all children (1)	I Sex		II Admission age		III Neurological status		IV Social position			V WISC Full IQ at admission				
		Males (2)	Females (3)	less than 8 years (4)	8 years or more (5)	Non organics (6)	Organics (7)	1 or 2 (8)	3 (9)	4 or 5 (10)	Below 46 (11)	46-69 (12)	70-89 (13)	90-109 (14)	Above 109 (15)
A. No. of children	39.	27.	12.	24.	15.	14.	25.	5.	15.	19.	5.	10.	14.	6.	4.
B. Annual scores															
Admission															
Mean	10.43	11.03	9.08	9.12	12.53	11.64	9.76	6.60	9.66	12.05	6.60	8.80	10.71	14.00	13.00
Std. Dev.	4.15	4.55	2.77	3.35	4.54	3.81	4.25	3.97	3.94	3.67	3.97	2.93	3.79	4.60	2.44
First year															
Mean	12.51	13.33	10.66	10.75	15.33	13.21	12.12	8.40	11.40	14.47	8.40	11.20	13.14	14.16	16.25
Std. Dev.	4.69	5.10	3.02	3.46	5.12	4.83	4.66	3.36	4.56	4.24	3.28	4.13	4.45	5.23	4.71
Second year															
Mean	14.58	15.70	12.08	13.20	16.80	15.35	14.16	11.60	14.00	15.84	11.40	11.60	15.85	16.50	18.75
Std. Dev.	4.93	5.17	3.28	4.01	5.58	5.04	4.92	2.50	5.38	4.79	1.14	3.43	4.92	6.31	3.86
Third year															
Mean	16.02	16.51	14.91	14.58	18.33	17.71	15.08	11.60	15.20	17.84	12.20	14.50	16.92	17.33	19.50
Std. Dev.	4.42	4.43	4.39	3.88	4.36	3.56	4.64	3.57	4.31	3.81	2.48	4.47	4.53	3.98	3.00
C. Linear trend equation															
Admission score	10.56	11.32	8.85	9.09	12.92	11.42	10.07	6.81	9.68	12.24	6.68	8.90	10.95	13.65	13.57
Annual change	1.88	1.88	1.89	1.88	1.88	2.03	1.80	1.82	1.92	1.87	1.98	1.75	2.13	1.23	2.20
Probability	0.0000	0.0000	0.0002	0.0000	0.0017	0.0004	0.0001	0.0121	0.0007	0.0001	0.0026	0.0023	0.0003	0.1782	0.0116
D. Sub groups within I to V															
Prob. equal slopes		*** 0.9851 ***		*** 0.9913 ***		*** 0.7258 ***		*****	*****	*****	*****	*****	*****	*****	*****
Prob. equal trends		*** 0.0019 ***		*** 0.0000 ***		*** 0.0226 ***		*****	*****	*****	*****	*****	*****	*****	*****
E. Friedman Anova															
Probability	0.0000	0.0000	0.0000	0.0000	0.0000	0.0000	0.0000	0.0001	0.0000	0.0000	0.0000	0.0000	0.0000	0.0000	0.0000

Table A-1-36. Wechsler Intelligence Scale for Children—Verbal

Variable	Total all children (1)	I Sex Males (2)	I Sex Females (3)	II Admission age less than 8 years (4)	II Admission age 8 years or more (5)	III Neurological status Non organics (6)	III Neurological status Organics (7)	IV Social position 1 or 2 (8)	IV Social position 3 (9)	IV Social position 4 or 5 (10)	V WISC Below 46 (11)	V WISC 46-69 (12)	V WISC 70-89 (13)	V WISC 90-109 (14)	V WISC Above 109 (15)
A. No. of children	40.	27.	13.	25.	15.	14.	26.	5.	15.	20.	6.	10.	14.	6.	4.
B. Annual scores															
Admission															
Mean	77.70	80.00	72.92	72.84	85.80	92.00	70.00	59.40	79.66	80.80	44.00	61.50	80.35	100.33	125.50
Std. Dev.	25.07	27.80	18.18	24.28	25.04	29.85	18.46	14.58	25.99	25.42	0.00	5.38	5.87	16.78	14.64
First year															
Mean	83.42	85.88	78.30	79.64	89.73	97.71	75.73	66.20	85.20	86.40	47.83	67.30	84.00	109.83	135.50
Std. Dev.	27.90	30.67	21.20	25.95	30.76	33.34	21.46	23.37	28.45	28.22	4.95	10.97	13.72	11.75	16.19
Second year															
Mean	85.65	89.29	78.07	83.08	89.93	98.78	78.57	69.40	86.40	89.15	49.83	70.10	85.71	113.33	136.50
Std. Dev.	28.79	31.27	22.00	27.80	30.88	32.43	24.45	25.10	29.91	28.76	10.72	13.17	16.12	14.78	15.00
Third year															
Mean	86.40	89.48	80.00	85.32	88.20	101.71	78.15	70.40	84.86	91.55	50.50	73.30	84.92	117.50	131.50
Std. Dev.	29.80	33.35	20.25	30.39	29.74	31.51	25.82	29.61	29.50	29.99	10.63	17.59	20.64	16.28	18.23
C. Linear trend equation															
Admission score	79.04	81.38	74.17	74.08	87.30	93.02	71.51	60.91	81.51	81.72	44.81	62.31	81.43	102.00	129.40
Annual change	2.83	3.18	2.10	4.08	0.74	3.02	2.73	3.62	1.68	3.50	2.15	3.82	1.54	5.50	1.90
Probability	0.1477	0.2267	0.5918	0.0891	0.8189	0.5726	0.1670	0.5631	0.6124	0.2092	0.1332	0.0318	0.6076	0.0460	0.5959
D. Sub groups within I to V															
Prob. equal slopes		*** 0.7912 ***		*** 0.5869 ***		*** 0.9376 ***		*****			*****				
Prob. equal trends		*** 0.0561 ***		*** 0.0672 ***		*** 0.0000 ***		*****			*****				
E. Friedman Anova															
Probability	0.0000	0.0000	0.0004	0.0000	0.1717	0.0000	0.0000	0.1808	0.0347	0.0000	0.0268	0.0002	0.7214	0.0000	0.0044

Table A-1-37. Wechsler Intelligence Scale for Children—Performance

Variable	Total all children (1)	I Sex — Males (2)	I Sex — Females (3)	II Admission age — less than 8 years (4)	II Admission age — 8 years or more (5)	III Neurological status — Non organics (6)	III Neurological status — Organics (7)	IV Social position — 1 or 2 (8)	IV Social position — 3 (9)	IV Social position — 4 or 5 (10)	V WISC Full IQ at admission — Below 46 (11)	V — 46-69 (12)	V — 70-89 (13)	V — 90-109 (14)	V — Above 109 (15)
A. No. of children	40.	27.	13.	25.	15.	14.	26.	5.	15.	20.	6.	10.	14.	6.	4.
B. Annual scores															
Admission															
Mean	77.77	77.40	78.53	72.92	85.86	97.07	67.38	65.80	77.06	81.30	48.50	62.40	77.71	101.83	124.25
Std. Dev.	24.58	25.47	23.60	22.35	26.72	23.34	18.39	31.82	24.70	22.94	13.47	11.41	6.96	13.55	10.30
First year															
Mean	81.90	81.96	81.76	78.12	88.20	98.35	73.03	68.00	83.26	84.35	54.00	64.70	82.71	108.33	124.25
Std. Dev.	24.61	25.95	22.58	23.19	26.41	22.06	21.42	32.00	26.63	21.14	15.49	14.00	8.15	11.79	5.90
Second year															
Mean	82.40	82.62	81.92	77.40	90.73	102.00	71.84	69.00	81.33	86.55	51.66	65.00	81.14	112.00	132.00
Std. Dev.	27.91	29.20	26.16	25.06	31.23	27.95	21.87	38.01	28.00	25.52	13.42	15.77	12.54	13.20	13.21
Third year															
Mean	83.25	83.51	82.69	79.40	89.66	104.00	72.07	66.80	82.26	88.10	53.66	65.70	84.42	109.16	128.50
Std. Dev.	26.55	27.37	25.84	24.97	28.71	21.44	22.13	35.22	27.29	23.25	17.92	16.41	11.18	13.24	11.47
C. Linear trend equation															
Admission score	78.79	78.52	79.33	74.15	86.52	96.69	69.15	66.80	78.93	81.68	49.98	62.91	78.71	103.98	124.17
Annual change	1.69	1.90	1.26	1.87	1.39	2.44	1.28	0.40	1.36	2.26	1.31	1.02	1.85	2.56	2.05
Probability	0.6422	0.5827	0.6782	0.6165	0.6703	0.6097	0.5098	0.9501	0.6586	0.6706	0.6309	0.6191	0.1177	0.2765	0.6174
D. Sub groups within I to V															
Prob. equal slopes		*** 0.8652 ***		*** 0.8925 ***		*** 0.7218 ***		*****	0.9386	*****	*****	*****	0.9822	*****	*****
Prob. equal trends		*** 0.9712 ***		*** 0.0055 ***		*** 0.0000 ***		*****	0.0216	*****	*****	*****	0.0000	*****	*****
E. Friedman Anova															
Probability	0.0000	0.0000	0.0210	0.0000	0.0014	0.0000	0.0000	0.8273	0.0013	0.0000	0.1739	0.5255	0.0000	0.0004	0.0212

Table A-1-38. Wechsler Intelligence Scale for Children—Full

Variable	Total all children (1)	I Sex Males (2)	I Sex Females (3)	II Admission age less than 8 years (4)	II Admission age 8 years or more (5)	III Neurological status Non organics (6)	III Neurological status Organics (7)	IV Social position 1 or 2 (8)	IV Social position 3 (9)	IV Social position 4 or 5 (10)	V WISC Full IQ Below 46 (11)	V WISC Full IQ 46-69 (12)	V WISC Full IQ 70-89 (13)	V WISC Full IQ 90-109 (14)	V WISC Full IQ Above 109 (15)
A. No. of children	40.	27.	13.	25.	15.	14.	26.	5.	15.	20.	6.	10.	14.	6.	4.
B. Annual scores															
Admission Mean	76.20	77.37	73.76	71.20	84.53	93.14	67.07	61.60	77.26	79.05	45.00	58.10	77.14	101.33	127.25
Std. Dev.	25.11	27.34	20.51	22.63	27.57	28.68	17.58	21.25	25.97	25.24	0.00	6.53	5.14	5.81	11.05
First year Mean	81.65	83.40	78.00	77.92	87.86	97.85	72.92	67.00	83.26	84.10	49.50	62.90	81.92	110.16	133.00
Std. Dev.	26.97	29.05	22.64	24.39	30.65	29.61	21.27	26.35	28.36	26.25	6.59	11.23	8.80	9.06	12.24
Second year Mean	83.60	86.22	78.15	80.16	89.33	100.07	74.73	69.00	83.06	87.65	50.50	64.80	82.07	116.16	136.75
Std. Dev.	29.16	31.70	23.21	27.08	32.49	31.76	23.84	29.60	30.31	28.47	9.20	13.18	12.63	9.80	16.64
Third year Mean	84.05	86.14	79.69	81.72	87.93	103.00	73.84	68.20	82.46	89.20	51.66	66.80	83.14	114.66	133.00
Std. Dev.	28.27	30.50	23.49	27.08	30.71	27.09	23.57	31.31	29.46	26.43	10.34	16.75	15.12	6.74	11.94
C. Linear trend equation															
Admission score	77.55	78.91	74.71	72.68	85.66	93.75	68.82	63.18	79.20	79.90	46.01	58.94	78.35	103.68	129.35
Annual change	2.55	2.91	1.79	3.38	1.16	3.17	2.21	2.18	1.54	3.40	2.10	2.80	1.81	4.60	2.10
Probability	0.1848	0.2515	0.5224	0.1322	0.7361	0.6373	0.2434	0.6812	0.6424	0.1970	0.1298	0.1085	0.1678	0.0053	0.5307
D. Sub groups within I to V															
Prob. equal slopes		*** 0.7821 ***		*** 0.5826 ***		*** 0.7851 ***		*****	0.9002	*****	*****	*****	0.8154	*****	*****
Prob. equal trends		*** 0.1994 ***		*** 0.0277 ***		*** 0.0000 ***		*****	0.0230	*****	*****	*****	0.0000	*****	*****
E. Friedman Anova Probability	0.0000	0.0000	0.0000	0.0000	0.0005	0.0000	0.0000	0.5078	0.0018	0.0000	0.1630	0.0004	0.0148	0.0000	0.0005

Table A-1-39. Communication—Voice and Speech

Variable	Total all children (1)	I Sex Males (2)	I Sex Females (3)	II Admission age less than 8 years (4)	II Admission age 8 years or more (5)	III Neurological status Non organics (6)	III Neurological status Organics (7)	IV Social position 1 or 2 (8)	IV Social position 3 (9)	IV Social position 4 or 5 (10)	V WISC Full IQ at admission Below 46 (11)	V WISC 46-69 (12)	V WISC 70-89 (13)	V WISC 90-109 (14)	V WISC Above 109 (15)
A. No. of children	40.	27.	13.	25.	15.	14.	26.	5.	15.	20.	6.	10.	14.	6.	4.
B. Annual scores															
Admission															
Mean	23.32	23.51	22.92	22.28	25.06	24.92	22.46	21.00	23.86	23.50	17.83	21.50	24.00	24.83	31.50
Std. Dev.	5.69	5.65	6.00	5.60	5.59	5.44	5.74	4.69	7.52	4.32	2.31	4.57	5.42	5.70	1.29
First year															
Mean	24.72	25.37	23.38	24.08	25.80	25.28	24.42	23.00	26.13	24.10	21.33	22.50	25.64	26.33	29.75
Std. Dev.	5.15	4.43	6.41	4.84	5.64	5.09	5.27	3.39	7.01	3.62	2.06	3.34	5.93	6.12	2.87
Second year															
Mean	25.35	26.03	23.92	24.96	26.00	26.78	24.57	24.80	25.73	25.20	21.83	24.20	25.14	28.16	30.00
Std. Dev.	5.10	4.89	5.42	5.64	4.14	4.50	5.31	4.08	7.09	3.54	4.53	3.70	4.97	5.63	5.35
Third year															
Mean	24.72	24.81	24.53	24.40	25.26	25.35	24.38	22.80	25.53	24.60	21.33	23.90	25.42	25.66	28.00
Std. Dev.	4.52	4.27	5.18	4.80	4.11	4.60	4.53	5.31	5.71	3.23	4.13	4.22	4.75	2.50	5.65
C. Linear trend equation															
Admission score	23.80	24.25	22.88	22.84	25.41	25.17	23.07	21.81	24.62	23.68	18.93	21.68	24.48	25.60	31.35
Annual change	0.48	0.45	0.53	0.72	0.08	0.27	0.59	0.72	0.46	0.44	1.10	0.89	0.37	0.43	-1.02
Probability	0.1821	0.2780	0.5469	0.1204	0.8820	0.6398	0.1953	0.5789	0.5665	0.2332	0.0911	0.1121	0.5529	0.6502	0.2613
D. Sub groups within I to V															
Prob. equal slopes		*** 0.9112 ***		*** 0.6080 ***		*** 0.6820 ***		*****	0.9701	*****	*****	*****	0.5292	*****	*****
Prob. equal trends		*** 0.1480 ***		*** 0.0522 ***		*** 0.0522 ***		*****	0.1697	*****	*****	*****	0.0000	*****	*****
E. Friedman Anova															
Probability	0.0000	0.0000	0.1090	0.0000	0.1717	0.0241	0.0001	0.0311	0.0000	0.1199	0.0001	0.0672	0.0148	0.0063	0.2549

Table A-1-40. Communication—Language

Variable	Total all children (1)	I Sex Males (2)	I Sex Females (3)	II Admission age less than 8 years (4)	II Admission age 8 years or more (5)	III Neurological status Non organics (6)	III Neurological status Organics (7)	IV Social position 1 or 2 (8)	IV Social position 3 (9)	IV Social position 4 or 5 (10)	V WISC Full IQ at admission Below 46 (11)	V WISC 46-69 (12)	V WISC 70-89 (13)	V WISC 90-109 (14)	V WISC Above 109 (15)
A. No. of children	40.	27.	13.	25.	15.	14.	26.	5.	15.	20.	6.	10.	14.	6.	4.
B. Annual scores															
Admission Mean	6.95	7.33	6.15	6.36	7.93	7.42	6.69	4.80	7.00	7.45	3.33	5.80	7.85	8.66	9.50
Std. Dev.	2.80	2.86	2.60	2.88	2.46	2.68	2.89	1.30	3.29	2.52	0.51	1.61	2.53	3.14	1.00
First year Mean	7.30	7.48	6.92	6.96	7.86	7.71	7.07	5.80	7.33	7.65	4.00	6.70	7.64	9.50	9.25
Std. Dev.	2.63	2.75	2.43	2.74	2.41	2.19	2.85	2.16	3.10	2.32	0.89	1.63	2.70	2.07	1.89
Second year Mean	8.07	8.29	7.61	7.92	8.33	8.92	7.61	7.80	7.66	8.45	4.83	7.40	8.28	10.83	9.75
Std. Dev.	2.51	2.49	2.59	2.76	2.09	2.30	2.54	2.77	2.87	2.23	1.32	1.89	2.26	1.32	1.25
Third year Mean	8.05	8.25	7.61	7.92	8.26	8.28	7.92	7.20	7.80	8.45	5.00	7.30	8.64	10.16	9.25
Std. Dev.	2.39	2.50	2.18	2.72	1.79	2.39	2.43	2.38	2.90	1.98	1.54	1.70	2.23	1.72	1.50
C. Linear trend equation															
Admission score	6.98	7.30	6.31	6.44	7.87	7.52	6.69	5.02	7.03	7.43	3.41	6.01	7.65	8.91	9.47
Annual change	0.40	0.35	0.50	0.56	0.14	0.37	0.42	0.92	0.27	0.38	0.58	0.52	0.30	0.58	-0.02
Probability	0.0253	0.1128	0.0932	0.0230	0.5680	0.1877	0.0694	0.0468	0.5611	0.0916	0.0082	0.0340	0.3023	0.1444	0.9334.
D. Sub groups within I to V															
Prob. equal slopes		*** 0.7046 ***		*** 0.2647 ***		*** 0.9030 ***		*****			*****				
Prob. equal trends		*** 0.0751 ***		*** 0.0513 ***		*** 0.0711 ***		*****			*****				
E. Friedman Anova Probability	0.000	0.0001	0.0003	0.0000	0.6593	0.0002	0.0001	0.0000	0.0251	0.0037	0.0000	0.0061	0.1600	0.0026	0.5575

TABLES A-2

Probability of No Annual Change for
Schizophrenic Children
(for Variables 1–40)

Table A-2-1. Ego Status: Probability of No Annual Change*

Variable	Years compared			
	Admission to 1st	1st to 2nd	2nd to 3rd	Admission to 3rd
Total (1) All children	.0115	.1986	.3143	.0003
I Sex				
(2) Males	.0863	.5316	.5474	.0159
(3) Females	.0514	.2056	.6136	.0033
II Admission age				
(4) less than 8 yrs.	.0195	.6658	.5345	.6658
(5) 8 yrs. or more	.2672	.5845	.5845	.0269
III Neurological status				
(6) Non organics	.5986	.1124	.2184	.0049
(7) Organics	.0155	.7406	.7496	.0087
IV Social position				
(8) 1 or 2	.5074	.5074	1.0000	.2225
(9) 3	.0614	1.0000	.2309	.0161
(10) 4 or 5	.1084	.1635	.7234	.0068
V WISC Full IQ at admission				
(11) Below 46	1.0000	1.0000	.5366	.5366
(12) 46–69	.0389	.6656	.6515	.0080
(13) 70–89	.0803	1.0000	.5986	.0418
(14) 90–109	.5366	.2473	1.0000	.1117
(15) Above 109	1.0000	.5278	1.0000	.5278

*Based on 2-tail Wilcoxon Matched Pairs Signed Ranks Test.

Table A-2-2. Metropolitan Achievement Test—Reading: Probability of No Annual Change*

Variable	Years compared			
	Admission to 1st	1st to 2nd	2nd to 3rd	Admission to 3rd
Total (1) All children	.0000	.0000	.0000	.0000
I Sex				
(2) Males	.0003	.0002	.0003	.0001
(3) Females	.0125	.0044	.0054	.0020
II Admission age				
(4) less than 8 yrs.	.0007	.0002	.0002	.0001
(5) 8 yrs. or more	.0045	.0049	.0116	.0013
III Neurological status				
(6) Non organics	.0023	.0013	.0045	.0013
(7) Organics	.0018	.0012	.0003	.0001
IV Social position				
(8) 1 or 2	.2225	.1015	.1015	.1015
(9) 3	.0082	.0037	.0082	.0011
(10) 4 or 5	.0010	.0007	.0008	.0004
V WISC Full IQ at admission				
(11) Below 46	1.0000	.2473	.2473	.2473
(12) 46–69	.0718	.0090	.0309	.0076
(13) 70–89	.0044	.0138	.0025	.0018
(14) 90–109	.0260	.0260	.0260	.0260
(15) Above 109	.0643	.0643	.5278	.0643

*Based on 2-tail Wilcoxon Matched Pairs Signed Ranks Test.

Table A-2-3. Metropolitan Achievement Test—Arithmetic: Probability of No Annual Change*

Variable	Years compared			
	Admission to 1st	1st to 2nd	2nd to 3rd	Admission to 3rd
Total (1) All children	.0000	.0000	.0000	.0000
I Sex				
(2) Males	.0003	.0002	.0005	.0001
(3) Females	.0165	.0025	.0049	.0020
II Admission age				
(4) less than 8 yrs.	.0007	.0004	.0013	.0001
(5) 8 yrs. or more	.0076	.0015	.0027	.0013
III Neurological status				
(6) Non organics	.0054	.0013	.0038	.0013
(7) Organics	.0007	.0007	.0009	.0001
IV Social position				
(8) 1 or 2	.2225	.1015	.8879	.1015
(9) 3	.0032	.0012	.0032	.0011
(10) 4 or 5	.0027	.0013	.0012	.0004
V WISC Full IQ at admission				
(11) Below 46	1.0000	.2473	.2473	.2473
(12) 46–69	.0718	.0123	.0309	.0076
(13) 70–89	.0025	.0020	.0198	.0018
(14) 90–109	.0710	.0558	.0337	.0260
(15) Above 109	.0643	.0643	.0643	.0643

*Based on 2-tail Wilcoxon Matched Pairs Signed Ranks Test.

Table A-2-4. Metropolitan Achievement Test—Total Achievement: Probability of No Annual Change*

Variable	Years compared			
	Admission to 1st	1st to 2nd	2nd to 3rd	Admission to 3rd
Total (1) All children	.0000	.0000	.0000	.0000
I Sex				
(2) Males	.0003	.0001	.0003	.0001
(3) Females	.0078	.0071	.0033	.0020
II Admission age				
(4) less than 8 yrs.	.0007	.0001	.0006	.0001
(5) 8 yrs. or more	.0032	.0035	.0027	.0013
III Neurological status				
(6) Non organics	.0023	.0013	.0049	.0013
(7) Organics	.0012	.0004	.0003	.0001
IV Social position				
(8) 1 or 2	.2225	.1015	.1015	.1015
(9) 3	.0051	.0030	.0037	.0011
(10) 4 or 5	.0010	.0004	.0010	.0004
V WISC Full IQ at admission				
(11) Below 46	1.0000	.2473	.9130	.2473
(12) 46–69	.0718	.0090	.0196	.0076
(13) 70–89	.0033	.0078	.0030	.0018
(14) 90–109	.0260	.0260	.0260	.0260
(15) Above 109	.0643	.0643	.0643	.0643

*Based on 2-tail Wilcoxon Matched Pairs Signed Ranks Test.

Table A-2-5. Vineland Social Maturity Scale—Social Age: Probability of No Annual Change*

Variable	Years compared			
	Admission to 1st	1st to 2nd	2nd to 3rd	Admission to 3rd
Total (1) All children	.0000	.0003	.0560	.0000
I Sex				
(2) Males	.0005	.0021	.0696	.0000
(3) Females	.0047	.0246	.5121	.0037
II Admission age				
(4) less than 8 yrs.	.0004	.0042	.1854	.0001
(5) 8 yrs. or more	.0086	.0049	.1200	.0027
III Neurological status				
(6) Non organics	.0018	.0040	.9426	.0022
(7) Organics	.0010	.0124	.0168	.0001
IV Social position				
(8) 1 or 2	.2225	.6888	.5759	.0757
(9) 3	.0054	.0059	.5515	.0022
(10) 4 or 5	.0005	.0029	.1378	.0003
V WISC Full IQ at admission				
(11) Below 46	.2473	.2473	.9130	.0436
(12) 46–69	.0120	.0343	.0343	.0052
(13) 70–89	.0055	.0352	.2216	.0026
(14) 90–109	.0404	.2225	.5965	.0404
(15) Above 109	.0643	.0643	.8494	.1401

*Based on 2-tail Wilcoxon Matched Pairs Signed Ranks Test.

Table A-2-6. Vineland Social Maturity Scale—Social Quotient: Probability of No Annual Change*

Variable	Years compared			
	Admission to 1st	1st to 2nd	2nd to 3rd	Admission to 3rd
Total (1) All children	.0039	.3093	.2700	.0072
I Sex				
(2) Males	.0383	.5781	.6091	.0141
(3) Females	.0308	.5410	.1942	.2858
II Admission age				
(4) less than 8 yrs.	.0057	.2006	.5705	.0019
(5) 8 yrs. or more	.6709	.6332	.5081	.8284
III Neurological status				
(6) Non organics	.0065	.6332	.0400	.1382
(7) Organics	.0775	.5001	.8358	.0270
IV Social position				
(8) 1 or 2	.5965	1.0000	.8879	.8879
(9) 3	.2056	.2473	.6306	.0309
(10) 4 or 5	.0056	.8505	.5972	.0503
V WISC Full IQ at admission				
(11) Below 46	.5934	.8284	.5366	.5300
(12) 46–69	.0343	.1099	.7579	.0266
(13) 70–89	.6702	.6075	.9675	.1219
(14) 90–109	.0404	.5074	.0757	.5759
(15) Above 109	.0962	.7161	.2726	1.0000

*Based on 2-tail Wilcoxon Matched Pairs Signed Ranks Test.

Table A-2-7. Activity Level: Probability of No Annual Change*

Variable	Years compared			
	Admission to 1st	1st to 2nd	2nd to 3rd	Admission to 3rd
Total (1) All children	.7844	.6619	.5261	.5131
I Sex				
(2) Males	1.0000	.8608	.5662	.5875
(3) Females	.6545	.6306	1.0000	.7027
II Admission age				
(4) less than 8 yrs.	.5611	.8449	.6064	.1982
(5) 8 yrs. or more	.7331	.6740	.7133	.6156
III Neurological status				
(6) Non organics	.2438	.6863	.7300	.3007
(7) Organics	.6264	.8432	.5919	1.0000
IV Social position				
(8) 1 or 2	1.0000	1.0000	.2225	.2225
(9) 3	.1013	.5503	.7133	.1692
(10) 4 or 5	.2154	.9069	.2455	.7763
V WISC Full IQ at admission				
(11) Below 46	.5366	.2473	1.0000	.6524
(12) 46–69	1.0000	.2188	1.0000	.1651
(13) 70–89	.6647	.6514	.1448	.3007
(14) 90–109	.6068	1.0000	1.0000	.6786
(15) Above 109	1.0000	.5278	.5278	.8494

*Based on 2-tail Wilcoxon Matched Pairs Signed Ranks Test.

Table A-2-8. Attentiveness: Probability of No Annual Change*

Variable	Years compared			
	Admission to 1st	1st to 2nd	2nd to 3rd	Admission to 3rd
Total (1) All children	.5840	.0969	.6363	.0424
I Sex				
(2) Males	.1913	.1750	.0333	.0364
(3) Females	.5727	.6332	.0964	.6786
II Admission age				
(4) less than 8 yrs.	.9220	.0720	.5345	.0223
(5) 8 yrs. or more	.5963	.6544	.5151	.5963
III Neurological status				
(6) Non organics	.5028	.6514	.6863	.0650
(7) Organics	.1966	.1832	.5781	.6706
IV Social position				
(8) 1 or 2	.2225	.2225	.5074	.5965
(9) 3	.5027	.5845	.9056	.2309
(10) 4 or 5	.1171	.2961	.0694	.1577
V WISC Full IQ at admission				
(11) Below 46	.5366	.1117	.5366	.0558
(12) 46–69	.1818	.6656	.5173	.6656
(13) 70–89	.2572	.2184	1.0000	.7745
(14) 90–109	.1117	.2473	.6068	.5934
(15) Above 109	.7161	.1982	1.0000	.5278

*Based on 2-tail Wilcoxon Matched Pairs Signed Ranks Test.

Table A-2-9. Sustained Effort: Probability of No Annual Change*

Variable	Years compared			
	Admission to 1st	1st to 2nd	2nd to 3rd	Admission to 3rd
Total (1) All children	.5499	.1625	.2267	.0038
I Sex				
(2) Males	.8901	.6944	.0295	.0067
(3) Females	.2327	.0767	.6709	.2189
II Admission age				
(4) less than 8 yrs.	.8771	.2031	.0742	.0037
(5) 8 yrs. or more	.2801	.5582	.7331	.6489
III Neurological status				
(6) Non organics	.2712	.8208	.1950	.0451
(7) Organics	.8735	.1171	.6787	.0372
IV Social position				
(8) 1 or 2	.2225	.5074	.5965	.6526
(9) 3	.5503	.5582	.2309	.0217
(10) 4 or 5	.9069	.2700	.6263	.0925
V WISC Full IQ at admission				
(11) Below 46	.1117	.1117	.8284	.0558
(12) 46–69	.0988	.1818	.1996	.1221
(13) 70–89	.6647	.0451	.5792	.0387
(14) 90–109	.2946	.2473	.9130	.9130
(15) Above 109	1.0000	.5278	.5278	.5278

*Based on 2-tail Wilcoxon Matched Pairs Signed Ranks Test.

Table A-2-10. Muscle Tone: Probability of No Annual Change*

Variable	Years compared			
	Admission to 1st	1st to 2nd	2nd to 3rd	Admission to 3rd
Total (1) All children	.7795	.8854	.2443	.5213
I Sex				
(2) Males	.6064	1.0000	.6217	.2514
(3) Females	.2327	.8284	.5300	.6545
II Admission age				
(4) less than 8 yrs.	.7268	.7056	.5604	.7699
(5) 8 yrs. or more	1.0000	.7133	.2672	.1882
I I Neurological status				
(6) Non organics	.5727	.7027	.1382	.1288
(7) Organics	.5907	.9220	.7648	.7363
IV Social position				
(8) 1 or 2	1.0000	.5074	1.0000	.5074
(9) 3	.6647	.6647	.5613	.6647
(10) 4 or 5	.0000	.7607	.6643	.5115
V WISC Full IQ at admission				
(11) Below 46	.6068	.6068	.5366	.9130
(12) 46–69	.1651	.6866	.6866	.1651
(13) 70–89	.6863	.6217	.2572	.5613
(14) 90–109	1.0000	.5278	.1982	.0962
(15) Above 109	.5278	1.0000	1.0000	.5278

*Based on 2-tail Wilcoxon Matched Pairs Signed Ranks Test.

Table A-2-11. Double Simultaneous Stimuli–Homologous–Eyes Open:
Probability of No Annual Change*

Variable	Years compared			
	Admission to 1st	1st to 2nd	2nd to 3rd	Admission to 3rd
Total (1) All children	.6180	.2897	.6032	.5906
I Sex				
(2) Males	.7363	.2132	.9768	.5084
(3) Females	.7271	.8838	.6136	.6306
II Admission age				
(4) less than 8 yrs.	.5558	.1955	.5183	.2973
(5) 8 yrs. or more	.9735	1.0000	1.0000	.9735
III Neurological status				
(6) Non organics	.6433	.6433	1.0000	.6433
(7) Organics	.7676	.6572	.5411	.5238
IV Social position				
(8) 1 or 2	1.0000	.5074	1.0000	.5074
(9) 3	.7300	.6217	.5801	.6004
(10) 4 or 5	.7042	.5241	1.0000	.6902
V WISC Full IQ at admission				
(11) Below 46	.0000	.1015	.5074	.1015
(12) 46–69	.3088	.1651	.6166	1.0000
(13) 70–89	.6647	.2184	.2184	.6647
(14) 90–109	.5366	.5366	.5366	.5366
(15) Above 109	1.0000	1.0000	1.0000	1.0000

*Based on 2-tail Wilcoxon Matched Pairs Signed Ranks Test.

Table A-2-12. Double Simultaneous Stimuli—Heterologous—Eyes Open: Probability of No Annual Change*

Variable	Years compared			
	Admission to 1st	1st to 2nd	2nd to 3rd	Admission to 3rd
Total (1) All children	.0033	.0007	.0106	.0000
I Sex				
(2) Males	.0677	.0062	.0256	.0003
(3) Females	.0138	.0260	.2056	.0078
II Admission age				
(4) less than 8 yrs.	.0057	.0012	.0727	.0002
(5) 8 yrs. or more	.2308	.1736	.0563	.0149
III Neurological status				
(6) Non organics	.0469	.0469	.6297	.0129
(7) Organics	.0223	.0044	.0150	.0002
IV Social position				
(8) 1 or 2	.8879	.0557	.5965	.1015
(9) 3	.0284	.0563	.2184	.0083
(10) 4 or 5	.0324	.0195	.0227	.0010
V WISC Full IQ at admission				
(11) Below 46	1.0000	.5074	.8879	.5074
(12) 46–69	.1496	.0205	.0389	.0080
(13) 70–89	.0418	.0242	.0284	.0032
(14) 90–109	.0558	.2473	.9130	.0337
(15) Above 109	1.0000	1.0000	1.0000	1.0000

*Based on 2-tail Wilcoxon Matched Pairs Signed Ranks Test.

Table A-2-13. Double Simultaneous Stimuli–Homologous–Eyes Closed:
Probability of No Annual Change*

Variable	Years compared			
	Admission to 1st	1st to 2nd	2nd to 3rd	Admission to 3rd
Total (1) All children	.8061	.0267	.5647	.0144
I Sex				
(2) Males	.7363	.1209	.6514	.0359
(3) Females	.9426	.1117	1.0000	.2056
II Admission age				
(4) less than 8 yrs.	.9756	.1054	.1955	.0180
(5) 8 yrs. or more	.6647	.1124	.6647	.5986
III Neurological status				
(6) Non organics	.6433	.6297	1.0000	.6297
(7) Organics	.0000	.0434	.6434	.0209
IV Social position				
(8) 1 or 2	.5074	.2225	.5074	.2225
(9) 3	.7081	.0563	.6647	.1124
(10) 4 or 5	.7322	.5366	.7042	.1551
V WISC Full IQ at admission				
(11) Below 46	.5074	.5759	.2225	.1015
(12) 46–69	.6381	.0205	1.0000	.0792
(13) 70–89	.6647	.6647	.6647	.5986
(14) 90–109	.5366	.5366	1.0000	.5366
(15) Above 109	1.0000	1.0000	1.0000	1.0000

*Based on 2-tail Wilcoxon Matched Pairs Signed Ranks Test.

Table A-2-14. Double Simultaneous Stimuli—Heterologous—Eyes Closed: Probability of No Annual Change*

Variable	Years compared			
	Admission to 1st	1st to 2nd	2nd to 3rd	Admission to 3rd
Total (1) All children	.0136	.0002	.0060	.0000
I Sex				
(2) Males	.0939	.0019	.0083	.0005
(3) Females	.0514	.0138	.6524	.0138
II Admission age				
(4) less than 8 yrs.	.0579	.0020	.0110	.0003
(5) 8 yrs. or more	.1124	.0149	.2438	.0284
III Neurological status				
(6) Non organics	.1924	.0238	.1924	.0238
(7) Organics	.0298	.0014	.0150	.0003
IV Social position				
(8) 1 or 2	1.0000	.2803	.5074	.5759
(9) 3	.0563	.0083	.6004	.0049
(10) 4 or 5	.0761	.0048	.0045	.0015
V WISC Full IQ at admission				
(11) Below 46	.0000	.5074	.8879	.5074
(12) 46–69	.5173	.0560	.0205	.0180
(13) 70–89	.0262	.0049	.0698	.0017
(14) 90–109	.1117	.0558	.5366	.0894
(15) Above 109	1.0000	1.0000	1.0000	1.0000

*Based on 2-tail Wilcoxon Matched Pairs Signed Ranks Test.

Table A-2-15. Double Simultaneous Stimuli—Total: Probability of No Annual Change*

Variable	Years compared			
	Admission to 1st	1st to 2nd	2nd to 3rd	Admission to 3rd
Total (1) All children	.0015	.0001	.0007	.0000
I Sex				
(2) Males	.0169	.0008	.0039	.0002
(3) Females	.0283	.0181	.0605	.0049
II Admission age				
(4) less than 8 yrs.	.0047	.0007	.0016	.0001
(5) 8 yrs. or more	.0985	.0262	.1448	.0307
III Neurological status				
(6) Non organics	.0564	.0238	.1789	.0129
(7) Organics	.0071	.0006	.0021	.0001
IV Social position				
(8) 1 or 2	.8879	.1015	.5074	.0557
(9) 3	.0698	.0032	.0605	.0035
(10) 4 or 5	.0063	.0150	.0023	.0010
V WISC Full IQ at admission				
(11) Below 46	.5074	.2225	.1740	.1015
(12) 46–69	.2611	.0120	.0266	.0091
(13) 70–89	.0098	.0106	.0049	.0017
(14) 90–109	.0337	.0558	.6786	.0558
(15) Above 109	1.0000	1.0000	1.0000	1.0000

*Based on 2-tail Wilcoxon Matched Pairs Signed Ranks Test.

Table A-2-16. Oculomotor Functioning—Eye Movement:
Probability of No Annual Change*

Variable	Years compared			
	Admission to 1st	1st to 2nd	2nd to 3rd	Admission to 3rd
Total (1) All children	.9448	.7795	.0267	.0915
I Sex				
(2) Males	.6861	.8143	.1114	.1421
(3) Females	.6786	.6136	.1117	.5300
II Admission age				
(4) less than 8 yrs.	.6616	.6801	.1176	.0545
(5) 8 yrs. or more	.5845	.2196	.1141	.7941
III Neurological status				
(6) Non organics	.9220	.8956	.3007	.5028
(7) Organics	.9050	.6264	.0602	.1266
IV Social position				
(8) 1 or 2	.5074	.7838	.8879	.6888
(9) 3	.5963	.6350	.0793	.1357
(10) 4 or 5	.9541	.5494	.0786	.1881
V WISC Full IQ at admission				
(11) Below 46	.8284	.6786	.1117	.1117
(12) 46–69	.9582	.6656	.6166	.5821
(13) 70–89	.6647	.6647	.6166	.1278
(14) 90–109	.9130	1.0000	.1117	.1693
(15) Above 109	.1982	.8494	.5278	.1982

*Based on 2-tail Wilcoxon Matched Pairs Signed Ranks Test.

Table A-2-17. Oculomotor Functioning–Dissociation of Head and Eye Movement: Probability of No Annual Change*

Variable	Years compared			
	Admission to 1st	1st to 2nd	2nd to 3rd	Admission to 3rd
Total (1) All children	.5784	.0556	.2819	.0014
I Sex				
(2) Males	.9507	.1913	.0433	.0014
(3) Females	.2056	.1584	.1038	.6524
II Admission age				
(4) less than 8 yrs.	.6658	.0223	.7363	.0037
(5) 8 yrs. or more	.9056	.9056	.1983	.1282
III Neurological status				
(6) Non organics	.1950	.6514	.6217	.0563
(7) Organics	.9866	.0921	.6503	.0071
IV Social position				
(8) 1 or 2	.5074	.1015	.5074	.2225
(9) 3	.5845	.2309	.1983	.2309
(10) 4 or 5	.9227	.5608	.0080	.0045
V WISC Full IQ at admission				
(11) Below 46	1.0000	1.0000	1.0000	1.0000
(12) 46–69	.6515	.0792	.9582	.0988
(13) 70–89	.8956	.6647	.2572	.0563
(14) 90–109	.5300	.0337	.5366	.0337
(15) Above 109	.5278	.5278	.5278	.5278

*Based on 2-tail Wilcoxon Matched Pairs Signed Ranks Test.

Table A-2-18. Whirling—Arms at Side: Probability of No Annual Change*

Variable	Years compared			
	Admission to 1st	1st to 2nd	2nd to 3rd	Admission to 3rd
Total (1) All children	.6400	.7602	.0210	.0326
I Sex				
(2) Males	.1913	.9789	.0079	.0192
(3) Females	.7271	.5597	.8022	.8838
II Admission age				
(4) less than 8 yrs.	.7081	.5433	.0480	.1082
(5) 8 yrs. or more	.3073	.5582	.2546	.1785
III Neurological status				
(6) Non organics	.5582	.6514	.0451	.0190
(7) Organics	.6223	.7496	.1510	.3042
IV Social position				
(8) 1 or 2	.6526	.8879	.2225	.2225
(9) 3	.1692	.1882	.1517	.2672
(10) 4 or 5	.6717	.0819	.1635	.0786
V WISC Full IQ at admission				
(11) Below 46	.5934	.9130	.8284	.1693
(12) 46–69	.6866	.5489	.2188	.1496
(13) 70–89	.5028	.5374	.0650	.1278
(14) 90–109	.2946	.5934	.6786	.0337
(15) Above 109	.5908	.7161	.1982	.2726

*Based on 2-tail Wilcoxon Matched Pairs Signed Ranks Test.

Table A-2-19. Whirling—Arms Outstretched and Parallel:
Probability of No Annual Change*

Variable	Years compared			
	Admission to 1st	1st to 2nd	2nd to 3rd	Admission to 3rd
Total (1) All children	.1625	.2576	.0007	.0003
I Sex				
(2) Males	.2629	.0529	.0022	.0009
(3) Females	.6136	.6136	.0767	.0894
II Admission age				
(4) less than 8 yrs.	.1887	.6217	.0039	.0018
(5) 8 yrs. or more	.5772	.5151	.0503	.0383
III Neurological status				
(6) Non organics	.7974	.8698	.0149	.0059
(7) Organics	.1548	.2059	.0115	.0087
IV Social position				
(8) 1 or 2	.0557	.1015	.5759	.0557
(9) 3	.8590	.9056	.0139	.0440
(10) 4 or 5	.5263	.5452	.0168	.0088
V WISC Full IQ at admission				
(11) Below 46	.5366	.5300	.9130	.0234
(12) 46–69	.6656	.5481	.0303	.5481
(13) 70–89	.6166	.8208	.0605	.0262
(14) 90–109	.6786	.2056	.5934	.2473
(15) Above 109	.8494	.7161	.0643	.0962

*Based on 2-tail Wilcoxon Matched Pairs Signed Ranks Test.

Table A-2-20. Romberg—Arms at Side: Probability of No Annual Change*

Variable	Years compared			
	Admission to 1st	1st to 2nd	2nd to 3rd	Admission to 3rd
Total (1) All children	.1334	.0417	.2882	.0010
I Sex				
(2) Males	.6861	.0472	.2472	.0026
(3) Females	.0514	.5831	.7767	.1200
II Admission age				
(4) less than 8 yrs.	.2456	.1795	.1312	.0044
(5) 8 yrs. or more	.6334	.1013	.5963	.0538
III Neurological status				
(6) Non organics	.1635	.0116	.2572	.0126
(7) Organics	.2919	.6005	.0972	.0127
IV Social position				
(8) 1 or 2	.6888	.5965	.2803	.6888
(9) 3	.3073	.7941	.2672	.1882
(10) 4 or 5	.5029	.0056	.6669	.0020
V WISC Full IQ at admission				
(11) Below 46	.1382	.5366	.6068	.5366
(12) 46–69	.5481	.7946	.0234	.0885
(13) 70–89	.5421	.6166	.5226	.0860
(14) 90–109	.7517	.1693	.5934	.0260
(15) Above 109	.5908	.0643	.6357	.1982

*Based on 2-tail Wilcoxon Matched Pairs Signed Ranks Test.

Table A-2-21. Romberg—Arms Outstretched and Parallel: Probability of No Annual Change*

Variable	Years compared			
	Admission to 1st	1st to 2nd	2nd to 3rd	Admission to 3rd
Total (1) All children	.1754	.7224	.0467	.0070
I Sex				
(2) Males	.5368	.6283	.0933	.0211
(3) Females	.1808	.9130	.2946	.1200
II Admission age				
(4) less than 8 yrs.	.3072	.8662	.1023	.0248
(5) 8 yrs. or more	.6489	.7735	.2546	.1210
III Neurological status				
(6) Non organics	.1950	.5374	.5792	.0418
(7) Organics	.5245	.9583	.0216	.0551
IV Social position				
(8) 1 or 2	.5759	.5965	.6888	.7838
(9) 3	.1013	.5209	.6740	.0187
(10) 4 or 5	.8036	.8913	.0152	.0665
V WISC Full IQ at admission				
(11) Below 46	.7517	.2473	.9130	.2056
(12) 46–69	.9154	.0080	.1651	.8731
(13) 70–89	.3162	.8956	.0563	.0418
(14) 90–109	.6524	.0260	.6786	.0894
(15) Above 109	.0643	.8494	.6357	.0962

*Based on 2-tail Wilcoxon Matched Pairs Signed Ranks Test.

Table A-2-22. Finger to Finger Test: Probability of No Annual Change*

Variable	Years compared			
	Admission to 1st	1st to 2nd	2nd to 3rd	Admission to 3rd
Total (1) All children	.1148	.8398	.2404	.0083
I Sex				
(2) Males	.3139	.5143	.1387	.0024
(3) Females	.1929	.1929	.8838	.8838
II Admission age				
(4) less than 8 yrs.	.5791	.6217	.6616	.0657
(5) 8 yrs. or more	.0655	.1357	.1785	.0503
III Neurological status				
(6) Non organics	.7745	.6647	.7521	.9220
(7) Organics	.0825	.6178	.1082	.0025
IV Social position				
(8) 1 or 2	.7838	.5074	.1015	.2803
(9) 3	.2425	.7941	.5772	.5676
(10) 4 or 5	.1946	.5608	.1577	.0119
V WISC Full IQ at admission				
(11) Below 46	.7517	.8284	.6068	.2946
(12) 46–69	.6515	.8731	.0440	.0266
(13) 70–89	.1199	.8956	.7745	.2184
(14) 90–109	.1117	.5366	.6524	.0337
(15) Above 109	.5278	.5278	.1982	.1982

*Based on 2-tail Wilcoxon Matched Pairs Signed Ranks Test.

Table A-2-23. Finger to Nose Test: Probability of No Annual Change*

Variable	Years compared			
	Admission to 1st	1st to 2nd	2nd to 3rd	Admission to 3rd
Total (1) All children	.0258	.8041	.2241	.0025
I Sex				
(2) Males	.0421	.7532	.0150	.0042
(3) Females	.6709	.5934	.1038	.2473
II Admission age				
(4) less than 8 yrs.	.0169	.5907	.1460	.0013
(5) 8 yrs. or more	.7532	.5676	.8590	.7331
III Neurological status				
(6) Non organics	.0563	.6217	.6217	.0605
(7) Organics	.1921	.5317	.2571	.0141
IV Social position				
(8) 1 or 2	.7838	.1015	.2225	.2225
(9) 3	.5151	.6790	.7331	.1517
(10) 4 or 5	.0194	.1521	.1694	.0072
V WISC Full IQ at admission				
(11) Below 46	.1117	.8284	.2473	.0558
(12) 46–69	.2842	.5149	.0792	.0266
(13) 70–89	.7300	.7081	.5170	.6004
(14) 90–109	.0558	1.0000	1.0000	.1117
(15) Above 109	1.0000	.5278	.5278	1.0000

*Based on 2-tail Wilcoxon Matched Pairs Signed Ranks Test.

Table A-2-24. Auditory Startle: Probability of No Annual Change*

Variable	Years compared			
	Admission to 1st	1st to 2nd	2nd to 3rd	Admission to 3rd
Total (1) All children	.6732	.7715	.5915	.2986
I Sex				
(2) Males	.6722	.5183	1.0000	.2059
(3) Females	.2105	.6307	.1789	.8891
II Admission age				
(4) less than 8 yrs.	.5181	.6010	.2593	.7919
(5) 8 yrs. or more	.5898	.0469	1.0000	.0194
III Neurological status				
(6) Non organics	.6136	.8284	.6524	.6332
(7) Organics	.5770	.8920	.7792	.5446
IV Social position				
(8) 1 or 2	.1015	.2225	1.0000	.1740
(9) 3	.5986	.5028	.7081	.9735
(10) 4 or 5	.0939	.0939	.5557	.0095
V WISC Full IQ at admission				
(11) Below 46	.5278	.1982	.1982	.5278
(12) 46–69	.2615	.6780	.1374	.6300
(13) 70–89	.8284	1.0000	.5140	.6786
(14) 90–109	.1117	.5366	.7517	.5366
(15) Above 109	.8494	.5278	.8494	.2726

*Based on 2-tail Wilcoxon Matched Pairs Signed Ranks Test.

Table A-2-25. Delayed Auditory Feedback—Voice and Speech: Probability of No Annual Change*

Variable	Years compared			
	Admission to 1st	1st to 2nd	2nd to 3rd	Admission to 3rd
Total (1) All children	.8030	.6160	.7078	.9352
I Sex				
(2) Males	.9684	.5748	.6178	.9684
(3) Females	.6166	.9582	1.0000	.7220
II Admission age				
(4) less than 8 yrs.	.5129	.6767	.1229	.9600
(5) 8 yrs. or more	.2572	.7745	.1950	.9485
III Neurological status				
(6) Non organics	.6702	.7803	.6721	.3085
(7) Organics	.9756	.7417	.8813	.5748
IV Social position				
(8) 1 or 2	.6357	.5908	.0962	.6357
(9) 3	.5986	.8449	.5582	.5028
(10) 4 or 5	.5608	.9464	.7741	.9805
V WISC Full IQ at admission				
(11) Below 46	.5278	.1982	.0643	.2726
(12) 46–69	.5481	.3088	.6381	.8328
(13) 70–89	.1200	.9426	.7027	.6332
(14) 90–109	.6888	.6526	.6888	.6526
(15) Above 109	.1982	.5908	.5908	.5908

*Based on 2-tail Wilcoxon Matched Pairs Signed Ranks Test.

Table A-2-26. Delayed Auditory Feedback—Language:
Probability of No Annual Change*

Variable	Years compared			
	Admission to 1st	1st to 2nd	2nd to 3rd	Admission to 3rd
Total (1) All children	.8825	.0457	.5082	.0222
I Sex				
(2) Males	.5705	.2254	.5931	.1876
(3) Females	.1996	.0988	.9582	.0343
II Admission age				
(4) less than 8 yrs.	.6321	.6686	.6321	.1691
(5) 8 yrs. or more	.7974	.0563	.6217	.0563
III Neurological status				
(6) Non organics	.9022	.2066	.9022	.2374
(7) Organics	.9050	.1258	.5444	.0442
IV Social position				
(8) 1 or 2	.0962	1.0000	.1982	.0962
(9) 3	.8208	.5421	.6863	.9735
(10) 4 or 5	.6674	.0402	.5868	.0197
V WISC Full IQ at admission				
(11) Below 46	.8494	.8494	.8494	.7161
(12) 46–69	.2188	.0440	.6166	.0630
(13) 70–89	.8022	.5300	.2056	.1200
(14) 90–109	.2225	.5074	.5074	.7838
(15) Above 109	.8494	.5278	.5908	.8494

*Based on 2-tail Wilcoxon Matched Pairs Signed Ranks Test

Table A-2-27. Delayed Auditory Feedback—Self Awareness:
Probability of No Annual Change*

Variable	Years compared			
	Admission to 1st	1st to 2nd	2nd to 3rd	Admission to 3rd
Total (1) All children	.6304	.2567	.1512	.0074
I Sex				
(2) Males	.6787	.6005	.6151	.0872
(3) Females	.6656	.5489	.2188	.0303
II Admission age				
(4) less than 8 yrs.	.7217	.2274	.1312	.0255
(5) 8 yrs. or more	.3162	.7521	.7081	.1278
III Neurological status				
(6) Non organics	.2713	.0954	.1924	.0176
(7) Organics	.7417	.6722	.6124	.1410
IV Social position				
(8) 1 or 2	.5074	.5965	.2803	.1015
(9) 3	.3117	.6545	1.0000	.1584
(10) 4 or 5	.9096	.1664	.1467	.0776
V WISC Full IQ at admission				
(11) Below 46	.5965	.5965	.5965	.6526
(12) 46–69	.6166	.6381	.6095	.0205
(13) 70–89	.5597	.5727	.5727	.0605
(14) 90–109	1.0000	.5278	.5278	.5278
(15) Above 109	.1982	1.0000	1.0000	.1982

*Based on 2-tail Wilcoxon Matched Pairs Signed Ranks Test.

Table A-2-28. Gottschaldt Embedded Figures Test:
Probability of No Annual Change*

Variable	Years compared			
	Admission to 1st	1st to 2nd	2nd to 3rd	Admission to 3rd
Total (1) All children	.0003	.0082	.0150	.0000
I Sex				
(2) Males	.0079	.0286	.0030	.0000
(3) Females	.0078	.1584	.5081	.0049
II Admission age				
(4) less than 8 yrs.	.0123	.0127	.0284	.0001
(5) 8 yrs. or more	.0051	.2801	.2672	.0016
III Neurological status				
(6) Non organics	.0106	.0387	.1361	.0017
(7) Organics	.0064	.0825	.0475	.0001
IV Social position				
(8) 1 or 2	.5074	.2225	.5074	.1015
(9) 3	.0699	.1282	.8151	.0022
(10) 4 or 5	.0015	.0611	.0084	.0003
V WISC Full IQ at admission				
(11) Below 46	1.0000	1.0000	.1117	.1117
(12) 46–69	.1651	.1651	.5797	.0205
(13) 70–89	.0083	.0418	.1841	.0015
(14) 90–109	.0260	.0894	.6068	.0260
(15) Above 109	.6357	.7161	.0962	.0962

*Based on 2-tail Wilcoxon Matched Pairs Signed Ranks Test

Table A-2-29. Street's Gestalt Completion Test: Probability of No Annual Change*

Variable	Years compared			
	Admission to 1st	1st to 2nd	2nd to 3rd	Admission to 3rd
Total (1) All children	.0001	.0018	.0018	.0000
I Sex				
(2) Males	.0033	.0053	.0592	.0000
(3) Females	.0049	.1382	.0049	.0020
II Admission age				
(4) less than 8 yrs.	.0086	.0003	.0787	.0001
(5) 8 yrs. or more	.0022	.9056	.0032	.0011
III Neurological status				
(6) Non organics	.0038	.2712	.0116	.0015
(7) Organics	.0052	.0032	.0328	.0000
IV Social position				
(8) 1 or 2	.5074	.0557	.1740	.0404
(9) 3	.0655	.0251	.2425	.0016
(10) 4 or 5	.0007	.0755	.0045	.0002
V WISC Full IQ at admission				
(11) Below 46	.5366	.0337	.1117	.0337
(12) 46–69	.0792	.1353	.0497	.0080
(13) 70–89	.0038	.0451	.0418	.0015
(14) 90–109	.0558	.1117	.7517	.0260
(15) Above 109	.1982	.8494	.2726	.0643

*Based on 2-tail Wilcoxon Matched Pairs Signed Ranks Test

Table A-2-30. Bender Gestalt Test: Probability of No Annual Change*

Variable	Years compared			
	Admission to 1st	1st to 2nd	2nd to 3rd	Admission to 3rd
Total (1) All children	.0000	.0012	.6059	.0000
I Sex				
(2) Males	.0001	.0043	.2545	.0002
(3) Females	.0707	.1221	.9582	.0497
II Admission age				
(4) less than 8 yrs.	.0013	.0003	.6109	.0002
(5) 8 yrs. or more	.0037	.8531	.8531	.1383
III Neurological status				
(6) Non organics	.0198	.0283	.5831	.0071
(7) Organics	.0003	.0109	.6203	.0006
IV Social position				
(8) 1 or 2	.0962	.0962	.8494	.0962
(9) 3	.0020	.0309	.5515	.0049
(10) 4 or 5	.0095	.0440	.5328	.0022
V WISC Full IQ at admission				
(11) Below 46	.1015	.0557	.5074	.0557
(12) 46–69	.6524	.0260	.5300	.0260
(13) 70–89	.0026	.1219	.2066	.0049
(14) 90–109	.0404	.0404	.5965	.0757
(15) Above 109	.0643	.8494	.7161	.5278

*Based on 2-tail Wilcoxon Matched Pairs Signed Ranks Test

Table A-2-31. Weigl Color Form Sorting Test: Probability of No
Annual Change*

Variable	Years compared			
	Admission to 1st	1st to 2nd	2nd to 3rd	Admission to 3rd
Total (1) All children	.1410	.0489	.9219	.0020
I Sex				
(2) Males	.0660	.0909	.5442	.0120
(3) Females	.8188	.6707	.2105	.0474
II Admission age				
(4) less than 8 yrs.	.8376	.2155	.7808	.0451
(5) 8 yrs. or more	.0614	.1210	.8820	.0111
III Neurological status				
(6) Non organics	.5300	.8284	.6136	.0964
(7) Organics	.1795	.0099	.5973	.0071
IV Social position				
(8) 1 or 2	.7838	.2225	.5965	.8879
(9) 3	.7745	.8956	.1539	.1278
(10) 4 or 5	.0796	.0324	.5115	.0056
V WISC Full IQ at admission				
(11) Below 46	.5759	1.0000	.5074	.5074
(12) 46–69	.1099	.0560	.0885	.0389
(13) 70–89	.6136	.1480	.5366	.0309
(14) 90–109	.1117	.6068	.2473	.7517
(15) Above 109	.1982	.5278	.5278	.1982

*Based on 2-tail Wilcoxon Matched Pairs Signed Ranks Test.

Table A-2-32. Orientation Test: Probability of No Annual Change*

Variable	Years compared			
	Admission to 1st	1st to 2nd	2nd to 3rd	Admission to 3rd
Total (1) All children	.0002	.0000	.0032	.0000
I Sex				
(2) Males	.0009	.0012	.0032	.0000
(3) Females	.0656	.0025	.6524	.0036
II Admission age				
(4) less than 8 yrs.	.0019	.0004	.0062	.0001
(5) 8 yrs. or more	.0139	.0082	.1517	.0011
III Neurological status				
(6) Non organics	.0149	.0070	.1448	.0013
(7) Organics	.0024	.0005	.0090	.0001
IV Social position				
(8) 1 or 2	.5074	.0557	.0557	.0557
(9) 3	.0161	.0065	.1603	.0044
(10) 4 or 5	.0014	.0026	.0358	.0002
V WISC Full IQ at admission				
(11) Below 46	.0337	.6524	.0337	.0894
(12) 46–69	.6166	.0060	.0792	.0091
(13) 70–89	.0149	.0049	.0307	.0015
(14) 90–109	.0260	.0558	.5934	.0260
(15) Above 109	.0643	.0000	.5278	.0643

*Based on 2-tail Wilcoxon Matched Pairs Signed Ranks Test

Table A-2-33. Lincoln-Oseretsky Motor Development Scale:
Probability of No Annual Change*

Variable	Years compared			
	Admission to 1st	1st to 2nd	2nd to 3rd	Admission to 3rd
Total (1) All children	.0005	.0130	.0002	.0000
I Sex				
(2) Males	.0065	.1560	.0004	.0000
(3) Females	.0283	.0337	.1480	.0020
II Admission age				
(4) less than 8 yrs.	.0048	.0223	.0024	.0001
(5) 8 yrs. or more	.0202	.2546	.0217	.0010
III Neurological status				
(6) Non organics	.0206	.0418	.0042	.0013
(7) Organics	.0079	.1299	.0074	.0001
IV Social position				
(8) 1 or 2	.5759	.1015	.5965	.1740
(9) 3	.0333	.0139	.0358	.0011
(10) 4 or 5	.0131	.6050	.0020	.0002
V WISC Full IQ at admission				
(11) Below 46	.5366	.1382	.6786	.1117
(12) 46–69	.0343	.2393	.1353	.0105
(13) 70–89	.1052	.5028	.0070	.0013
(14) 90–109	.0260	.0436	.2946	.0260
(15) Above 109	.5278	.5278	.0643	.0643

*Based on 2-tail Wilcoxon Matched Pairs Signed Ranks Test

Table A-2-34. Railwalking: Probability of No Annual Change*

Variable	Years compared			
	Admission to 1st	1st to 2nd	2nd to 3rd	Admission to 3rd
Total (1) All children	.0258	.0161	.0445	.0000
I Sex				
(2) Males	.0304	.0011	.1560	.0001
(3) Females	.5727	.5081	.1382	.0710
II Admission age				
(4) less than 8 yrs.	.0720	.0095	.6339	.0005
(5) 8 yrs. or more	.1603	.5582	.0174	.0051
III Neurological status				
(6) Non organics	.1736	.7521	.0149	.0042
(7) Organics	.0921	.0082	.6264	.0007
IV Social position				
(8) 1 or 2	.2225	.1015	.1740	.1015
(9) 3	.5963	.1076	.5582	.0471
(10) 4 or 5	.0393	.1635	.0131	.0003
V WISC Full IQ at admission				
(11) Below 46	.5366	.0558	.6786	.1117
(12) 46–69	.9154	.7946	.0180	.0180
(13) 70–89	.0698	.2065	.9735	.0242
(14) 90–109	.1117	.0260	.7517	.0260
(15) Above 109	.7161	.5908	.0643	.0643

*Based on 2-tail Wilcoxon Matched Pairs Signed Ranks Test

Table A-2-35. Dynamometer: Probability of No Annual Chnage*

Variable	Years compared			
	Admission to 1st	1st to 2nd	2nd to 3rd	Admission to 3rd
Total (1) All children	.0001	.0001	.0027	.0000
I Sex				
(2) Males	.0003	.0006	.1229	.0000
(3) Females	.0804	.0514	.0044	.0029
II Admission age				
(4) less than 8 yrs.	.0042	.0012	.0055	.0001
(5) 8 yrs. or more	.0037	.0150	.1076	.0011
III Neurological status				
(6) Non organics	.0486	.0070	.0161	.0015
(7) Organics	.0005	.0024	.0371	.0000
IV Social position				
(8) 1 or 2	.0557	.0557	.5965	.0557
(9) 3	.0333	.0017	.0471	.0010
(10) 4 or 5	.0026	.0435	.0150	.0003
V WISC Full IQ at admission				
(11) Below 46	.0557	.0757	.5759	.0404
(12) 46–69	.0205	.5821	.0080	.0060
(13) 70–89	.0116	.0023	.1052	.0013
(14) 90–109	.8284	.0894	.6068	.0337
(15) Above 109	.0962	.0643	.8494	.0643

*Based on 2-tail Wilcoxon Matched Pairs Signed Ranks Test

Table A-2-36. Wechsler Intelligence Scale for Children—Verbal:
Probability of No Annual Change*

Variable	Years compared			
	Admission to 1st	1st to 2nd	2nd to 3rd	Admission to 3rd
Total (1) All children	.0021	.1011	.9448	.0010
I Sex				
(2) Males	.0120	.0313	.6944	.0093
(3) Females	.0605	.7767	.6068	.0165
II Admission age				
(4) less than 8 yrs.	.0041	.0618	.5611	.0017
(5) 8 yrs. or more	.1435	.7941	.2935	.2309
III Neurological status				
(6) Non organics	.0486	.5613	.7081	.0116
(7) Organics	.0166	.1473	.7051	.0196
IV Social position				
(8) 1 or 2	.5759	.2225	.7838	.5759
(9) 3	.0655	.7735	.2801	.1882
(10) 4 or 5	.0138	.1264	.6845	.0037
V WISC Full IQ at admission				
(11) Below 46	.1117	.5934	.5300	.1117
(12) 46–69	.0560	.1496	.5797	.0303
(13) 70–89	.6681	.7521	.7081	.6647
(14) 90–109	.0710	.2946	.5300	.0260
(15) Above 109	.1401	.7161	.0962	.1401

*Based on 2-tail Wilcoxon Matched Pairs Signed Ranks Test

Table A-2-37. Wechsler Intelligence Scale for Children—Performance: Probability of No Annual Change*

Variable	Years compared			
	Admission to 1st	1st to 2nd	2nd to 3rd	Admission to 3rd
Total (1) All children	.0019	.6990	.7747	.0001
I Sex				
(2) Males	.0067	.5875	.9507	.0004
(3) Females	.0829	.0000	.7271	.0767
II Admission age				
(4) less than 8 yrs.	.0028	.5257	.1982	.0004
(5) 8 yrs. or more	.2546	.1357	.3073	.0383
III Neurological status				
(6) Non organics	.3162	.1736	.6166	.0025
(7) Organics	.0025	.5494	.6612	.0066
IV Social position				
(8) 1 or 2	.8879	.7838	.5759	.5965
(9) 3	.0120	.5845	.5582	.0471
(10) 4 or 5	.0375	.2014	.7234	.0004
V WISC Full IQ at admission				
(11) Below 46	.1117	.2473	.9130	.2473
(12) 46–69	.5797	.9582	.7579	.1818
(13) 70–89	.0126	.7974	.2712	.0149
(14) 90–109	.0894	.6524	.5300	.0436
(15) Above 109	.8494	.1401	.5278	.0962

*Based on 2-tail Wilcoxon Matched Pairs Signed Ranks Test

Table A-2-38. Wechsler Intelligence Scale for Children—Full:
Probability of No Annual Change*

Variable	Years compared			
	Admission to 1st	1st to 2nd	2nd to 3rd	Admission to 3rd
Total (1) All children	.0001	.1011	.7555	.0002
I Sex				
(2) Males	.0011	.0643	.5143	.0021
(3) Females	.0138	.9130	.5597	.0198
II Admission age				
(4) less than 8 yrs.	.0005	.2572	.6431	.0008
(5) 8 yrs. or more	.0358	.6174	.2801	.0503
III Neurological status				
(6) Non organics	.0126	.1736	.6342	.0042
(7) Organics	.0011	.2800	.1626	.0090
IV Social position				
(8) 1 or 2	.2225	.5759	.5965	.5759
(9) 3	.0202	.7532	.5845	.0614
(10) 4 or 5	.0017	.0393	.6717	.0008
V WISC Full IQ at admission				
(11) Below 46	.1117	.7517	.9130	.2473
(12) 46–69	.0266	.1818	.9582	.0303
(13) 70–89	.0359	.9735	1.0000	.1278
(14) 90–109	.0260	.1117	.7517	.0260
(15) Above 109	.1401	.5278	.1401	.0643

*Based on 2-tail Wilcoxon Matched Pairs Signed Ranks Test

Table A-2-39. Communication—Voice and Speech: Probability of No
Annual Change*

Variable	Years compared			
	Admission to 1st	1st to 2nd	2nd to 3rd	Admission to 3rd
Total (1) All children	.0115	.5931	.6546	.0385
I Sex				
(2) Males	.0159	.5633	.0660	.0736
(3) Females	.6524	.8284	.2946	.2946
II Admission age				
(4) less than 8 yrs.	.0095	.6293	.5170	.0152
(5) 8 yrs. or more	.5845	.7941	.5209	.8590
III Neurological status				
(6) Non organics	.5374	.6681	.1635	.2572
(7) Organics	.0069	.9479	.8944	.0639
IV Social position				
(8) 1 or 2	.1740	.2225	.2803	.5074
(9) 3	.0233	.6156	.6936	.0844
(10) 4 or 5	.6157	.5452	.6157	.2535
V WISC Full IQ at admission				
(11) Below 46	.0436	.9130	.7517	.0337
(12) 46–69	.2393	.1996	.7220	.1818
(13) 70–89	.1124	.5028	.5374	.2065
(14) 90–109	.2473	.5300	.2946	.5934
(15) Above 109	.2726	.8494	.1401	.6357

*Based on 2-tail Wilcoxon Matched Pairs Signed Ranks Test

Table A-2-40. Communication—Language: Probability of No Annual Change*

Variable	Years compared			
	Admission to 1st	1st to 2nd	2nd to 3rd	Admission to 3rd
Total (1) All children	.2035	.0027	.7795	.0031
I Sex				
(2) Males	.6365	.0079	.8802	.0304
(3) Females	.1038	.1382	.8022	.0260
II Admission age				
(4) less than 8 yrs.	.0618	.0032	.9220	.0013
(5) 8 yrs. or more	.7331	.6489	.5772	.6544
III Neurological status				
(6) Non organics	.6217	.0116	.2184	.1950
(7) Organics	.2305	.0696	.5748	.0056
IV Social position				
(8) 1 or 2	.2225	.0404	.1015	.0557
(9) 3	.6489	.5845	.5209	.1603
(10) 4 or 5	.6975	.0298	.7234	.0470
V WISC Full IQ at admission				
(11) Below 46	.1117	.0558	.8284	.0337
(12) 46–69	.0885	.1996	.8731	.0389
(13) 70–89	.5582	.2184	.5028	.2857
(14) 90–109	.6524	.0558	.0558	.2056
(15) Above 109	.5908	.5278	.1982	.7161

*Based on 2-tail Wilcoxon Matched Pairs Signed Ranks Test

TABLES A-3

Percentage Distribution by Average
Age for Schizophrenic Children
(for Variables 1–40)

Table A-3-1. Ego Status—for Average Age Groups: Percentage Distribution* of Schizophrenic Children

	Age (years)			
Score	7	8	9	10
1	20.0	12.5	12.5	10.0
2	55.0	42.5	32.5	27.5
3	25.0	45.0	52.5	60.0
4	0.0	0.0	2.5	2.5
5	0.0	0.0	0.0	0.0

*N = 40.

Table A-3-2. Metropolitan Achievement Test—Reading—for Average Age Groups: Percentage Distribution* of Schizophrenic Children

	Age (years)			
Score	7	8	9	10
65	68.4	34.2	15.8	10.5
66–90	2.6	2.6	2.6	5.3
91–115	7.9	28.9	21.1	13.2
116–140	10.5	18.4	28.9	18.4
141–165	2.6	5.3	21.1	23.7
166–190	5.3	5.3	0.0	18.4
191–215	2.6	5.3	5.3	2.6
216–240	0.0	0.0	5.3	7.9

*N = 38.

Table A-3-3. Metropolitan Achievement Test—Arithmetic—for Average Age Groups: Percentage Distribution* of Schizophrenic Children

	Age (years)			
Score	7	8	9	10
105	68.4	34.2	13.2	10.5
106–130	7.9	31.6	23.7	15.8
131–155	18.4	18.4	44.7	47.4
156–180	2.6	10.5	7.9	5.3
181–205	2.6	5.3	5.3	10.5
206–230	0.0	0.0	5.3	7.9
231–255	0.0	0.0	0.0	2.6

*N = 38.

Table A-3-4. Metropolitan Achievement Test—Total Achievement—for Average Age Groups: Percentage Distribution* of Schizophrenic Children

	Age (years)			
Score	7	8	9	10
75	68.4	34.2	15.8	10.5
76–100	0.0	2.6	2.6	5.3
101–125	15.8	28.9	21.1	15.8
126–150	7.9	18.4	36.8	23.7
151–175	5.3	10.5	13.2	23.7
176–200	0.0	2.6	2.6	10.5
201–225	2.6	2.6	5.3	5.3
226–250	0.0	0.0	2.6	5.3

*N = 38.

Table A-3-5. Vineland Social Maturity Scale—Social Age—for Average Age Groups: Percentage Distribution* of Schizophrenic Children

	Age (years)			
Score	7	8	9	10
Below 46	24.3	10.8	5.4	2.7
46–69	43.2	24.3	18.9	13.5
70–89	21.6	37.8	40.5	29.7
90–109	10.8	18.9	13.5	32.4
110–129	0.0	8.1	21.6	13.5
130 and over	0.0	0.0	0.0	8.1

*N = 37.

Table A-3-6. Vineland Social Maturity Scale—Social Quotient—for Average Age Groups: Percentage Distribution* of Schizophrenic Children

	Age (years)			
Score	7	8	9	10
Below 46	13.5	8.1	2.7	2.7
46–69	35.1	21.6	24.3	35.1
70–89	29.7	40.5	43.2	29.7
90–109	21.6	18.9	18.9	27.0
110–129	0.0	10.8	10.8	5.4
130 and over	0.0	0.0	0.0	0.0

*N = 37.

Table A-3-7. Activity Level—for Average Age Groups: Percentage Distribution* of Schizophrenic Children

Rating	Age (years)			
	7	8	9	10
1	27.5	22.5	25.0	20.0
2	52.5	57.5	60.0	57.5
3	20.0	20.0	15.0	22.5

*$N = 40$.

Table A-3-8. Attentiveness—for Average Age Groups: Percentage Distribution* of Schizophrenic Children

Rating	Age (years)			
	7	8	9	10
1	12.5	10.0	2.5	10.0
2	37.5	40.0	42.5	25.0
3	7.5	22.5	12.5	20.0
4	40.0	20.0	32.5	25.0
5	2.5	7.5	10.0	20.0

*$N = 40$.

Table A-3-9. Sustained Effort—for Average Age Groups: Percentage Distribution* of Schizophrenic Children

Rating	Age (years)			
	7	8	9	10
1	22.5	15.0	10.0	12.5
2	22.5	30.0	27.5	17.5
3	27.5	25.0	27.5	17.5
4	27.5	25.0	35.0	52.5
5	0.0	5.0	0.0	0.0

*$N = 40$.

Table A-3-10. Muscle Tone—for Average Age Groups: Percentage Distribution* of Schizophrenic Children

Rating	Age (years)			
	7	8	9	10
1	13.2	2.6	10.5	10.5
2	50.0	65.8	50.0	63.2
3	36.8	31.6	39.5	26.3

*$N = 38$.

Table A-3-11. Double Simultaneous Stimuli—Homologous—Eyes Open—for Average Age Groups: Percentage Distribution* of Schizophrenic Children

Score	Age (years)			
	7	8	9	10
0	15.8	18.4	5.2	5.2
1	2.6	0.0	2.6	2.6
2	2.6	5.2	5.2	2.6
3	2.6	2.6	10.5	7.9
4	76.3	73.7	76.3	81.6

*$N = 38$.

Table A-3-12. Double Simultaneous Stimuli—Heterologous—Eyes Open—for Average Age Groups: Percentage Distribution* of Schizophrenic Children

Score	Age (years)			
	7	8	9	10
0–2	42.0	31.8	23.6	15.8
3–5	7.8	10.5	0.0	7.9
6–8	26.3	18.4	15.7	0.0
9–10	23.7	39.5	60.5	76.3

*$N = 38$.

Table A-3-13. Double Simultaneous Stimuli—Homologous—Eyes Closed—for Average Age Groups: Percentage Distribution* of Schizophrenic Children

	Age (years)			
Score	7	8	9	10
0	21.1	15.8	7.9	5.2
1	0.0	5.2	0.0	0.0
2	2.6	7.9	2.6	5.2
3	10.5	7.9	7.9	2.6
4	65.8	63.2	81.6	86.8

*$N = 38$.

Table A-3-14. Double Simultaneous Stimuli—Heterologous—Eyes Closed—for Average Age Groups: Percentage Distribution* of Schizophrenic Children

	Age (years)			
Score	7	8	9	10
0–2	55.2	42.1	23.6	15.8
3–5	10.5	2.6	2.6	7.8
6–8	7.8	18.3	23.6	2.6
9–10	26.3	36.8	50.0	73.7

*$N = 38$.

Table A-3-15. Double   Simultaneous   Stimuli—Total—for Average Age Groups: Percentage Distribution* of Schizophrenic Children

	Age (years)			
Score	7	8	9	10
0–12	44.5	34.0	23.4	15.6
13–14	5.2	5.2	0.0	0.0
15–16	5.2	5.2	0.0	5.2
17–18	7.8	0.0	0.0	2.6
19–20	5.2	0.0	2.6	0.0
21–22	0.0	7.8	2.6	0.0
23–24	7.8	13.1	10.4	0.0
25–26	2.6	7.9	23.6	7.9
27–28	21.0	26.5	36.8	68.4

*N = 38.

Table A-3-16. Oculomotor Functioning—Eye Movement— for Average Age Groups: Percentage Distribution* of Schizophrenic Children

	Age (years)			
Score	7	8	9	10
4	12.5	5.0	12.5	2.5
5	10.0	20.0	5.0	7.5
6	5.0	7.5	20.0	20.0
7	15.0	12.5	10.0	5.0
8	27.5	20.0	25.0	25.0
9	7.5	15.0	2.5	7.5
10	22.5	20.0	25.0	32.5

*N = 40.

Table A-3-17. Oculomotor Functioning—Dissociation of Head and Eye Movement—for Age Groups: Percentage Distribution* of Schizophrenic Children

	Age (years)			
Score	7	8	9	10
0	72.5	55.0	47.5	37.5
1	7.5	20.0	10.0	12.5
2	5.0	10.0	15.0	7.5
3	15.0	15.0	27.5	42.5

*$N = 40$.

Table A-3-18. Whirling—Arms at Side—for Age Groups: Percentage Distribution* of Schizophrenic Children

	Age (years)			
Score	7	8	9	10
5–15	37.5	32.5	37.5	20.0
16	2.5	7.5	7.5	2.5
17	10.0	2.5	10.0	7.5
18	12.5	17.5	5.0	7.5
19	12.5	17.5	2.5	5.0
20	7.5	7.5	7.5	22.5
21	7.5	7.5	20.0	20.0
22	5.0	7.5	10.0	12.5
23	0.0	0.0	0.0	2.5
24	5.0	0.0	0.0	0.0

*$N = 40$.

Table A-3-19. Whirling—Arms Outstretched and Parallel—for Average Age Groups: Percentage Distribution* of Schizophrenic Children

Score	Age (years)			
	7	8	9	10
3–6	45.0	37.5	35.0	15.0
7	17.5	7.5	2.5	10.0
8	5.0	20.0	5.0	20.0
9	7.5	5.0	15.0	2.5
10	7.5	7.5	20.0	10.0
11	5.0	10.0	12.5	12.5
12	10.0	12.5	10.0	12.5
13	2.5	0.0	0.0	17.5

*$N = 40$.

Table A-3-20. Romberg—Arms at Side—for Average Age Groups: Percentage Distribution* of Schizophrenic Children

Score	Age (years)			
	7	8	9	10
6–19	52.5	57.5	45.0	27.5
20	5.0	0.0	7.5	5.0
21	15.0	0.0	2.5	12.5
22	2.5	0.0	7.5	7.5
23	5.0	2.5	0.0	5.0
24	10.0	15.0	5.0	10.0
25	5.0	10.0	2.5	10.0
26	5.0	7.5	10.0	12.5
27	0.0	7.5	15.0	7.5
28	0.0	0.0	5.0	2.5

*$N = 40$.

Table A-3-21. Romberg—Arms Outstretched and Parallel—for Average Age Groups: Percentage Distribution* of Schizophrenic Children

	Age (years)			
Score	7	8	9	10
4	35.0	22.5	30.0	17.5
5	5.0	7.5	5.0	5.0
6	15.0	15.0	2.5	7.5
7	7.5	12.5	10.0	12.5
8	7.5	2.5	5.0	2.5
9	0.0	5.0	7.5	7.5
10	2.5	7.5	7.5	7.5
11	7.5	2.5	5.0	7.5
12	5.0	10.0	12.5	7.5
13	5.0	2.5	5.0	10.0
14	10.0	5.0	0.0	5.0
15	0.0	7.5	2.5	2.5
16	0.0	0.0	7.5	7.5

*$N = 40$.

Table A-3-22. Finger to Finger Test—for Age Groups: Percentage Distribution* of Schizophrenic Children

	Age (years)			
Score	7	8	9	10
0	25.0	17.5	15.0	7.5
1	10.0	7.5	5.0	5.0
2	5.0	5.0	20.0	22.5
3	35.0	30.0	22.5	20.0
4	25.0	40.0	37.5	45.0

*$N = 40$.

Table A-3-23. Finger to Nose Test—for Average Age Groups: Percentage Distribution* of Schizophrenic Children

	Age (years)			
Score	7	8	9	10
0	22.5	10.0	7.5	5.0
1	0.0	0.0	2.5	0.0
2	15.0	22.5	12.5	2.5
3	27.5	12.5	25.0	37.5
4	35.0	55.0	52.5	55.0

*N = 40.

Table A-3-24. Auditory Startle—for Average Age Groups: Percentage Distribution* of Schizophrenic Children

	Age (years)			
Score	7	8	9	10
0	2.9	0.0	0.0	0.0
1	2.9	11.4	14.3	8.6
2	8.6	11.4	11.4	14.3
3	20.0	14.3	11.4	17.1
4	40.0	45.7	48.6	40.0
5	8.6	8.6	8.6	14.3
6	17.1	8.6	5.7	5.7

*N = 35.

Table A-3-25. Delayed Auditory Feedback—Voice and Speech—for Average Age Groups: Percentage Distribution* of Schizophrenic Children

Rating	Age (years)			
	7	8	9	10
9–11	8.3	16.7	8.3	2.8
12–14	19.4	8.3	19.4	16.7
15–17	22.2	16.7	11.1	19.4
18–20	8.3	13.9	16.7	22.2
21–23	13.9	16.7	13.9	19.4
24–26	13.9	22.2	27.8	13.9
27–32	13.9	5.6	2.8	5.6

*N = 36.

Table A-3-26. Delayed Auditory Feedback—Language—for Average Age Groups: Percentage Distribution* of Schizophrenic Children

Rating	Age (years)			
	7	8	9	10
3	5.6	8.3	16.7	22.2
4	5.6	2.8	5.6	8.3
5	11.1	13.9	8.3	8.3
6	16.7	16.7	13.9	16.7
7–8	30.5	27.7	38.8	25.0
9–10	13.9	19.5	11.2	13.9
11–12	16.7	11.2	5.6	5.6

*N = 36.

Table A-3-27. Delayed Auditory Feedback—Self Awareness—for Average Age Groups: Percentage Distribution* of Schizophrenic Children

Rating	Age (years)			
	7	8	9	10
1	41.7	47.2	61.1	69.4
2	33.3	33.3	27.8	30.6
3	25.0	19.4	11.1	0.0

*N = 36.

Table A-3-28. Gottschaldt Embedded Figures Test—for Average Age Groups: Percentage Distribution* of Schizophrenic Children

Score	Age (years)			
	7	8	9	10
0–1	72.5	55.0	40.0	35.0
2–3	5.0	12.5	17.5	12.5
4–5	5.0	7.5	7.5	7.5
6–7	2.5	5.0	10.0	10.0
8–9	5.0	0.0	5.0	7.5
10–11	5.0	2.5	2.5	0.0
12–13	2.5	10.0	10.0	12.5
14–15	2.5	7.5	7.5	15.0

*$N = 40$.

Table A-3-29. Street's Gestalt Completion Test—for Average Age Groups: Percentage Distribution* of Schizophrenic Children

Score	Age (years)			
	7	8	9	10
0–1	7.5	5.0	0.0	0.0
2–3	25.0	12.5	10.0	2.5
4–5	32.5	25.0	25.0	22.5
6–7	30.0	35.0	35.0	37.5
8–9	5.0	17.5	17.5	17.5
10–11	0.0	5.0	12.5	17.5
12–13	0.0	0.0	0.0	2.5

*$N = 40$.

Table A-3-30. Bender Gestalt Test—for Average Age Groups: Percentage Distribution* of Schizophrenic Children

	Age (years)			
Score	7	8	9	10
5–14	18.8	9.4	6.3	6.3
15–24	21.9	12.5	6.3	6.3
25–34	34.4	40.6	37.5	21.9
35–44	18.8	18.8	28.1	56.3
45–54	6.3	18.8	21.9	9.4

*N = 32.

Table A-3-31. Weigl Color Form Sorting Test—for Average Age Groups: Percentage Distribution* of Schizophrenic Children

	Age (years)			
Score	7	8	9	10
0	36.8	21.1	13.2	15.8
1	13.2	18.4	7.9	7.9
2	18.4	5.3	21.1	18.4
3	5.3	10.5	7.9	13.2
4	7.9	18.4	13.2	2.6
5	2.6	2.6	2.6	2.6
6	0.0	5.3	7.9	2.6
7	0.0	0.0	0.0	0.0
8	15.8	18.4	26.3	36.8

*N = 38.

Table A-3-32. Orientation Test—for Average Age Groups: Percentage Distribution* of Schizophrenic Children

	Age (years)			
Score	7	8	9	10
0–4	20.0	17.5	7.5	10.0
5–9	15.0	12.5	7.5	2.5
10–14	27.5	22.5	15.0	7.5
15–19	15.0	12.5	10.0	15.0
20–24	20.0	10.0	27.5	12.5
25–29	2.5	25.0	32.5	52.5

*N = 40.

Table A-3-33. Lincoln-Oseretsky Motor Development Scale—for Average Age Groups: Percentage Distribution* of Schizophrenic Children

Score	Age (years)			
	7	8	9	10
0–9	62.5	35.0	40.0	25.0
10–19	17.5	27.5	15.0	20.0
20–29	7.5	17.5	12.5	7.5
30–39	7.5	15.0	25.0	22.5
40–49	5.0	2.5	2.5	17.5
50–59	0.0	2.5	5.0	7.5

*N = 40.

Table A-3-34. Railwalking—for Average Age Groups: Percentage Distribution* of Schizophrenic Children

Score	Age (years)			
	7	8	9	10
0–9	40.0	37.5	40.0	22.5
10–19	20.0	10.0	2.5	5.0
20–29	10.0	12.5	10.0	17.5
30–39	15.0	20.0	10.0	15.0
40–49	5.0	2.5	2.5	12.5
50–59	2.5	5.0	12.5	0.0
60–69	2.5	7.5	7.5	0.0
70–79	2.5	2.5	5.0	10.0
80–89	2.5	0.0	7.5	7.5
90–99	0.0	2.5	0.0	0.0
100–109	0.0	0.0	0.0	0.0
110–119	0.0	0.0	2.5	5.0
120–129	0.0	0.0	0.0	5.0

*N = 40.

Table A-3-35. Dynamometer—for Average Age Groups: Percentage Distribution* of Schizophrenic Children

Score	Age (years)			
	7	8	9	10
0–4	5.1	2.6	0.0	0.0
5–9	38.5	23.1	12.8	10.3
10–14	43.6	51.3	41.0	35.9
15–19	10.3	12.8	28.2	28.2
20–24	2.6	10.3	12.8	25.6
25–29	0.0	0.0	5.1	0.0

*N = 39.

Table A-3-36. Wechsler Intelligence Scale for Children—Verbal—for Average Age Groups: Percentage Distribution* of Schizophrenic Children

Score	Age (years)			
	7	8	9	10
Below 46	15.0	7.5	10.0	7.5
46–69	25.0	27.5	20.0	25.0
70–89	35.0	25.0	30.0	27.5
90–109	12.5	22.5	17.5	17.5
110–129	7.5	12.5	15.0	10.0
130 and over	5.0	5.0	7.5	12.5

*N = 40.

Table A-3-37. Wechsler Intelligence Scale for Children—Performance—for Average Age Groups: Percentage Distribution* of Schizophrenic Children

Score	Age (years)			
	7	8	9	10
Below 46	12.5	10.0	15.0	12.5
46–69	25.0	15.0	20.0	17.5
70–89	37.5	42.5	27.5	37.5
90–109	10.0	15.0	17.5	15.0
110–129	12.5	15.0	15.0	12.5
130 and over	2.5	2.5	5.0	5.0

*N = 40.

Table A-3-38. Wechsler Intelligence Scale for Children—Full—for Average Age Groups: Percentage Distribution* of Schizophrenic Children

Age (years)				
Score	7	8	9	10
Below 46	15.0	7.5	12.5	12.5
46–69	25.0	30.0	27.5	22.5
70–89	35.0	30.0	25.0	32.5
90–109	15.0	17.5	15.0	5.0
110–129	7.5	10.0	10.0	22.5
130 and over	2.5	5.0	10.0	5.0

*$N = 40$.

Table A-3-39. Communication—Voice and Speech—for Average Age Groups: Percentage Distribution* of Schizophrenic Children

Age (years)				
Rating	7	8	9	10
9–20	40.0	17.5	17.5	17.5
21–23	15.0	27.5	17.5	25.0
24–26	17.5	20.0	30.0	25.0
27–29	10.0	25.0	20.0	15.0
30–32	10.0	2.5	5.0	15.0
33–35	5.0	2.5	7.5	2.5
36–38	2.5	5.0	2.5	0.0
39–41	0.0	0.0	0.0	0.0
42–44	0.0	0.0	0.0	0.0

*$N = 40$.

Table A-3-40. Communication—Language—for Average Age Groups: Percentage Distribution* of Schizophrenic Children

Age (years)				
Rating	7	8	9	10
3–7	62.5	50.0	37.5	35.0
8	2.5	15.0	15.0	17.5
9	12.5	15.0	12.5	17.5
10	10.0	10.0	15.0	17.5
11	7.5	2.5	17.5	7.5
12	2.5	5.0	0.0	2.5
13	2.5	2.5	2.5	2.5
14	0.0	0.0	0.0	0.0
15	0.0	0.0	0.0	0.0

*$N = 40$.

TABLES A-4

Annual Means and Standard Deviations
by Age for Normal Children
(for Variables Tested)

Table A-4-7. Activity Level: Annual Mean and
Standard Deviation by Age for Normal Children

Age (years)	Mean	Std. Dev.
6	2.4	0.7
7	2.4	0.5
8	2.6	0.5
9	3.0	0.0
10	2.8	0.4
11	2.8	0.4

Table A-4-8. Attentiveness: Annual Mean and
Standard Deviation by Age for Normal Children

Age (years)	Mean	Std. Dev.
6	3.9	0.8
7	4.0	0.8
8	4.3	0.5
9	4.6	0.7
10	4.7	0.6
11	4.8	0.4

Table A-4-9. Sustained Effort: Annual Mean and
Standard Deviation by Age for Normal Children

Age (years)	Mean	Std. Dev.
6	3.2	0.4
7	3.7	0.5
8	3.7	0.5
9	4.0	0.4
10	4.0	0.5
11	3.8	0.7

Table A-4-10. Muscle Tone: Annual Mean and
Standard Deviation by Age for Normal Children

Age (years)	Mean	Std. Dev.
6	2.9	0.3
7	2.4	0.7
8	2.7	0.5
9	3.0	0.0
10	2.8	0.4
11	2.9	0.3

Table A-4-11. Double Simultaneous Stimuli—
Homologous—Eyes Open: Annual Mean and
Standard Deviation by Age for Normal Children

Age (years)	Mean	Std. Dev.
6	4.0	0.0
7	4.0	0.0
8	4.0	0.0
9	4.0	0.0
10	4.0	0.0
11	3.9	0.3

Table A-4-12. Double Simultaneous Stimuli—
Heterologous—Eyes Open: Annual Mean and
Standard Deviation by Age for Normal Children

Age (years)	Mean	Std. Dev.
6	8.4	2.0
7	9.7	0.9
8	9.3	0.6
9	9.6	0.7
10	9.9	0.3
11	9.8	0.6

Table A-4-13. Double Simultaneous Stimuli—
Homologous—Eyes Closed: Annual Mean and
Standard Deviation by Age for Normal Children

Age (years)	Mean	Std. Dev.
6	3.9	0.7
7	3.9	0.3
8	3.9	0.3
9	3.9	0.3
10	4.0	0.0
11	4.0	0.0

Table A-4-14. Double Simultaneous Stimuli—
Heterologous—Eyes Closed: Annual Mean and
Standard Deviation by Age for Normal Children

Age (years)	Mean	Std. Dev.
6	4.2	3.8
7	7.1	2.9
8	6.2	3.9
9	7.3	3.8
10	8.9	1.6
11	8.3	3.0

Table A-4-15. Double Simultaneous Stimuli—
Total: Annual Mean and Standard Deviation by
Age for Normal Children

Age (years)	Mean	Std. Dev.
6	20.5	5.6
7	24.7	3.5
8	23.4	3.4
9	24.8	4.3
10	26.9	1.5
11	26.0	3.5

Table A-4-16. Oculomotor Functioning–Eye Movement: Annual Mean and Standard Deviation by Age for Normal Children

Age (years)	Mean	Std. Dev.
6	9.0	0.9
7	8.9	1.4
8	9.1	1.2
9	9.5	0.5
10	9.1	1.0
11	9.5	1.3

Table A-4-17. Oculomotor Functioning–Dissociation of Head and Eye Movement: Annual Mean and Standard Deviation by Age for Normal Children

Age (years)	Mean	Std. Dev.
6	1.8	1.0
7	2.3	1.9
8	2.6	0.5
9	2.4	0.9
10	2.9	0.2
11	3.0	0.0

Table A-4-18. Whirling–Arms at Side: Annual Mean and Standard Deviation by Age for Normal Children

Age (years)	Mean	Std. Dev.
6	20.8	1.9
7	20.2	1.6
8	20.5	1.9
9	20.9	1.2
10	21.7	1.5
11	21.8	1.5

Table A-4-19. Whirling—Arms Outstretched and Parallel: Annual Mean and Standard Deviation by Age for Normal Children

Age (years)	Mean	Std. Dev.
6	9.6	1.8
7	10.2	2.2
8	9.5	2.3
9	11.2	1.5
10	11.6	1.7
11	11.3	1.8

Table A-4-20. Romberg—Arms at Side: Annual Mean and Standard Deviation by Age for Normal Children

Age (years)	Mean	Std. Dev.
6	24.9	3.0
7	22.6	4.4
8	24.6	2.2
9	26.0	2.5
10	26.4	2.0
11	26.8	1.7

Table A-4-21. Romberg—Arms Outstretched and Parallel: Annual Mean and Standard Deviation by Age for Normal Children

Age (years)	Mean	Std. Dev.
6	10.9	3.1
7	8.5	2.7
8	9.2	3.6
9	12.4	1.6
10	11.8	2.5
11	13.6	1.2

Table A-4-22. Finger to Finger Test: Annual Mean and Standard Deviation by Age for Normal Children

Age (years)	Mean	Std. Dev.
6	3.6	0.7
7	3.7	0.5
8	3.8	0.4
9	3.7	0.6
10	3.9	0.5
11	3.9	0.3

Table A-4-23. Finger to Nose Test: Annual Mean and Standard Deviation by Age for Normal Children

Age (years)	Mean	Std. Dev.
6	3.6	0.5
7	3.8	0.6
8	3.9	0.3
9	4.0	0.0
10	4.0	0.0
11	4.0	0.0

Table A-4-24. Auditory Startle: Annual Mean and Standard Deviation by Age for Normal Children

Age (years)	Mean	Std. Dev.
6	4.2	1.1
7	3.4	1.4
8	3.3	1.0
9	3.1	1.2
10	3.6	1.4
11	3.3	1.4

Table A-4-25. Delayed Auditory Feedback—
Voice and Speech: Annual Mean and Standard
Deviation by Age for Normal Children

Age (years)	Mean	Std. Dev.
6	16.3	3.7
7	18.8	2.9
8	17.9	4.7
9	19.2	3.6
10	20.1	3.7
11	18.4	3.4

Table A-4-26. Delayed Auditory Feedback—
Language: Annual Mean and Standard Deviation
by Age for Normal Children

Age (years)	Mean	Std. Dev.
6	4.3	0.8
7	4.9	1.1
8	5.2	1.7
9	4.5	1.0
10	4.2	0.9
11	4.2	0.8

Table A-4-27. Delayed Auditory Feedback—Self
Awareness: Annual Mean and Standard Deviation
by Age for Normal Children

Age (years)	Mean	Std. Dev.
6	1.2	0.4
7	1.5	1.0
8	1.2	0.6
9	1.1	0.3
10	1.0	0.0
11	1.1	0.3

Table A-4-28. Gottschaldt Embedded Figures
Test: Annual Mean and Standard Deviation by
Age for Normal Children

Age (years)	Mean	Std. Dev.
6	2.1	2.7
7	4.3	4.0
8	7.8	3.6
9	7.7	4.4
10	9.5	3.3
11	12.0	3.9

Table A-4-29. Street's Gestalt Completion Test:
Annual Mean and Standard Deviation by Age
for Normal Children

Age (years)	Mean	Std. Dev.
6	5.9	1.4
7	6.6	1.6
8	6.9	2.0
9	6.5	1.6
10	6.9	1.5
11	8.4	2.0

Table A-4-31. Weigl Color Form Sorting Test:
Annual Mean and Standard Deviation by Age
for Normal Children

Age (years)	Mean	Std. Dev.
6	4.8	2.4
7	2.9	2.1
8	6.8	2.0
9	7.3	1.6
10	5.7	2.2
11	6.6	1.6

Table A-4-32. Orientation Test: Annual Mean
and Standard Deviation by Age for Normal
Children

Age (years)	Mean	Std. Dev.
6	16.1	4.9
7	22.9	4.0
8	26.4	2.6
9	25.5	2.3
10	27.8	1.3
11	28.5	0.7

Table A-4-34. Railwalking: Annual Mean and
Standard Deviation by Age for Normal Children

Age (years)	Mean	Std. Dev.
6	44.1	20.2
7	43.9	18.4
8	53.2	24.7
9	50.4	20.8
10	76.2	22.9
11	81.0	17.3

Table A-4-35. Dynamometer: Annual Mean and
Standard Deviation by Age for Normal Children

Age (years)	Mean	Std. Dev.
6	10.5	3.1
7	14.4	2.5
8	15.0	3.2
9	18.1	3.1
10	18.1	3.3
11	22.8	3.7

Table A-4-36. Wechsler Intelligence Scale for Children—Verbal: Annual Mean and Standard Deviation by Age for Normal Children

Age (years)	Mean	Std. Dev.
6	108.0	11.4
7	105.5	6.8
8	113.2	10.8
9	109.7	8.5
10	108.7	9.9
11	110.6	7.4

Table A-4-37. Wechsler Intelligence Scale for Children—Performance: Annual Mean and Standard Deviation by Age for Normal Children

Age (years)	Mean	Std. Dev.
6	103.2	15.1
7	103.4	15.7
8	106.7	5.9
9	99.6	8.9
10	98.9	15.0
11	105.4	15.4

Table A-4-38. Wechsler Intelligence Scale for Children—Full: Annual Mean and Standard Deviation by Age for Normal Children

Age (years)	Mean	Std. Dev.
6	106.1	12.4
7	105.1	10.1
8	111.0	8.9
9	106.1	8.3
10	104.4	12.9
11	109.0	11.4

Table A-4-39. Communication—Voice and Speech:
Annual Mean and Standard Deviation by Age for
Normal Children

Age (years)	Mean	Std. Dev.
6	33.6	5.3
7	32.4	3.8
8	33.6	5.1
9	32.9	4.4
10	36.7	3.9
11	38.6	2.0

Table A-4-40. Communication—Language: Annual
Mean and Standard Deviation by Age for Normal
Children

Age (years)	Mean	Std. Dev.
6	11.7	2.4
7	12.2	1.6
8	11.8	2.6
9	13.4	2.4
10	13.2	1.6
11	13.4	1.6

TABLES A-5

Percentage Distribution by Age
for Normal Children
(for Variables Tested)

Table A-5-7. Activity Level—for Age Groups: Percentage Distribution of Normal Children

Rating	Age (years)					
	6	7	8	9	10	11
1	10.0	0.0	0.0	0.0	0.0	0.0
2	40.0	60.0	40.0	0.0	20.0	20.0
3	50.0	40.0	60.0	100.0	80.0	80.0

Table A-5-8. Attentiveness—for Age Groups: Percentage Distribution of Normal Children

Rating	Age (years)					
	6	7	8	9	10	11
1	0.0	0.0	0.0	0.0	0.0	0.0
2	0.0	0.0	0.0	0.0	0.0	0.0
3	40.0	30.0	0.0	10.0	6.6	0.0
4	30.0	40.0	70.0	20.0	13.3	20.0
5	30.0	30.0	30.0	70.0	80.0	80.0

Table A-5-9. Sustained Effort—for Age Groups: Percentage Distribution of Normal Children

Rating	Age (years)					
	6	7	8	9	10	11
1	0.0	0.0	0.0	0.0	0.0	0.0
2	0.0	0.0	0.0	0.0	0.0	10.0
3	80.0	30.0	30.0	10.0	13.3	10.0
4	20.0	70.0	70.0	80.0	73.3	70.0
5	0.0	0.0	0.0	10.0	13.3	10.0

Table A-5-10. Muscle Tone—for Age Groups: Percentage Distribution of Normal Children

Rating	\multicolumn{6}{c}{Age (years)}
	6	7	8	9	10	11
---	---	---	---	---	---	---
1	0.0	10.0	0.0	0.0	0.0	0.0
2	10.0	40.0	30.0	0.0	20.0	10.0
3	90.0	50.0	70.0	100.0	80.0	90.0

Table A-5-11. Double Simultaneous Stimuli—Homologous—Eyes Open—for Age Groups: Percentage Distribution of Normal Children

Score	\multicolumn{6}{c}{Age (years)}
	6	7	8	9	10	11
---	---	---	---	---	---	---
0	0.0	0.0	0.0	0.0	0.0	0.0
1	0.0	0.0	0.0	0.0	0.0	0.0
2	0.0	0.0	0.0	0.0	0.0	0.0
3	0.0	0.0	0.0	0.0	0.0	10.0
4	100.0	100.0	100.0	100.0	100.0	90.0

Table A-5-12. Double Simultaneous Stimuli—Heterologous—Eyes Open—for Age Groups: Percentage Distribution of Normal Children

Score	\multicolumn{6}{c}{Age (years)}
	6	7	8	9	10	11
---	---	---	---	---	---	---
0–2	0.0	0.0	0.0	0.0	0.0	0.0
3–5	20.0	0.0	0.0	0.0	0.0	0.0
6–8	20.0	10.0	10.0	10.0	0.0	10.0
9–10	60.0	90.0	90.0	90.0	99.9	90.0

Table A-5-13. Double Simultaneous Stimuli—Homologous—Eyes Closed—for Age Groups: Percentage Distribution of Normal Children

	Age (years)					
Score	6	7	8	9	10	11
0	0.0	0.0	0.0	0.0	0.0	0.0
1	0.0	0.0	0.0	0.0	0.0	0.0
2	10.0	0.0	0.0	0.0	0.0	0.0
3	0.0	10.0	10.0	10.0	0.0	0.0
4	90.0	90.0	90.0	90.0	100.0	100.0

Table A-5-14. Double Simultaneous Stimuli—Heterologous—Eyes Closed—for Age Groups: Percentage Distribution of Normal Children

	Age (years)					
Score	6	7	8	9	10	11
0–2	50.0	10.0	20.0	20.0	0.0	0.0
3–5	10.0	20.0	10.0	10.0	6.6	0.0
6–8	10.0	20.0	40.0	0.0	26.6	0.0
9–10	30.0	50.0	30.0	70.0	66.6	0.0

Table A-5-15. Double Simultaneous Stimuli—Total—for Age Groups: Percentage Distribution of Normal Children

	Age (years)					
Score	6	7	8	9	10	11
0–12	0.0	0.0	0.0	0.0	0.0	0.0
13–14	30.0	0.0	0.0	0.0	0.0	0.0
15–16	0.0	0.0	0.0	10.0	0.0	0.0
17–18	10.0	10.0	20.0	10.0	0.0	0.0
19–20	10.0	10.0	0.0	0.0	0.0	20.0
21–22	10.0	0.0	0.0	10.0	0.0	0.0
23–24	10.0	20.0	50.0	0.0	13.2	0.0
25–26	0.0	10.0	10.0	10.0	20.0	0.0
27–28	30.0	50.0	20.0	60.0	66.6	80.0

Table A-5-16. Oculomotor Functioning—Eye Movement—for Age Groups: Percentage Distribution of Normal Children

Score	Age (years)					
	6	7	8	9	10	11
4	0.0	0.0	0.0	0.0	0.0	0.0
5	0.0	0.0	0.0	0.0	0.0	0.0
6	0.0	10.0	10.0	0.0	0.0	10.0
7	11.1	10.0	0.0	0.0	13.3	0.0
8	22.2	10.0	20.0	10.0	20.0	0.0
9	22.2	20.0	10.0	30.0	13.3	10.0
10	44.4	50.0	60.0	60.0	53.3	80.0

Table A-5-17. Oculomotor Functioning—Dissociation of Head and Eye Movement—for Age Groups: Percentage Distribution of Normal Children

Score	Age (years)					
	6	7	8	9	10	11
0	11.1	20.0	0.0	10.0	0.0	0.0
1	33.3	0.0	0.0	0.0	0.0	0.0
2	33.3	10.0	40.0	30.0	6.6	0.0
3	22.2	70.0	60.0	60.0	93.3	100.0

Table A-5-18. Whirling—Arms at Side—for Age Groups: Percentage Distribution of Normal Children

Score	Age (years)					
	6	7	8	9	10	11
5–15	0.0	0.0	0.0	0.0	0.0	0.0
16	10.0	0.0	0.0	0.0	0.0	0.0
17	0.0	10.0	10.0	0.0	0.0	0.0
18	0.0	0.0	10.0	0.0	6.6	0.0
19	10.0	20.0	10.0	20.0	0.0	10.0
20	0.0	30.0	10.0	10.0	13.3	20.0
21	40.0	20.0	30.0	40.0	20.0	0.0
22	30.0	10.0	10.0	20.0	33.3	30.0
23	10.0	10.0	20.0	10.0	13.3	30.0
24	0.0	0.0	0.0	0.0	13.3	10.0

Table A-5-19. Whirling—Arms Outstretched and Parallel—for Age Groups: Percentage Distribution of Normal Children

Score	Age (years)					
	6	7	8	9	10	11
3–6	0.0	10.0	10.0	0.0	0.0	0.0
7	10.0	0.0	20.0	0.0	6.6	0.0
8	20.0	10.0	0.0	10.0	0.0	10.0
9	20.0	10.0	20.0	0.0	0.0	0.0
10	30.0	20.0	10.0	20.0	20.0	30.0
11	0.0	20.0	10.0	20.0	6.6	10.0
12	10.0	30.0	30.0	30.0	26.6	10.0
13	10.0	0.0	0.0	20.0	40.0	40.0

Table A-5-20. Romberg—Arms At Side—for Age Groups: Percentage Distribution of Normal Children

Score	Age (years)					
	6	7	8	9	10	11
6–19	0.0	20.0	0.0	0.0	0.0	0.0
20	10.0	0.0	0.0	10.0	0.0	0.0
21	0.0	10.0	10.0	0.0	0.0	0.0
22	20.0	10.0	10.0	0.0	6.6	0.0
23	10.0	0.0	10.0	0.0	6.6	0.0
24	0.0	10.0	20.0	10.0	6.6	20.0
25	10.0	20.0	10.0	10.0	0.0	0.0
26	10.0	30.0	20.0	20.0	13.3	20.0
27	10.0	0.0	10.0	10.0	26.6	0.0
28	30.0	0.0	10.0	40.0	40.0	60.0

Table A-5-21. Romberg—Arms Outstretched and Parallel—for Age Groups: Percentage Distribution of Normal Children

Score	Age (years)					
	6	7	8	9	10	11
4	0.0	10.0	0.0	0.0	0.0	0.0
5	0.0	10.0	0.0	0.0	0.0	0.0
6	10.0	0.0	20.0	0.0	6.6	0.0
7	10.0	20.0	30.0	0.0	0.0	0.0
8	0.0	10.0	10.0	0.0	6.6	0.0
9	20.0	0.0	0.0	0.0	0.0	0.0
10	10.0	20.0	20.0	10.0	13.3	0.0
11	0.0	20.0	0.0	20.0	13.3	10.0
12	0.0	10.0	0.0	30.0	6.6	0.0
13	30.00	0.0	0.0	10.0	20.0	30.0
14	10.0	0.0	0.0	20.0	33.3	40.0
15	10.0	0.0	10.0	10.0	0.0	20.0
16	0.0	0.0	10.0	0.0	0.0	0.0

Table A-5-22. Finger to Finger Test—for Age Groups: Percentage Distribution of Normal Children

Score	Age (years)					
	6	7	8	9	10	11
0	0.0	0.0	0.0	0.0	0.0	0.0
1	0.0	0.0	0.0	0.0	0.0	0.0
2	10.0	0.0	0.0	10.0	6.7	0.0
3	20.0	30.0	20.0	10.0	0.0	10.0
4	70.0	70.0	80.0	80.0	93.3	90.0

Table A-5-23. Finger to Nose Test—for Age Groups: Percentage Distribution of Normal Children

Score	Age (years)					
	6	7	8	9	10	11
0	0.0	0.0	0.0	0.0	0.0	0.0
1	0.0	0.0	0.0	0.0	0.0	0.0
2	0.0	10.0	0.0	0.0	0.0	0.0
3	40.0	0.0	10.0	0.0	0.0	0.0
4	60.0	90.0	90.0	100.0	100.0	100.0

Table A-5-24. Auditory Startle—for Age Groups: Percentage Distribution of Normal Children

	Age (years)					
Score	6	7	8	9	10	11
0	0.0	0.0	0.0	0.0	0.0	0.0
1	0.0	0.0	0.0	0.0	0.0	0.0
2	11.1	44.4	25.0	40.0	33.3	44.4
3	11.1	0.0	37.5	30.0	20.0	11.1
4	22.2	22.2	25.0	10.0	0.0	11.1
5	55.6	33.3	12.5	20.0	46.7	33.3
6	0.0	0.0	0.0	0.0	0.0	0.0

Table A-5-25. Delayed Auditory Feedback—Voice and Speech—for Age Groups: Percentage Distribution of Normal Children

	Age (years)					
Rating	6	7	8	9	10	11
9–11	10.0	0.0	10.0	0.0	0.0	0.0
12–14	20.0	10.0	20.0	0.0	6.6	20.0
15–17	50.0	20.0	10.0	30.0	20.0	10.0
18–20	0.0	50.0	20.0	40.0	26.6	50.0
21–23	20.0	20.0	30.0	20.0	26.6	10.0
24–26	0.0	0.0	10.0	10.0	20.0	10.0
27–32	0.0	0.0	0.0	0.0	0.0	0.0

Table A-5-26. Delayed Auditory Feedback—Language—for Age Groups: Percentage Distribution of Normal Children

	Age (years)					
Rating	6	7	8	9	10	11
3	10.0	0.0	10.0	10.0	26.6	20.0
4	60.0	50.0	30.0	50.0	33.3	40.0
5	20.0	20.0	30.0	20.0	33.3	40.0
6	10.0	20.0	10.0	20.0	6.6	0.0
7–8	0.0	10.0	20.0	0.0	0.0	0.0
9–10	0.0	0.0	0.0	0.0	0.0	0.0
11–12	0.0	0.0	0.0	0.0	0.0	0.0

Table A-5-27. Delayed Auditory Feedback—Self Awareness—for Age Groups: Percentage Distribution of Normal Children

	Age (years)					
Rating	6	7	8	9	10	11
1	80.0	70.0	90.0	90.0	100.0	90.0
2	20.0	30.0	0.0	10.0	0.0	10.0
3	0.0	0.0	10.0	0.0	0.0	0.0

Table A-5-28. Gottschaldt Embedded Figures Test—for Age Groups: Percentage Distribution of Normal Children

	Age (years)					
Score	6	7	8	9	10	11
0–1	50.0	40.0	0.0	10.0	0.0	0.0
2–3	30.0	0.0	0.0	20.0	6.6	10.0
4–5	10.0	20.0	40.0	0.0	0.0	0.0
6–7	0.0	10.0	20.0	0.0	26.6	0.0
8–9	10.0	20.0	10.0	30.0	13.2	20.0
10–11	0.0	10.0	10.0	20.0	19.9	0.0
12–13	0.0	0.0	10.0	20.0	20.0	10.0
14–15	0.0	0.0	10.0	0.0	13.2	60.0

Table A-5-29. Street's Gestalt Completion Test—for Age Groups: Percentage Distribution of Normal Children

	Age (years)					
Score	6	7	8	9	10	11
0–1	0.0	0.0	0.0	0.0	0.0	0.0
2–3	10.0	0.0	0.0	0.0	0.0	0.0
4–5	30.0	30.0	40.0	30.0	13.2	0.0
6–7	40.0	30.0	20.0	30.0	60.0	40.0
8–9	20.0	40.0	40.0	40.0	20.0	30.0
10–11	0.0	0.0	0.0	0.0	6.6	20.0
12–13	0.0	0.0	0.0	0.0	0.0	10.0

Table A-5-34. Railwalking—for Age Groups: Percentage Distribution of Normal Children

Age (years)						
Score	6	7	8	9	10	11
0–9	0.0	10.0	0.0	0.0	0.0	0.0
10–19	10.0	0.0	0.0	0.0	0.0	0.0
20–29	0.0	0.0	30.0	20.0	0.0	0.0
30–39	50.0	40.0	0.0	20.0	13.3	0.0
40–49	10.0	10.0	0.0	10.0	0.0	10.0
50–59	0.0	10.0	40.0	30.0	13.3	10.0
60–69	0.0	30.0	10.0	0.0	13.3	0.0
70–79	30.0	0.0	10.0	10.0	13.3	20.0
80–89	0.0	0.0	0.0	0.0	13.3	30.0
90–99	0.0	0.0	0.0	10.0	13.3	20.0
100–109	0.0	0.0	10.0	0.0	20.0	10.0
110–119	0.0	0.0	0.0	0.0	0.0	0.0
120–129	0.0	0.0	0.0	0.0	0.0	0.0

Table A-5-35. Dynamometer—for Age Groups: Percentage Distribution of Normal Children

Age (years)						
Score	6	7	8	9	10	11
0–4	0.0	0.0	0.0	0.0	0.0	0.0
5–9	30.0	0.0	0.0	0.0	0.0	0.0
10–14	60.0	66.6	50.0	20.0	20.0	0.0
15–19	10.0	33.3	40.0	40.0	26.6	20.0
20–24	0.0	0.0	10.0	40.0	53.3	50.0
25–29	0.0	0.0	0.0	0.0	0.0	20.0
30–34	0.0	0.0	0.0	0.0	0.0	10.0

Table A-5-36. Wechsler Intelligence Scale for Children—Verbal—for Age Groups: Percentage Distribution of Normal Children

Score	Age (years)					
	6	7	8	9	10	11
Below 46	0.0	0.0	0.0	0.0	0.0	0.0
46–69	0.0	0.0	0.0	0.0	0.0	0.0
70–89	10.0	0.0	10.0	0.0	0.0	0.0
90–109	40.0	60.0	10.0	50.0	60.0	40.0
110–129	50.0	40.0	80.0	50.0	33.2	60.0
130 and over	0.0	0.0	0.0	0.0	6.6	0.0

Table A-5-37. Wechsler Intelligence Scale for Children—Performance—for Age Groups: Percentage Distribution of Normal Children

Score	Age (years)					
	6	7	8	9	10	11
Below 46	0.0	0.0	0.0	0.0	0.0	0.0
46–69	0.0	0.0	0.0	0.0	0.0	0.0
70–89	20.0	30.0	0.0	10.0	26.6	20.0
90–109	40.0	20.0	60.0	60.0	46.6	30.0
110–129	40.0	50.0	40.0	30.0	26.6	50.0
130 and over	0.0	0.0	0.0	0.0	0.0	0.0

Table A-5-38. Wechsler Intelligence Scale for Children—Full—for Age Groups: Percentage Distribution of Normal Children

Score	Age (years)					
	6	7	8	9	10	11
Below 46	0.0	0.0	0.0	0.0	0.0	0.0
46–69	0.0	0.0	0.0	0.0	0.0	0.0
70–89	20.0	10.0	0.0	0.0	13.3	10.0
90–109	30.0	60.0	40.0	70.0	40.0	40.0
110–129	50.0	30.0	60.0	30.0	40.0	50.0
130 and over	0.0	0.0	0.0	0.0	6.6	0.0

Table A-5-39. Communication—Voice and Speech—for Age Groups: Percentage Distribution of Normal Children

	Age (years)					
Rating	6	7	8	9	10	11
9–20	0.0	0.0	0.0	0.0	0.0	0.0
21–23	10.0	0.0	0.0	0.0	0.0	0.0
24–26	0.0	10.0	10.0	10.0	0.0	0.0
27–29	0.0	10.0	10.0	20.0	6.6	0.0
30–32	30.0	40.0	30.0	10.0	13.3	0.0
33–35	10.0	20.0	10.0	30.0	20.0	0.0
36–38	50.0	10.0	20.0	20.0	13.3	50.0
39–41	0.0	10.0	10.0	10.0	40.0	50.0
42–44	0.0	0.0	10.0	0.0	6.6	0.0

Table A-5-40. Communication—Language—for Age Groups: Percentage Distribution of Normal Children

	Age (years)					
Rating	6	7	8	9	10	11
3–7	0.0	0.0	10.0	0.0	0.0	0.0
8	10.0	0.0	0.0	0.0	0.0	0.0
9	10.0	0.0	0.0	10.0	0.0	0.0
10	20.0	10.0	10.0	0.0	6.6	10.0
11	0.0	30.0	30.0	20.0	13.3	0.0
12	20.0	30.0	0.0	20.0	6.6	20.0
13	10.0	0.0	20.0	20.0	20.0	10.0
14	20.0	20.0	20.0	20.0	33.3	30.0
15	10.0	10.0	10.0	10.0	20.0	30.0